OXFORD MONOGRAPHS ON LABOUR LAW

General Editors: PAUL DAVIES, KEITH EWING, MARK FREEDLAND

A Right to Care?

Unpaid Care Work in European Employment Law

OXFORD MONOGRAPHS ON LABOUR LAW

General Editors: Paul Davies, Fellow of Jesus College and Allen and Overy Professor of Corporate Law in the University of Oxford; Keith Ewing, Professor of Public Law at King's College, London; and Mark Freedland, Fellow of St. John's College, and Professor of Employment Law in the University of Oxford.

This series has come to reperesent a significant contribution to the literature of British, European, and international labour law. The series recognizes the arrival not only of a renewed interest in labour law generally, but also the need for fresh approaches to the study of labour law following a period of momentous change in the UK and Europe. The series is concerned with all aspects of labour law, including traditional subjects of study such as collective labour law and individual employment law, but it also includes works which concentrate on the growing role of human rights and the combating of discrimination in employment, and others which examine the law and economics of the labour market and the impact of social security law and of national and supranational employment policies upon patterns of employment and the employment contract. Two of the authors contributing to the series, Lucy Vickers and Diamond Ashiagbor, have received awards from the Society of Legal Scholars in respect of their books.

Titles already published in this series

Freedom of Speech and Employment Strategy
LUCY VICKERS

Regulating Flexible Work
DEIRDRE McCANN

The Law of the Labour Market
SIMON DEAKIN AND FRANK WILKINSON

The Presonal Employment Contract
MARK FREEDLAND

The European Employment
DIAMOND ASHIAGBOR

EU Intervention in Domestic Labour Law
PHIL SYRPIS

Towards a Flexible Labour Market
PAUL DAVIES AND MARK FREEDLAND

Welfare to Work
AMIR PAZ-FUCHS

A Right to Care?

Unpaid Care Work in European Employment Law

NICOLE BUSBY

OXFORD
UNIVERSITY PRESS

OXFORD
UNIVERSITY PRESS

Great Clarendon Street, Oxford, OX2 6DP,
United Kingdom

Oxford University Press is a department of the University of Oxford.
It furthers the University's objective of excellence in research, scholarship,
and education by publishing worldwide. Oxford is a registered trade mark of
Oxford University Press in the UK and in certain other countries

First published 2011

Published in the United States of America by Oxford University Press
198 Madison Avenue, New York, NY 10016, United States of America

British Library Cataloguing in Publication Data
Data available

Library of Congress Control Number: 2011924626

ISBN 978–0–19–957902–0

Series Editors' Preface

The aim of our series of labour law monographs has been to publish works which are, on the one hand, of the highest quality of scholarship, and, on the other hand, innovative or experimental, serving to expand the boundaries of the subject or to throw bright new light upon established areas of discussion. We feel sure that the present work will be regarded as maintaining that by now established tradition, and as continuing the progressive extension of the series from labour law, as previously understood, towards a wider understanding of the discipline.

Nicole Busby begins this work with the arresting but not exaggerated assertion that '[t]he reconciliation of paid work and unpaid care is arguably the most pressing problem currently facing labour law'. By so doing, she immediately locates her work within two greatly intersecting genres of labour law studies which are currently very prominent and which are well represented in our series, that is to say the genre which is focused upon the issue of flexibility and atypical employment, and the genre which is focused upon the situation of women in the workplace.

In that situation, we are, as Series Editors, inevitably concerned to ensure that monographs presented within those genres have fresh contributions to make to an already impressive body of literature. We have felt fully satisfied that this criterion of inclusion in our series has been amply fulfilled. The author's idea of canvassing the possibilities of developing a 'right to care' in European employment law is a fruitful and topical one.

The work is all the more significant for being presented not in the traditional sense of a right on the part of the dependent person to be cared for, but in the very different though interestingly correlative sense of a right on the part of the would-be carer to be enabled to discharge her or his caring responsibilities. The author's decision to survey the regulatory scene from that particular perspective of inquiry is validated by the freshness and liveliness of approach which is sustained through the work.

So we warmly welcome this work into our series and look forward to the debates and the policy developments which we think it will serve to provoke.

Paul Davies, Keith Ewing, and Mark Freedland

Preface

Although this book started its life in a period which preceded the current economic crisis, the relevance of the subject matter has only been enhanced by the circumstances of the last two years. The recession which has swept through Europe, predicated by the meltdown of financial institutions and accompanied by high unemployment rates, and the inevitable threat to further economic integration has left the future of European social policy vulnerable to budgetary restrictions and protective practices by Member States. In times of economic downturn, the pursuit of workplace equality is likely to suffer as the types of work undertaken by groups of vulnerable workers become more precarious. However, at the same time, the current circumstances in which the European Union finds itself do offer all of Europe's citizens an opportunity for reflection and a chance to reassess the future priorities of the integration project. In taking stock of the EU's achievements so far and in identifying and prioritizing future goals, it is at least possible that we might engage in the reassessment of work and the different values attributed to its various components in order to provide a law and policy framework capable of encompassing all aspects of individual effort and achievement. I hope that the ideas presented in this book might, in some small way, contribute to that task.

During the writing of this book, the Lisbon Treaty came into force and the changes that it made to EU law, including the renaming of European Court of Justice as the Court of Justice of the European Union and the renumbering of the pre-existing Treaties and, in the case of the EC Treaty, its renaming as the Treaty on the Functioning of the EU (TFEU), have been incorporated into the text as appropriate. The law is stated as at 1 December 2010. All errors and omissions are entirely my own.

It is not possible to list all of those who, in various ways, have contributed to the book and to the wider project from which it originated and I thank all of those whose ideas have been incorporated and who have offered assistance and support over the years. However, I must pay specific tribute to some key individuals. This book started out as a PhD thesis and, although little remains of that original work in this text, the ideas formulated here have their roots in my postgraduate studies. Mike Sanderson has provided a valuable and enduring friendship throughout. Noreen Burrows has remained a source of inspiration and I will always be in her debt for providing an early opportunity that has enabled me to pursue a career that I love. My supervisor and friend Jane Mair deserves special thanks for her invaluable support and advice. Evelyn Ellis and Rosa Greaves provided useful feedback and encouragement. In recent years, the participants and discussants at various streams and panels of the Socio-Legal Studies Association's annual conferences have provided a friendly yet challenging environment for the testing and development of new ideas. My gratitude is due to Grace James and Morag McDermont who, as good friends and collaborators, have provided tireless assistance and enthusiasm for various offshoots enabling the continuing development of certain aspects of the work presented here.

I am indebted to the editorial team at OUP for their encouragement and support, not least the editors of the Oxford Monographs on Labour Law series, Paul Davies, Keith Ewing, and Mark Freedland, for adopting and endorsing the text. Two anonymous reviewers provided insightful comments that enabled me considerably to refine the original proposal. Gwen Booth and Chris Champion assisted at an earlier stage and Natasha Knight, Ela Kotkowska, and Ceri Warner have been extremely helpful and patient in guiding the manuscript towards publication.

Finally, my greatest debt is to my family who have lived with this book for as long as I have. My daughters Eve, Eleanor, and Màiri have kept me grounded and have helped me to experience at first hand the value of giving and receiving care within a supportive environment. I dedicate this book to them and to my husband Calum who, through his love and encouragement, has made it possible to achieve both personal and professional fulfilment.

Nicole Busby
The Stirling Law School
February 2011

Contents

Table of Cases

COURT OF JUSTICE OF THE EUROPEAN UNION

UNITED KINGDOM

UNITED STATES

Table of Legislation

DOMESTIC

EUROPEAN UNION

INTERNATIONAL CONVENTIONS

1

Unpaid Care and Paid Work in European Employment Law

Introduction

The reconciliation of paid work and unpaid care is arguably the most pressing problem currently facing labour law. The need to develop suitable legal strategies that enable individuals to combine informal care-giving with paid employment matters to the individuals themselves, the recipients of their care, employers, and the State. It matters to society as a whole, to each and every citizen and is of fundamental importance in ensuring the continued sustainability of developed economies. Recognition of the need to facilitate informal care-giving within formal workplace structures has led to the development of a plethora of laws and associated policies aimed at providing support for carers to remain in paid employment, largely by assimilating into established practices and procedures. As a result, there is now a greater number of pre-school childcare places available in the EU than at any time[1] and the provision of paid or partially paid periods of maternity leave available following the birth of a child has increased incrementally at the EU level over the last 20 years.[2] Rather than resulting from a new political awareness of the needs of worker-carers, such recent additions to the law and policy mix are part of a slow, incremental movement towards targeted State support for the management of unpaid care and paid employment within a social welfare framework. However, despite the development of a complex and apparently sophisticated web of law and policy, worker-carers face an ongoing conflict between meeting the requirements of those for whom they care and the demands of an often inflexible working environment. In attempting to meet these competing demands, carers themselves face a deficit in support which can have many negative effects on their personal well-being. This discord between the two facets of an individual's life can be labelled 'the

[1] Eurofound (2006) *Childcare Services in the EU—What Future?*, available at <http://www.eurofound.europa.eu/emcc/content/source/eu06015a.htm?p1=ef_publication&p2=null> accessed 7 December 2010.

[2] At the time of writing, a proposal for a directive to further extend the minimum period of paid maternity leave from 14 to 18 weeks is working its way through the EU legislative process. See *Proposal for a directive of the European Parliament and the Council amending Council Directive 93/85/EEC*, COM (2008) 600/4, discussed in Chapter 5.

unpaid care/paid work conflict' and it is finding a sustainable solution to this conflict that presents labour law with its greatest challenge.

Aims of the Book

This book considers how paid work and unpaid care can be reconciled by exploring the potential for the development of a right to care in European employment law. The specific aim is to explore EU law's response to changes that have taken place in the employment context since the Community's inception and to assess its overall contribution to the reconciliation of the unpaid care/paid work conflict. A central claim is that the constitutional provisions of EU law already endorse a responsive approach to this conflict which, although merely implicit in the existing provisions at the present time, has the potential to be effectively utilized to provide individuals with a clear right to reconcile paid work and unpaid care. The main hurdle to be overcome is in the requirement for a change of approach to the current conceptualization of the conflict which necessitates a shift of focus from the employment rights of carers to the provision of caring rights for those who engage in paid work. It is asserted that the proposal outlined in the book, rather than requiring a complete overhaul of existing law and policy, could be incorporated into the current regulatory framework in order to bring cohesion to that framework and, if used to full effect, could have a far-reaching impact on the future of unpaid and paid work reconciliation.

Background to the Unpaid Care/Paid Work Conflict

Despite the existence of a broad and comprehensive range of relevant policies intended to assist in the reconciliation of personal and professional life, EU citizens still experience and observe dissatisfaction through related conflicts that are manifested in various ways. Within organizations, such conflict may result in inefficient working practices and, for government agencies and departments responsible for setting labour market targets, in disappointingly low economic activity rates among some sectors. In the wider society, it is possible to discern a general sense that personal and collective interests are not being adequately addressed. For the individual worker-carer, the impact of this conflict can be acute and can result in the non-achievement of personal goals and aspirations as well as in a high financial cost through low wages, lost opportunities for career advancement, and poor pension entitlement at the end of the working life.

These are all typical features of women's labour market experiences due to the fact that worker-carers are overwhelmingly female, the largest group being comprised of mothers and, in particular, of pre-school or school-age children. Thus, the unpaid care/paid employment conflict is severely gendered although not all worker-carers are women and not all of those for whom they care are dependent children. Furthermore, contemporary family units come in many shapes and sizes reflecting a myriad of finely tuned care and paid work arrangements which are subject to wide diversity even where such units correspond with the traditional nuclear family within which the main provider of care is a mother of young children. This variety of needs on the part of carers and those for whom they care poses a particular challenge in the search for a successful legal strategy. The success of individual policies is difficult to ascertain and relies on their measurement against a subjective set of criteria which will vary depending on the prioritization of particular outcomes: in short, the reconciliation of paid labour and unpaid care matters to different stakeholders for different reasons. Consequently, it is necessary to find a unifying feature on which all relevant parties might agree as the starting point in developing a suitable strategy.

This can be problematic in the wider context of social inquiry as stakeholders in many socio-economic institutions often have little common ground so that progress can founder on as elementary a pursuit as identifying what the basics are. However, where the provision of care is concerned, there are few variables: we all experience dependency on others for our survival from birth and throughout the lifecycle. All human beings have participated in the care relationship, either as recipients or as both carer and recipient, providing an innate insight into the importance of that relationship. Although we may disagree about the relative importance of the parent/child bond to the future emotional maturity of an individual, we cannot deny the reliance of an infant on another human being for basic survival at the physiological level and for varying degrees of emotional and psychological support through the various stages of development up to full maturity as an independent and autonomous individual. The common unifying feature then is our humanity and it is on this universal basis and its moral expression that the case presented in this book is founded.

The Care Component of Labour Law

Over the last 30 years, the concept of paid work has undergone a transformation in terms of how it is comprised, what it entails, and who engages in it.[3] Patterns of employment have changed, as have working arrangements so that, for example, all EU Member States have witnessed significant increases in part-time work.[4] What has been characterized as the 'feminization of the workforce' has taken place with more women continuing to work during the childbearing and rearing years than ever before. Added to this, developments in medical science have led to an increase in life expectancy, improved child mortality even for those born with serious disabilities, and enhanced survival rates for what were once classified as terminal illnesses, leading to a rise in the number of people requiring high levels of care. As a result of these changes, increasing numbers of workers now have competing

[3] A. Supiot, 'The Transformation of Work and the Future of Labour Law in Europe: A Multidisciplinary Perspective', *International Labour Review*, 138/1 (1999), 32.

[4] See Chapter 4.

responsibilities outside of their professional life due to their roles within dependency relationships.

This reconfiguration of work has, by and large, not been accompanied by any radical change to or overhaul of the regulatory framework within which the employment relationship operates. The accommodation of 'difference', identified by comparison with the standard worker model, has largely been attempted through protection against discrimination on the grounds of such difference rather than through the development of self-standing rights which seek to ensure its normalization.[5] More recent additions to EU legislation aimed at prohibiting specific practices such as discrimination against part-time workers have been added to the existing framework so that the resulting system of employment and social law represents an incremental consolidation of various legal and policy instruments.[6] This is not necessarily a criticism as the evolution of a legal system typically depends on weeding out the ineffective and supplementing and amending the tried and tested, thus enabling the emergence of a dynamic and adaptable set of rules capable of responding to future challenges without compromising its adherence to fundamental principles and so ensuring legal certainty and legitimate expectation. However, the system that emerges is not merely a product of what is legally effective, but is also shaped by external factors which emanate from the political, social, and economic system within which it operates. These factors are based on subjective decision-making which, in turn, is guided by the over-riding ideology to which their architects subscribe. This is particularly so in the case of Community law which was originally intended to regulate a specific and narrow range of activities in order to achieve a particular set of objectives. The primary aims of what has now become EU law were grounded in its economic imperative and thus conformed to the market-based notions of commercial expediency and commodification of all relevant units of exchange. In political terms, this adherence to a market order is reflected in an underlying liberal ideology within which the prioritization of certain competing factions has occurred.

The Liberal Foundations of EU Law

Despite the reorientation of EU law to embrace social as well as economic aspirations, it is this market-led philosophy that has dominated any perceived or actual conflict between the economic and the social goals of the European Union. As appealing as it may be to imagine ways in which this apparent deadlock might be broken by the institutional rejection of liberal ideology, it is simply not possible for the EU to detach itself from the very foundations on which it is based and, besides, there is much to commend further economic and social integration in the current context particularly in relation to the development of workers' rights as a means of overcoming disadvantage and discrimination. It is, therefore, more productive to

5 See, for example, the prohibition of discrimination on the grounds of sex, discussed in Chapter 5.
6 See Chapter 5.

take a pragmatic view by seeking ways in which existing structures might be adapted and utilized in order to achieve compelling social objectives. This book aims to do that by articulating a right to care which would, in fact, enhance and give effect to the current legal and policy framework by integrating and consolidating the relevant provisions and by making them accessible to those at whom they are targeted. This proposal is, thus, compatible with the political liberalism which characterizes policy and law-making within the EU context.

Although it may seem unquestionable that any proposed amendment to a legal system should correspond with the underlying ethos on which that system is predicated, the market liberalism which characterizes EU law and policy has traditionally been viewed as irreconcilable with the qualities and values associated with care-giving. This has been perceived as presenting an insurmountable hurdle in effectively utilizing the corresponding legal system as a means of recognizing and responding to the unpaid care/paid work conflict on the basis that attempts to prioritize commercial expediency and the unyielding yet non-commodifiable demands of the care relationship within a market order will always result in the predomination of the former. However, as this book will argue, the apparent mismatch between liberalism and the reconciliation of unpaid care and paid employment is largely based on a particular conception of liberal ideology as *neo*-liberal which, when considered from the care-giver's often neglected perspective, is unsustainable. Furthermore, the polarization of the competing demands of paid work and unpaid care as opposing sides of an irreconcilable dichotomy vastly oversimplifies the relationship between the two components of an individual's life. The difficulties that arise from attempts to provide unpaid care alongside paid employment are by no means confined to a small minority of the population. On the contrary, the care relationship is neither a novel nor an alien concept but rather one with which we are all familiar and from which we have all, albeit to varying degrees, benefited. Furthermore, evidence based on labour market participation rates and predicted levels of unpaid care,[7] suggests that more of us will have to adapt to the demands of the simultaneous provision of both in the future.

Although EU law and policy does, to some extent, recognize and seek to remedy the unpaid care/paid work conflict,[8] its economic foundation has meant that attempts at its resolution have routinely placed emphasis on the 'paid work' side of the equation to the detriment of the 'unpaid care' aspect. The contention that such undue focus on one particular aspect of socio-economic policy is a result of choices made on ideological grounds by those to whom society has delegated decision-making is a central tenet of the analysis presented in this book. Such ideology is itself the product of perceptions concerning the relationship between care and employment and the low value ascribed to the former which are rooted in the characteristics of those who traditionally engage in both.

[7] See, for example, European Commission, *Health and Long-Term Care in the European Union*, Special Eurobarometer 283 (Luxembourg: 2007).

[8] See Chapter 5.

The Gender Effect

Woman's association with care arises from her biological difference and the traditional assumption that nature has better equipped the female sex for unpaid work within the family. In Greek philosophy, on which many of our contemporary conceptions of gender are based, Plato's conviction that the 'female bears and the male begets'[9] encapsulates the belief that the different natures of men and women result in a fundamental predisposition for their respective roles within the family. Aristotle, whose formula that 'likes should be treated alike'[10] is the premise on which current anti-discrimination law is based, was of the view that the male was 'more fitted to rule than the female'[11] placing women within the private confines of the home.

As outdated as the dichotomization expounded by the Greek School may appear in current analyses of gender relations, the ideological doctrine intended to explain the relative social positions of women and men is endemic in the philosophy underpinning contemporary social arrangements and supporting institutions. The welfare systems of most industrialized countries are stubbornly predicated on the assumption that the division of labour within families will place men in the position of main earner or 'breadwinner' and women in that of primary carer and 'home-maker', at least during the childbearing and rearing years. That such ideology continues to inform policy-making is not necessarily intentional: there are very few who would claim that men are better suited to participation in paid work than women as well-established sex discrimination legislation demonstrates. However, such beliefs are so entrenched in our psyches that they inform our individual and collective actions and enable our unquestioning acceptance of rules and institutions founded on discriminatory criteria which exist at all levels of society. Furthermore, the relationship between certain social groups and the development of legal systems has led to the furtherance of particular interests through the medium of the law. Male dominance in the 'public sphere', particularly within political institutions, has led to the furtherance of male interests[12] and a corresponding adherence to the *status quo* in unpaid care arrangements despite overwhelming evidence that family formation and labour market participation have irrevocably changed.[13]

[9] Plato, *The Republic*, R. Waterfield (trans) (Oxford: Oxford University Press, 1993), Bk V 454e.

[10] The 'Aristotelian formula'—Aristotle, *Nicomachean Ethics*, V. 3 1131a10-b15; *The Politics*, III.9.1280 a8–15, III.12.1282b18–23.

[11] *The Nicomachean Ethics*, D. Ross (trans) (Oxford: Oxford University Press, 1925): *The Politics*, Bk 1 xii, 1259a 37.

[12] The polarization of the 'private' and 'public' spheres of civil society, discussed in Chapter 2, actually derives from the Greek school, which drew a distinction between the *polis* (public) and *oikis* (private), see further J. Swanson, *The Public and The Private in Aristotle's Political Philosophy* (Ithaca, NY and London: Cornell University Press, 1992).

[13] R. Crompton (ed), *Restructuring Gender Relationships and Employment: The Decline of the Male Breadwinner* (Oxford: Oxford University Press, 1999); *Employment and the Family* (Cambridge: Cambridge University Press, 2006).

The Care Relationship

In recent years, EU-level attempts to address the so-called 'work-life balance' have tended to focus on increasing the amount of paid work undertaken by women[14] and, consequently, on reducing the level of unpaid care that takes place within families. The resulting 'outsourcing' of care, categorized as de-familialization,[15] has been articulated through specific policies with increasing emphasis on formal care provision for both children and adult dependants. Through such means, care is commodified and put onto the market place, thus enabling furtherance of the dual goals of economic growth and competitiveness through both its exchange and the enhanced labour market activity of its former (female) providers. Such strategic policy-making implicitly recognizes the inequalities that persist in relation to the division of paid work and unpaid care within families and the resulting difficulties encountered by those who attempt to combine both. However, its reliance on economic growth as its underlying rationale means that much which is imperative to the nature of the care relationship, and the attachment to it of those who participate in it, is overlooked.

Contemporary investigators of the relationship[16] concur that the intrinsically intimate nature of the exchange that takes place between a carer and a recipient of care demonstrate the inalienability of certain aspects. This central component of the relationship is crucial to the well-being of both parties and is, thus, non-commodifiable. This claim forms a basic tenet on which much of the analysis presented in this book is founded. As will become clear, the position adopted is not that care should not or cannot be commodified, but rather that 'the full commodification of care is not possible'.[17] This, coupled with recognition of the importance of individual autonomy, informs the nature of the book's central investigation which is to find ways in which unpaid care can successfully be combined with paid work. This does not entail a prescriptive view that, once uncovered, such a formula should be pursued by all of those with caring responsibilities. On the contrary it is the exercise of *real choice* that is of paramount concern. Nevertheless, recognition of the shift towards the adult worker model family demands the development of appropriate strategies to enable and facilitate such choice.

Whether performed within the private domain of the family or contracted out in the market place as a unit of exchange, care is undervalued and its importance to the well-being of all participants is overlooked. This leaves carers, who are predominantly female, with a narrow range of options regarding their life choices. What is required

[14] See Chapter 5.

[15] G. Esping-Andersen, D. Gaillie, A. Hemerijck, and J. Myles, *Why We Need a New Welfare State* (Oxford: Oxford University Press, 2002).

[16] Such as Eva Feder Kittay, Martha Fineman and Kathleeen Lynch *et al*, all of whose work is considered in Chapter 3.

[17] S. Giullari and J. Lewis, *The Adult Worker Model Family, Gender Equality and Care: The Search for New Policy Principles, and the Possibilities and Problems of a Capabilities Approach*, United Nations Research Institute, Social Policy and Development Programme (2005) Paper No 19, at 8.

in order to successfully counter the current neglect of such issues is a viable strategy which seeks to equalize, as far as possible, the contributions made by men and women to the informal provision of care[18] whilst, at the same time, recognizing the value of the care relationship to society as a whole. This requires the simultaneous maintenance of the particular protections that exist in response to the inequality experienced by women in their dual role as carer and employee and the separation of care and gender within the legal and policy framework. It is only by challenging its association with low paid 'women's work' that care will acquire an enhanced status and that the paid, often precarious, work undertaken alongside it will be normalized. This, it is asserted, is possible by the application of a legally recognized right to care aimed at providing a solution to the current conflict.

Justifying a 'Right' to Care

In contemporary society the language of rights is everywhere. We refer without question to our right to a specific status, for example, the right to freedom and to express ourselves in a particular way as articulated by our rights to free speech and to religious belief. The claim, conferment, and expression of rights are the processes by which our fundamental values are acknowledged. Rights are developed and invoked as a means of protecting aspects of life that, as a society, we view as being central to our individual and collective well-being. Furthermore, rights can be used to prevent harm being done to members of society on the basis of personal characteristics, such as sexuality, disability, or race or because of imbalances in power between contracting parties, so that vulnerable workers are protected against certain potential forms of exploitation by employing organizations. All of the foregoing examples of the uses to which rights might be put have currency in the current context. In its simplest form, a right is a claim on others which can be justified by its adherence to a particular standard which is acknowledged and recognized by society. In subscribing to an acceptable standard, society makes a value judgement about how we want to live which encompasses, among other things, a moral component which is defensible, not in the individual views of each and every member of society, but in collective terms by the majority.

In relation to the unpaid work of caring, it is undeniable that the effort expended in the provision of that care corresponds, at least on its face, with the necessary components for recognition as a justified claim on others. Its moral property, based on the expression of selfless love for its recipient, surely meets the necessary ethical standard. We all, to varying degrees, have gained in our well-being from 'love labour', usually through our experiences as dependent infants and children but also, in many cases, as the givers of such care who share in the mutually beneficial exchange of emotional support that the care relationship engenders. However, such

[18] See C. McGlynn, 'Work, Family and Parenthood: The European Union Agenda' in J. Conaghan and K. Rittich (eds), *Labour Law, Work and Family* (Oxford: Oxford University Press, 2005), in which the author asserts the need to develop EU policies which facilitate 'equal parenting'.

relationships also exact a high price from those engaged in the provision of care. The constant requirement to anticipate and meet the needs of others can be extremely demanding both physically and emotionally; much of the effort is expended in the completion of non-intellectually challenging repetitive tasks—washing, cooking, cleaning—which add nothing to the sense of personal achievement or self-actualization of the individual undertaking them but are, nonetheless, crucial to the well-being of those in her care.

The undervaluing of care means that women, who more often than not are the providers of such unpaid work, are likely to earn significantly less in employment over their life-cycles than their male counterparts and are also less likely to be able to benefit from work-related benefits. In old age, many women bear the financial consequences of time away from the labour market or years spent in part-time and precarious work through reduced and, in some cases, non-existent, pensions. These inequalities persist, despite the longevity of well-established laws designed to protect against discrimination on the grounds of sex. The law may be sex-aware, but it is gender-blind and, thus, inadequate in addressing the unequal division of labour that takes place within families and the corresponding penalties meted out against those who provide the unpaid work of caring. If such penalties were exacted against a group of individuals on the basis of, for example, the colour of their skin or their sexuality, the sense of moral outrage felt by the wider society in such enlightened times and the resulting call for rights would surely resonate with even the most traditional legislature.

It would be misleading to suggest that the complexities inherent in attempting to provide legislative protection for those engaged in the work/care equation have been completely overlooked by the EU legislature. Alongside a well-developed framework of rights in respect of equal pay and treatment for men and women,[19] EU law also provides directives aimed at protecting against discrimination on the grounds of part-time working[20] and temporary contractual status.[21] The shortcomings of these legal instruments in the current context will be considered at length in Chapter 5. What is necessary at this juncture is to distinguish them from the right encapsulated within the current proposal and to identify what the introduction of a specific right to care would add to the pre-existing framework of rights that would facilitate its effectiveness in this regard. The answer lies in its conceptual basis which, rather than acting as a replacement for such provisions, would supplement them by consolidating what already exists and identifying what is currently lacking.

[19] Now largely consolidated by Directive 2006/54/EC of the European Parliament and of the Council on the implementation of the principle of equal opportunities and equal treatment of men and women in matters of employment and occupation (recast), OJ 2006 L 204/23, which is assessed in Chapter 5.

[20] Council Directive 97/81/EC of 15 December 1997 concerning the framework agreement on part-time work concluded by UNICE, CEEP and the ETUC, OJ 1997 L 14/9, see Chapter 5.

[21] Council Directive 1999/70/EC of 28 June 1999 concerning the framework agreement on fixed-term work concluded by ETUC, UNICE and CEEP, OJ 1999 L 244/64 and Directive 2008/104/EC of the European Parliament and of the Council of 19 November 2008 on temporary agency work, OJ 2008 L 327/9, which Member States have until December 2011 to implement.

The Conceptual Foundations of the Right to Care and European Union Law

The positioning of such a right within the pre-existing framework of EU law raises questions regarding care's perceived incompatibility with liberalism and associated market ideology. However, there is a considerable body of literature in law and associated disciplines which is supportive of—and indeed has informed—the case presented here which is that the traditional values of liberalism are in fact well suited to the legal recognition of care within a legal system which is intended to regulate interplay between the individual and the institutions supporting paid work. In reorienting the regulation of paid work in line with liberalism's core values of autonomy, freedom, and equality, it is quite possible—in fact necessary—to extend its reach to take account of the impact of unpaid care in the formulation of law and policy. Furthermore, although EU law may appear to be an unwieldy mechanism for effecting rapid social change, previous experiences over its relatively short life demonstrate that it can be surprisingly responsive and quick to adapt at times of necessity.[22] This is such a time—the current approaches in this area are simply not effective and require reworking as a matter of urgency. It is hoped that the ideas presented in this book will contribute to that task.

The particular conception of liberalism advocated in this book is founded on the notion of sustainable social development rather than the high yield short-termism more usually associated with liberal ideology, particularly in its political neo-liberal incarnation, which is justified through adherence to a business model. Under the latter, the development of creative policy-making is often thwarted unless immediate economic benefits can be identified. The proposed alternative places greater emphasis on the social cost of not valuing care-giving appropriately which, although more difficult to quantify in the context of a business model, is rationalized on the basis of long-term sustainable development. Such an approach at least attempts to address related social problems such as the relationship between time and income poverty[23] and related social outcomes such as child poverty and declining fertility rates. This, in turn, counters the vulnerability of measures rationalized solely by an economic imperative, the maintenance of which relies on the vagaries of the market as their justification is grounded on the assumption that they are 'good for business'. In economic downturns, such measures are often the first to go due to their reliance on fulfilling the criteria of 'affordability' which, in times of market fluctuation, is a moveable feast. This marks such territory out as fertile grounds for the development of rights which are aimed at protecting the vulnerable from exploitation.

[22] See, for example, the Court of Justice's early jurisprudence on the interpretation of Art 119/EEC discussed in Chapter 6.

[23] See T. Burchardt, *Time and Income Poverty* (LSE: Centre for Analysis of Social Exclusion, 2008) available <http://sticerd.lse.ac.uk/dps/case/cr/CASEreport57.pdf> accessed 7 December 2010.

Intellectually, this approach has its roots in moral and political philosophy[24] rather than in economics and, thus, is able to free itself from much of the frustration expressed with the shortcomings of that discipline as a means of identifying solutions to the issues under review.[25] However, despite the dark and at times, obtuse, contributions of economists to debates around the issues of paid work and informal care-giving, the main source of light in recent years has been cast by a scholar working ostensibly, albeit with inter- and multi-disciplinary methods, in that very discipline. In his work on the capabilities approach, Armatya Sen has offered the most exciting innovation in recent years in the broad fields of equality and justice. Sen's and Martha Nussbaum's work on the application of the capability approach to the area of gender equality offers important insights into the reconciliation of unpaid care and paid work and the division of labour within families. In Chapters 2 and 7 their work is specifically utilized to assist in establishing the philosophical foundations and practical development of a right to care.

Scope and Structure of the Book

Rather than treading the well-worn path of EU law-making by situating the unpaid care/paid employment conflict in the context of the need to facilitate family responsibility within pre-existing work-based structures, the proposal outlined in this book takes a wider perspective. The development of a specific right to provide care alongside paid employment necessitates primary consideration of the needs of those on whom others depend for such care, whether that dependency is based on the traditional parent/child relationship, the relationship within which the provision of care for a disabled or terminally ill partner or relative takes place, or on the provision of elder care.

As outlined above, the book's focus is on the response of labour law and, as a consequence, the relevant issues are situated within that particular paradigm. However, there is also a case to be made for entitlement to State support for those who, on the basis of their caring responsibilities, do not engage in paid employment. Whilst direct consideration of this aspect is outside of the scope of this text, it is hoped that many of the ideas presented here, particularly in relation to caring labour's ethical nature and its corresponding social and economic value, can also be used in support of that case. The analysis focuses on the EU legal order, with particular consideration of the jurisprudence of the Court of Justice (CoJ) because of that legal system's specific potential is this context, but it is anticipated that much of that analysis and the case presented here in support of the development of a specific right to care will have application within other legal systems.

[24] See E. Feder Kittay, 'A Feminist Public Ethic of Care Meets the New Communitarian Family Policy', *Ethics*, 111 (2001), 3.

[25] See S. Fredman, *Women and the Law* (Oxford: Oxford University Press, 1997), 405 *et seq.*

In Chapter 2 consideration is given to the theoretical basis on which a right to care might be grounded. The liberal tradition which supports the notion of individual autonomy central to the current proposal is explored by an historical analysis of its development and application through the work of leading theorists. The early exponents' acceptance of the notion of a social contract entered into freely between a people and the State as a means of expressing the relationship between those who govern and those who are governed. The movement has its origins in seventeenth century European society when the dissolution of the feudal system and the emergence of capitalism were accompanied by a focus on the concepts of individual autonomy and equality before the law. In political terms, the notion of individual consent became paramount so that the State retreated in matters involving personal decision-making, its main function being 'to act as a neutral umpire between conflicting interests'.[26] In terms of legal intervention, this model of the liberal State can be seen as the basis for the public–private divide, in which 'the "public" State should intrude as little as possible into the sphere of individual autonomy or the "private" sphere'.[27] The public–private divide and the emergence of legal abstentionism have had a particular and enduring relevance in the development of law and policy within the current context but their relationship to the area under review is more reflective of pre-existing divisions along gender lines, particularly within the 'private' sphere of the family, than indicative of some indefinably prescient ability on the part of the original social contract theorists to forecast the future.

In Chapter 3 the causes of the unpaid care/paid work conflict are explored, specifically in the context of the gendered nature of paid work within segregated labour markets and of the unregulated division of labour within families. The existing literature in this area, particularly that written from a labour law perspective, provides useful insights into the 'paid work' side of the equation but has tended to neglect the 'unpaid care' component except where it provides an explanation for deviation from the 'standard worker' norm. The reasons for such demarcation are explored and the care relationship itself is considered in light of its effect on carers' labour market activity and in relation to its diversity in terms of levels of dependency and corresponding support required. It is argued that care should be recognized as an essential and everyday human activity that carries a heavy social burden which should be the subject of shared responsibility.

The gender dimension of unpaid care is considered in order to determine how best to overcome the resulting segregation of paid work along gender lines. It is argued that, as well as providing some much-needed protection for vulnerable workers, the provision of a specific right to care, which is not derived from the prohibition of sex discrimination, is important if we wish to overcome the problems associated with the 'ghettoization' of women's work through the engagement of men in the provision of care and the resultant changes in working arrangements required for its accommodation. Through such reorientation, the

[26] Ibid, 6. [27] Ibid, 7.

'atypical' becomes normative and the precariousness associated with part-time and/or temporary work or that based on tripartite arrangements is confronted head-on. The conferment of rights in a specific area legitimizes the claims of those able to benefit. The legal recognition of care's value to the whole of society through the provision of an individual right to protection against discrimination on the grounds of caring responsibilities would also provide an enhanced status for carers capable of encouraging and facilitating men's engagement in unpaid care and, thus, lifting it out of the confines of gender role ascription.

The main aim of Chapter 4 is to identify the appropriate form and content of the proposed right to care which should be situated within European employment law. Although it is asserted that such a right is compatible with the prerequisites for a contract between citizens and the State, the recognition of carers' dependency, full or partial, through a public ethos of care supported by State means would require the acknowledgement of a wider social responsibility than is usual in employment policy models. This positions the contractual nexus between the carer and the State in its agency role on society's behalf so that the burden of support becomes part of a wider social responsibility which has both contractual and moral implications.[28] The enhanced intervention by the State may seem at odds with classic liberalism and its adherence to the concept of rational, autonomous decision-making. However, this proposal sits comfortably with the move towards the reconfiguration of social and labour rights[29] which is at the heart of the current phase of the EU's integration project within which the concept of citizenship is of central concern. Furthermore, as contemporary advocates of traditional welfare capitalism have noted, the dual concepts of autonomy and rationality, which are often heralded as the founding principles of liberalism, have limited application in the present context.[30] As Chapter 4 argues, traditional liberal theory actually supports the assertion that recognition of responsibility for care is properly positioned within a rights framework. This is because such an approach acknowledges the need for social rights which extend beyond liberal and political rights and which are based on community membership.

In Chapter 5 the current provisions of EU law are assessed in order to consider the 'fit' of the proposed right to care within the pre-existing framework. It is asserted that what is proposed is not merely compatible with many of the current provisions of that framework but is in fact necessary to provide cohesion between the various strands that, together, constitute the relevant body of law and, in doing

[28] West has posited the existence of an intrinsic right to care which is implicit in the rights conferred on the subjects of constitutional democracies. Although West's analysis focuses on the US constitution, her argument has resonance in the context of EU law, particularly in the relationship between the Treaties and the Court of Justice, see R. West, 'The Right to Care' in E. Feder Kittay and E. Feder (eds), *The Subject of Care: Feminist Perspectives on Dependency* (New York: Rowman and Littlefield, 2002).

[29] See Chapter 4 and the discussion of the EU Charter of Fundamental Rights in Chapter 5.

[30] Eg M. Fineman, *The Autonomy Myth: A Theory of Dependency* (New York: The New Press, 2004); S. Moller Okin, *Justice, Gender and the Family* (New York: Basic Books, 1989).

so, to give them effect. The apparently subtle reframing of the work/care equation required in order to provide legal recognition of carer status would of course require a significant cultural shift within workplaces which is nevertheless in tune with the current move towards the recognition of diversity and the reconfiguration of working arrangements. Furthermore, although certain provisions of EU law provide a suitable base for such development,[31] their current application in this respect depends on the appropriate interpretation by the Court of Justice. That the Court will be willing and able to rise to such a challenge is by no means a foregone conclusion. For one thing the current policy framework has moved the fulfilment of the EU's social aims away from a litigation-based approach towards the bottom-up co-ordination of national policies enforced through compliance with soft law guidance. Furthermore, the Court's decision-making in the area of work/family reconciliation has not always been as progressive or consistent as it has been in other areas.

In the consideration of the Court's jurisprudence presented in Chapter 6, it appears that the opportunity for creative judicial decision-making in this context has long been available through the referral of questions concerning the rights of so-called 'atypical' workers by national courts under the Article 267 TFEU procedure. The main difficulty inherent in attempting to mould rights to individual circumstances lies in the diversity of needs that vary, not only on the basis of specific circumstances, but over time as levels of dependency change and, in some cases, disappear. In the EU context, this challenge could potentially be met by the creative approach that is at least possible on the part of the Court through its interpretive methods which enable it to develop responsive solutions to specific issues by drawing on a wide range of legislative and policy instruments. In this respect the Court's engagement in progressive decision-making is enabled through its teleological reasoning based on the constitutional provisions of the Treaty, some of which are suitably aspirational in tone, and the non-binding nature of its judgments. The usefulness of the Court's jurisprudence to the regulatory function of the EU institutions has been seen in other areas of social policy, for example, through Directive 2004/38's codification of its decision-making on the right of residence in order to give meaning to the provision of free movement of workers under what is now Article 45 TFEU. It might, thus, be expected that the Court's apparently progressive stance on gender equality could be usefully harnessed to give effect to a right to care through its articulation of EU law's implicit acceptance of such a right. However, as the survey of cases involving attempts by workers to combine paid employment with caring responsibilities demonstrates,[32] the reasoning underpinning the Court's jurisprudence in this area has often lacked the necessary degree of insight and empathy.

Chapter 7 concludes that, given the Court's apparent reluctance to engage in the creative application of Treaty provisions in this context, the required shift in

[31] See Art 3 TEU for the general provision; Arts 157 and 151–3 TFEU and Chapter III CFR on equality; and Art 33 CFR on the reconciliation of family and professional life.

[32] See Chapter 6.

emphasis could be facilitated by further regulatory activity at European level, either by legislative or soft law means. This is possible through the preservation of the existing legal framework and appropriate implementing legislation within Member States. The review of current legal provision in this area is not out of step with the over-riding strategy of the EU as the development of the policy and legislative framework relating to the reconciliation of work and family life is permanently on the EU's political agenda.[33] In relation to the Member States' implementing legislation, the incorporation of a specific right to care would depend on the regulatory model in operation. Some existing models are considered in order to identify what a specific right to care might look like. The UK's Disability Discrimination Act 1995 confers a duty on employers to take account of an individual's particular disability as a basis for adapting work-related practices and procedures to suit individual needs which has been shaped through judicial interpretation of the 'reasonable adjustment' requirement.[34] Legislation introduced by the Australian states of New South Wales and Victoria provides an example of carer-specific protection which, like the UK provisions relating to disability, places an obligation on employers to reasonably accommodate the needs of carers through workplace adjustments. The sort of adjustments relevant to the current context would include flexible work arrangements such as compressed hours, home working, and carer's leave.

The needs-based approach amounts to what has been termed 'responsive'[35] or 'reflexive'[36] regulation which places emphasis on the involvement of those at whom it is targeted. As Hepple has argued, such engagement with stakeholders is crucial for the development of workable regulation which can be effectively enforced. The targeted approach suggested, whereby the legislative framework enables a specific response to be made to each request based on the particular needs of the individual concerned, is truly reflexive. The approach advocated, which places the needs of the carer and the recipient of care at its centre, requires legislation which is both wide in scope (in terms of both carers and needs) and conceptually flexible.

The strength of the proposal which is set out in the remaining chapters of this book lies in its flexibility and adaptability, which enable it to meet the often diverse and varying needs of those who combine unpaid care with paid employment. However, this reflexive quality also poses the greatest threat to the legal recognition of such a right which is apparently at odds with the carefully drafted and detailed legislative responses with which we are generally more familiar, particularly at national level. This aspect provides further cause for the positioning of such a

[33] See, for example, COM (2008) 635 final in which the Commission sets out its plans in respect of the achievement of '[a] better work-life balance: stronger support for reconciling professional, private and family life'.

[34] Provided by the Disability Discrimination Act 1995 (as amended) in judgments such as that by the House of Lords in *Archibald v Fife Council* [2004] UKHL 32.

[35] B. Hepple, M. Coussey, and T. Choudhury, *Equality: A New Framework* (Oxford: Hart Publishing, 2000); see also I. Ayres and J. Braithwaite, *Responsive Regulation: Transcending the Deregulation Debate* (Oxford: Oxford University Press, 1992).

[36] C. McCrudden, 'Equality Legislation and Reflexive Regulation: A Response to the Discrimination Law Review', *Industrial Law Journal*, 36 (2007), 255.

right at the European level at which directives are generally aspirational rather than definitive in content. Although it would still be necessary to find ways in which the right could be incorporated into the national legal systems of the Member States without losing any of its flexibility, it is submitted that, rather than obscuring the legal entitlement of the individual by adding further detail to an already complex system of rights, such an approach would improve legal certainty for employers and employees by making current provisions more accessible and cohesive.

2

Theoretical Perspectives on Work and Care

Introduction

This chapter will identify a suitable theoretical perspective from which to develop the proposal for a right to care. This necessitates the location of a conceptual approach which is capable of recognizing and valuing carers' participation in both the 'public' sphere as paid workers and the 'private' domain of the family, as well as acknowledging and responding to the diverse needs of those for whom they care. As the vast majority of carers are women, any proposed perspective must take full account of the *de facto* gender dimension of the unpaid care/paid employment conflict whilst avoiding the prescriptive classification of care as a 'women's issue'. In order to demonstrate how the proposed right to care is firmly grounded in the liberal tradition, the applicability of established liberal theories of equality and distributive justice will be considered, as will the corresponding conceptualizations of the terms 'equality', 'autonomy', and 'freedom' which are commonly perceived as liberalism's ultimate goals. It is asserted that the specific interpretation of these terms has shifted over the last 30 years, so that their contemporary conceptualization is grounded, not in traditional liberalism, but in a particular strain of neo-liberal economic theory which has come to predominate socio-economic thinking in both academic and policy circles. In seeking to reassert the original and arguably more sustainable conception of liberalism, reference will be made to the work of leading liberal theorists such as Dworkin and Rawls. This analysis is intended to show that the theoretical basis of the proposed right to care is perfectly compatible with liberal ideology as it does, in fact, rely on the central tenets of that tradition. The implication of this on its situation within the pre-existing EU legal order will be considered.

A common thread in the work of the liberal theorists considered is that, despite the undeniable importance of their contributions in the fields of social and economic justice, many have ignored or dismissed the importance of gender in their analyses of human and/or institutional behaviour. This point is further explored through a review of the work of contemporary feminist critiques of established liberal theory from across a broad spectrum of disciplines encompassing political theory, philosophy, and law. This review reveals substantial shortcomings in the established theories of justice which make their application to the current context unsatisfactory. As an alternative, the Capabilities Approach (CA), as expounded by the economist Amartya Sen and philosopher Martha Nussbaum, is considered to determine whether it provides a suitable framework within which to evaluate law and policy aimed at resolving the unpaid care/paid work conflict in order to develop a right to care.

The Place of Gender in the Unpaid Care/Paid Work Equation

The construction of a theoretical framework within which to argue the case for a right to care requires a number of considerations. The particular meanings ascribed to terms such as equality and freedom must be determined to enable their application in the development of practical solutions. It is necessary to consider the treatment of and corresponding status afforded to unpaid care in contemporary theory and to identify how that status has been reached over time. A suitable framework should provide a means of defining and meeting the needs of carers and of those for whom they care within the institutional arrangements surrounding paid employment. As a necessary precondition, it must examine and evaluate the structures which support and sustain those arrangements. Feminist theorists have long argued that the institutions on which liberal society depends[1] are inherently hostile to women generally and to care-givers in particular and these compelling accounts must be carefully incorporated into any intended response to the unpaid care/paid employment conflict.

As set out in Chapter 1, the issue of gender is a key determinant in the development of a full understanding of the dynamics surrounding the care relationship and its current low status within the legal and political institutions which regulate employment arrangements. However, as the following exploration of the emergence of liberal theory demonstrates, women's position within society has not been served particularly well by those concerned with furthering our philosophical understanding of society and its institutions. The Greek school's overemphasis of biological difference as a means of justification for men and women's relative roles within the family has endured in many respects. The early social contract theorists' failure to consider whether the personal freedom that emerged from the new social arrangements of the eighteenth century extended to women has been of central concern to feminist theorists' attempts to put women into the picture ever since.[2] These examples demonstrate the lack of attention that has been paid to women's perspective, particularly within the complex context of the family which, in turn, has led to a denial of the economic and social value of those aspects of life closely associated with womanhood and has resulted in an enduring failure to acknowledge the care relationship as an essential human activity.

[1] See, for example, S. Moller Okin, *Justice, Gender and the Family* (New York: Basic Books, 1989) on the unjust nature of the family and C. Pateman's critique of the social contract and women's position within liberal society in *The Sexual Contract* (Cambridge: Polity Press, 1988).

[2] For example, in the context of political theory, see the work of Pateman and Okin (above) and, in legal theory, S. Fredman, *Women and the Law* (Oxford: Oxford University Press, 1997).

Although the provision of care is by no means an exclusively female pursuit, woman's association with it is inextricably linked to the construction of a female identity. Denial of this association only serves to perpetuate the myth that there is nothing particularly valuable about the care relationship. In order to elevate unpaid care it to its rightful place within the socio-economic order, full recognition should be given to it at all available opportunities. To do so is to acknowledge the valuable contributions of those who for generations have engaged and continue to engage in the hard work of caring. Such recognition, particularly if articulated through the development of a legal right to employment protection on the basis of competing prior interests, has a normative effect so that men will be enabled and encouraged to participate in care-taking. Thus, the cross-disciplinary task of putting women into the picture painted by theorists of social justice inherently involves recognizing and prioritizing central concerns such as dependency and care-taking otherwise missing from standard accounts of liberal society.

The Dichotomization of 'Alternatives'

Theorists have long grappled with the settlement of participation in public life alongside the provision of care within households and the corresponding appropriation of State involvement. In the earliest days of philosophical reasoning, scholars of the Greek school opined that the differences in men's and women's biological states should be reflected in the division of labour within families, with women better suited to the private sphere of the household and men to the public world of work. Aristotle saw the biological differences between the sexes as justification for women's subordination. Woman's physical difference from man was proof of her inferiority as he, by nature, is 'more fitted to rule than the female'.[3] In *The Politics,* he argued that the father should retain absolute authority and power over his family, the form of which should be preserved, with women remaining the 'property' of their husbands alongside other proprietal arrangements.[4] Much of Aristotle's schema originated from a set of assumptions relating to the association of 'form' with the rational mind and reason, and 'matter' with the non-rational: rather the object of rational thought and knowledge. Within this framework, the Greek theorists[5] dichotomized alternatives and this binary method of analysis, although rejected by feminist jurists for its misogyny,[6] nevertheless

[3] *The Nicomachean Ethics*, D. Ross (trans) (Oxford University Press, 1925): *The Politics* Bk 1 xii, 1259a 37.

[4] Ibid.

[5] See also Plato, *The Republic*, R. Waterfield (trans) (Oxford University Press, 1993) in which, although divergent in other respects, there is a similar approach to the dichotimization of form and matter to that taken by Aristotle.

[6] Most notably in the work of Okin, see, for example, *Women in Western Political Thought* (Princeton: Princeton University Press, 1979), Chapter 4; *Justice, Gender and the Family*, n 1 above, 52–60; 'On Plato' in M. L. Shanley and C. Pateman (eds), *Feminist Interpretations and Political Theory* (Cambridge: Polity Press, 1991).

emerges as the foundation on which certain contemporary institutional arrangements are based. Fredman argues that the 'polarisation of alternatives' as a means of explaining the different experiences of men and women, is unhelpful in that 'the dichotomy obscures the possibility of elements of both poles in the same individual'.[7] Likewise, de Beauvoir rightly questions Aristotle's logic thus: '[I]f matter and form must co-operate in all action, there is no necessity for the active and passive principles to be separated in two different categories of individuals.'[8] Furthermore, to focus on women's sameness or difference from men only serves to contribute to the perpetuation of 'man' as the standard against which 'woman' should be judged, so that 'He is the Subject, he is the Absolute—she is the Other.'[9]

In the current context, the most important of Aristotle's dicta is that 'likes should be treated alike',[10] meaning that if two persons have equal status in at least one normatively relevant respect, they must be treated equally in this respect. This principle has been used as a starting point for legal intervention targeted at the attainment of formal equality between different social groups and, in the context of sex discrimination law, its application necessitates the identification of differences and similarities between the sexes. Aside from those related to biology, such differences might better be explained as the products of socially constructed gender norms so that the distinction between sex and gender is a central concern in any analysis of women's experience in the family and in the labour market. The fact of woman's ability to bear children has provided the rationalization for her role as primary carer within the family and that of breadwinner to man. Institutions have been created and further developed in support of this arrangement, so that man's space has become the public and woman's the private. While assisting in a general understanding of the sexually divisive nature of society, this simplistic analysis ignores the fact of women's participation in the public sphere as well as overlooking the actual and potential contribution of men in the private. Although familial arrangements and corresponding gender roles may explain the different positions of men and women within contemporary labour markets, they do not assist in reaching an understanding of why such differences persist nor do they offer a way out of the unpaid care/paid work conflict. Furthermore, if the ascription of women to the private and men to the public spheres is indeed a socially constructed phenomenon, the State's reluctance to intervene in the private arrangements of the family can be seen to have contributed to the continuing subordination of women.[11]

7 Fredman, n 2 above, 4.

8 S. de Beauvoir, *The Second Sex* (trans H. M. Parshley) (New York: Vintage, 1949), 38.

9 Ibid, 16.

10 The 'Aristotelian formula'—Aristotle, *Nicomachean Ethics*, V. 3 1131a10–b15; *The Politics*, III.9.1280 a8–15, III.12. 1282b18–23.

11 See Okin, n 1 above.

A Woman's Place in the Social Contract

The political and economic changes that swept through European society during the seventeenth and eighteenth centuries gave rise to a new political philosophy in which the State's regulation of the public and private spheres was of particular concern.[12] The dissolution of the feudal system and the emergence of capitalism were accompanied by a focus on the concepts of individual autonomy, freedom, and equality before the law. Individuals were no longer the subjects of a preordained hierarchy with their position dependent on whichever level was their birthright, rather, in the words of Locke, 'Men [are] by Nature all free, equal and independent.'[13] In political terms, the notion of 'individual consent'[14] became paramount so that the State retreated in matters involving personal decision-making, its main function being 'to act as a neutral umpire between conflicting interests'.[15] The promise of greater individual freedom did not extend to women who, on the basis of the rationality criterion, were denied full participation in political life. Furthermore, the public–private divide was reinforced through the perceived role of law which determined that the State should not interfere with individual autonomy nor intrude in the private sphere of the family. In the contemporary context, adherence to legal abstentionism is based on the belief that the market is self-regulatory.

The Hobbesian separation of God's law from that of man[16] saw man's subordination to God replaced by an alternative ruler, albeit one granted the power to command through the consent of the governed under the auspices of the sovereign state. In asserting that a contract between the sovereign and his subjects engendered no individual freedom of choice whether to enter the contract, Filmer observed that, rather than being born free, each individual was ascribed a 'preordained subject status'.[17] For man, this took the form of subjection to the Monarch and, for woman, subjection to the Monarch, her father, and her husband. Although Locke rejected most of Filmer's thesis in his *Two Treatises on Government*,[18] he retained his ambivalence towards woman by accepting her naturally inferior social status but arguing that such 'natural disabilities' could be overcome. In Locke's

[12] In the context of rights-based legal instruments, the period from the early seventeenth until the late eighteenth century witnessed landmarks such as the English Petition of Rights (1627), the Habeas Corpus Act (1679), the American Declaration of Independence (1776), the United States Constitution (1787), the American Bill of Rights (1791), and the French Declaration of the Rights of Man and Citizen (1789). These instruments, based on the concepts of individual rights and popular sovereignty, form the basis for the international standards still applied today as encapsulated by modern-day instruments such as the Universal Declaration of Human Rights.

[13] John Locke, *Two Treatises of Government*, P. Laslett (ed) (Cambridge: Cambridge University Press, 1988), 'The Second Treatise', para 95.

[14] Ibid.

[15] Fredman, n 2 above, 6.

[16] T. Hobbes, *The Leviathan* (1651), R. Tuck (ed) (Cambridge: Cambridge University Press, 1991).

[17] Sir R. Filmer, *Patriarcha and Other Writings*, J. P. Sommerville (ed) (Cambridge: Cambridge University Press, 1991).

[18] See n 13 above.

analysis of marital relations, the husband retained overall power through operation of the 'last Determination' which gave him ultimate decision-making on matters pertaining to jointly held properties and interests. This right was based on his 'ability and strength' and a husband's exercise and potential abuse of it separated marital relations from monarchical rule on the basis that the wife had 'in many cases, a Liberty to separate from him; where natural Right or their contract allows it'.[19]

Locke's views on women 'contradict his proclamations of freedom and equality for all' and, his 'apparent rejection of patriarchy'[20] which, made largely in response to Filmer's work in the context of absolute monarchy, related to man's subjection to a Monarch and not men's power over women. Locke's position on women's equality with men, demonstrable through his recognition of a voluntary marriage contract, is obscured by his promotion of the 'last Determination' and his separation of political activity from family life. Although he opposed patriarchy in the political context of civil society on the grounds that subjection to a Monarch was in conflict with the freedom to enter a contract voluntarily, Locke did not apply the same standard of justification to the exercise of power within the family. This separation preserves women's subordinated status within the private sphere and leaves public life and political participation the domain of men.[21] Furthermore, Locke's categorization of 'conjugal society' as a voluntary contract between husband and wife gives it 'a measure of legitimacy on his own terms'.[22]

In the contemporary context, the term 'patriarchy' refers to a form of political power which lies at the heart of the feminist critique of traditional jurisprudence,[23] but the concept itself is both conceptually and analytically complex. As Pateman has noted, despite the resurgence of debates among political theorists regarding the legitimacy and justification of political power, 'the patriarchal form has been largely ignored in the twentieth century'.[24] Pateman questions Locke's acceptance of the marriage contract as a necessary transaction when, in his hypothesis, 'women are declared to be naturally subject to men. There are other ways in which a union between man and his natural subordinate could be established, but, instead, Locke holds that it is brought into being through contract, which is an agreement between two equals.'[25]

Rousseau continued the tradition of biological essentialism in his work which was highly influential over the development of social contract theory during the late seventeenth century. Rousseau posited that the formation of the social contract was the moment of creation of the law and, as such, 'a moment of distinct rationality, in

[19] Locke, n 13 above, 82.
[20] Fredman, n 2 above, 8.
[21] Pateman, n 1 above, 21 and Chapter 4.
[22] Fredman n 2 above, 8.
[23] Ibid.
[24] Pateman, n 1 above, 19. The concept of patriarchy is a recurring theme throughout Pateman's text, but of particular interest in this context are Chapter 2 'Patriarchal Confusions' and Chapter 4 'Genesis, Fathers and the Political Liberty of Sons'.
[25] Pateman, n 1 above, 54.

which nature becomes a society, and human beings become persons, as citizens under law'.[26] The subject of gender was certainly under discussion at this time and was the focus of great deliberation in the work of Rousseau and that of his contemporaries.[27] The replacement of superstition with reason led theorists of the time to question human beings' capacity for rationality over the pull of nature. Rather than questioning the continued subjection of women, however, Rousseau sought to justify it as being based on the division between mind and biology, with women's role determined by the latter:

> The male is male only at certain moments; the female is female her whole life . . . everything constantly recalls her sex to her, and to fulfil its function, an appropriate physical constitution is necessary to her . . . she needs a soft sedentary life to suckle her babies.[28]

Rousseau's view that woman's position in society was determined solely by her physical capability entrenched the notion that women's place was the private sphere of home and family and men's the public sphere of political and economic participation. Such division was justified on the basis that women were less rational and, thus, less suited to public life and were more usefully engaged in the caring and nurturing role better matched to their biological state.[29] Lacey notes that, 'liberal and Enlightenment thinking has been associated with an intensification of feminist analysis'[30] and the work of Wollstonecraft provides clear evidence of this. Writing in response to the views of Rousseau and others, Wollstonecraft drew parallels between the subjection of women and that of slaves, arguing 'if women are by nature inferior to men, their virtues must be the same in quality, if not in degree, or virtue is a relative idea . . . virtue has only one eternal standard'.[31]

The social contract theorists analysed a new way of organizing society's relations by means of a contract between the ruler and the ruled under the auspices of the Sovereign state. From the outset, women were not party to that contract and their absence from the new political order went largely unnoticed. It seems likely that the diminishing influence of patriarchal relations in subsequent considerations of political and social theory is linked to the emergence of what was perceived to be a more egalitarian form of society. That theorists overlooked the continuation of women's subordination is itself illustrative of the dominance of a male perspective in analyses of the new civil society as 'a patriarchal social order'.[32] Furthermore, the patriarchal right or 'sex right' defined as 'the power that men exercise over

[26] S. Baer, 'Citizenship in Europe and the Construction of Gender by Law' in K. Knopp (ed) *Gender and Human Rights* (Oxford: Oxford University Press, 2004), 89.

[27] For example, David Hume and Immanuel Kant.

[28] J.-J. Rousseau, *Emile* (1762) A. Bloom (trans) (Penguin, 1991), 450.

[29] It should be noted that not all Enlightenment writers shared Rousseau's views on women, and stark contrasts can be drawn between his writings and the work of Voltaire and Montesquieu who believed women to be capable of equality with men.

[30] N. Lacey, 'Feminist Legal Theory and the Rights of Women' in Knopp (ed), n 26 above, 14. The most notable feminist writer of the time was Mary Wollstonecraft, whose *Vindication of the Rights of Women* was published in 1792 (Prometheus Books, reprinted 1989).

[31] Wollstonecraft, n 30 above, 108.

[32] Pateman, n 1 above, 1.

women'[33] extends through civil society. Attempts to separate the public and private spheres, so that the former becomes the domain of the 'social contract' and the latter the subject of the 'sexual contract', are misleading as the spheres are both separate and inseparable with an understanding of either dependent on the inter-relationship between the two, so that '[c]ivil freedom depends on patriarchal right'.[34]

Liberalism's Flaw: Concept or Conceptualization?

Pateman's complete rejection of liberalism is tempered by the work of other feminist theorists who stress its potential for individual freedom as being beneficial to women whose access to the advantages it offers is blocked or restricted, not by the inherent nature of liberalism itself, but by the institutions which have developed under the patriarchal enactment of civil society. In her ground-breaking feminist account of distributive justice, Okin[35] opined that the power relations played out within families have been largely overlooked in contemporary analyses and that it is the enduring and unequal distribution of unpaid labour within families that makes women vulnerable.[36] In Okin's view, it is not the liberal ideals of personal autonomy and freedom themselves that are damaging to women but rather the interpretation given to their realization within modern liberal society and how that interpretation is played out within the family and associated institutions that is itself 'deeply and pervasively gender-structured'.[37] Okin's attention is largely focused on providing a critique of Rawls's *A Theory of Justice*[38] which she argues is capable of leading us 'to challenge fundamentally the gender system of our society' which 'in [Rawls's] account of his theory... is barely hinted at, much less developed'.[39]

Rawls's use of the 'original position' to rationalize or explain the quest for equality in the context of political and personal freedoms and cooperative arrangements,[40] is firmly rooted in the liberal tradition and offers a contemporary application of the social contract as a basis for civil society providing guiding principles of justice and accompanying criteria for a 'nearly just society'. In the original position, free and rational beings acting as representatives of real persons are placed behind a 'veil of ignorance' so that they do not know the sex, race, physical disabilities, social class, or 'conception of the good' of the persons they represent, although they are aware that such characteristics exist. The representatives also possess a good knowledge of economic systems and human psychology. The aim of the representatives is to choose principles of justice that are suitable to govern a just and fair social order. 'Since all are similarly situated and no one is able to design principles to

[33] Ibid. [34] Ibid, 4. [35] Okin, n 1 above, see further Chapter 3 below.
[36] Ibid. [37] Ibid, 89.
[38] John Rawls, *A Theory of Justice* (Oxford: Oxford University Press, 1972).
[39] Okin, n 1 above, 89. [40] Rawls, n 38 above.

favour his particular position, the principles of justice are the result of a fair agreement or bargain.'[41] From this artificial stance, stripped of self-knowledge, the representatives must make decisions about which societal rules best cater to all potential members of society, rather than those favouring a particular individual or group interest. Under these conditions, rationality dictates that the best way to optimize the interests of the represented is to rule out discrimination on the basis of any of the possible characteristics in order to prevent any resulting disadvantage.

From their original position, the representatives prioritize individual liberty over equality with each citizen having an equal right to the 'most extensive basic liberty compatible with a similar liberty for others'.[42] Under the 'difference principle', social and economic differences must be equally distributed under conditions of equality of opportunity and should provide the greatest benefit to the least advantaged members of society. This might require the giving of more power, income, or status to some persons provided that certain conditions are met, basically that life will be made better for those who are currently 'worst off' and that access to the positions of privilege are not blocked by discrimination based on irrelevant criteria.

Rawls's theory has attracted criticism on the ground that his promotion of the individual as an atomistic being fails to consider his or her place within the political community. Without her connections to others, the individual has no shared identity, rendering the ascription of group rights impossible.[43] Rawls's denial of the importance of community has particular resonance in the context of unpaid care as its omission from the construction of a theory of justice represents a denial of the intrinsic connection between mother and child and, by extension, between carer and cared for.[44] Moreover, the principles upon which much feminist methodology is predicated require deep consideration of the shared experiences of individuals, so that techniques which take account of connection and interdependency are deemed particularly useful as a means of identifying and articulating women's viewpoints. In short, Rawls's individualistic approach is unhelpful when placed in the wider context of what he is trying to do, that is, to identify principles for community life.

Fredman finds it 'striking' that Rawls does not expressly address women's position in society in *A Theory of Justice*[45] and this apparent lack of concern may be attributable, at least in part, to his methodology, so that the level of abstraction required in the creation of the original position 'proves nothing and clouds our

[41] Ibid, 12.

[42] Ibid, 60. The equal basic liberties (specified at 291) include 'freedom of thought and liberty of conscience; the political liberties and freedom of association, as well as the freedoms specified by the liberty and integrity of the person; and finally, the rights and liberties covered by the rule of law'.

[43] See M. Sandel, *Liberalism and the Limits of Justice* (Cambridge: Cambridge University Press, 1982), A. MacIntyre, *After Virtue: A Study in Moral Theory* (London: Duckworth, 1984).

[44] See D. Cornell, 'Beyond Tragedy and Complacency', *Northwestern University Law Review*, 81 (1987), 693; 'The Doubly Prized World: Myth, Allegory and the Feminine', *Cornell Law Review*, 75 (1990), 644.

[45] Fredman, n 2 above, 23.

vision'[46] or creates a 'logical abstraction of such rigour that nothing happens here'.[47] Rather than enabling identification of the principles of justice required to create a fair society, the level of ignorance required by Rawls's original position makes any understanding of the influences on each individual's perspective impossible. The needs of the individual members of disadvantaged groups can only be met by their inclusion in the decision-making process[48] so that adequate account can be taken of the experiences that have made them who they are. However, the exclusion of gender analysis from Rawls's principles of justice cannot be attributed to his choice of methodology alone. His subsequent consideration of other social, economic, and political institutions[49] makes the fact that he omits to apply his theory to the family unsatisfactory, and shows that he is 'trapped into the traditional mode of thinking that life within the family and relations between the sexes are not properly to be regarded as part of the subject matter of a theory of social justice'.[50] The sharing of care within the family is key to the distribution of justice between men and women within individual relationships and also in the context of the wider society. If men shared equally in the provision of care, the impact would be felt in the workplace where women *and* men would require periods of care-related leave and flexible working arrangements. Eradication of the relevance of gender from the care equation would expose children to a process of socialization that encompasses the principles of justice and it is in this context that Rawls's theory has much to offer through its elimination of individual characteristics in the ascription of tasks which are distributed justly rather than on the basis of individuals' perceived suitability. This is a particularly useful device in the deconstruction of concepts such as gender, as it enables preconceptions to be stripped away.

Notwithstanding its shortcomings in the present context, much can be deduced from Rawls's theory about the nature of justice in abstraction, primarily that, subject to modifications,[51] his particular conception of liberalism is compatible with the achievement of 'justice between the sexes, within the family and in society at large'.[52] Indeed, there is much comfort for those committed to the attainment of such a goal in Rawls's ultimate conclusion that distributive justice works to ensure

[46] M. Matsuda, 'Liberal Jurisprudence and Abstracted Visions of Human Nature: a Feminist Critique of Rawls' Theory of Justice', *New Mexico Law Review*, 16 (1986), 613, 624.

[47] Pateman, n 1 above, 43.

[48] N. Lacey, 'Theories of Justice and the Welfare State', *Social and Legal Studies*, Vol 1 (1992), 323, 338.

[49] J. Rawls, *Political Liberalism* (New York: Columbia University Press, 1996), 11.

[50] Okin, n 1 above, 184.

[51] Such as those proposed by Okin who identifies Rawls's failure to apply the principles of justice to 'the realms of human nurturance' as the central flaw in his work but nevertheless contends that 'the feminist potential of Rawls's method of thinking and his conclusions is considerable', Okin, n 1 above, 108 and M. Nussbaum on the modification of the primary goods to take account purely of the basic capabilities in 'The Future of Feminist Liberalism' in E. Feder Kittay and E. Feder, *The Subject of Care: Feminist Perspectives on Dependency* (New York: Rowan and Littlefield, 2002), 186, 192.

[52] Okin, n 1 above, 109.

equal outcomes. The transference of this contemporary liberal perspective into a suitable legal and policy framework with identifiable outcomes requires an articulation of the specific terminology commonly used as a means of confronting existing inequalities. Due consideration must be paid to the conceptions of difference and sameness in an attempt to explain the nature and causes of inequality in order that the appropriate standard of equality might be identified and promoted as a desirable goal.

Putting Distributive Justice into a Rights Framework

The need for equality between different societal groups has long been acknowledged. In 1867 Mill made his first parliamentary speech in favour of votes for women and continued to call for legal recognition of equality between the sexes in his writing.[53] Mill's call was not new—the concepts of 'Liberté, egalité, fraternité' had served as the ideals of the body politic ever since the French Revolution. However, the concept of equality is contested[54] and the term 'equal' can be both descriptive and/or prescriptive depending on the context in which it is used.[55] For example, although society may accept, fundamentally, that individual members are equal, it must also recognize that certain social processes and practices lead to inequalities between individuals that might be remedied through the application of normative rules. Resources may be distributed unevenly so that some are in receipt of greater quantities and prosper at the expense of others. One way of attempting to rectify such inequality is through the use of legal intervention aimed at ensuring equal distribution. In attempting to implant the concept of equality into a legal system, the key issues become identification of the persons or processes to whom the concept might be applied and the areas and degrees of similarity which provide a basis for application of the equality principle. In the current context, legal intervention intended to provide an adequate response to the unpaid care/paid employment conflict can be manifested as a right, based on our shared humanity, to the equal distribution of resources on the basis of an individual's contribution in labour market terms and in respect of the unpaid provision of care.

[53] J. S. Mill, *The Subjection of Women* (London: Longman, 1869) in which he wrote: 'I am convinced that social arrangements which subordinate one sex to the other by law are bad in themselves and form one of the principle obstacles which oppose human progress; I am convinced that they should give way to perfect equality.' For considerations of Mill's contributions to the application of liberalism to the feminist cause, see M. Nussbaum, *Sex and Social Justice* (New York: Oxford University Press, 1999), 64–5 and Okin (1979), n 6 above, 282.

[54] As Dworkin has noted, 'People who praise it or disparage it disagree about what they are praising or disparaging.' R. Dworkin, *Sovereign Virtue: The Theory and Practice of Equality* (Cambridge MA: Harvard University Press, 2000), 2.

[55] F. Oppenheim, 'Egalitarianism as a Descriptive Concept' in L. Pojman and R. Westmoreland (eds), *Equality: Selected Readings* (Oxford: Oxford University Press, 1997), 55–65.

Equal Treatment or Treatment as an Equal?

The equal treatment model is based on the Aristotelian formula that 'likes should be treated alike' and, thus, bestows the same treatment on individuals regardless of individual circumstances or group membership. Although falling somewhat short of the complete disregard for biological or socially constructed differences expounded by the assimilationist ideal,[56] equal treatment nonetheless explicitly disregards such differences in favour of the application of the 'merit principle'. This assumes that, given equal access to the same opportunities, individuals will achieve success through personal effort enabling benefits to be distributed according to merit. The problem with this approach is that it fails to take into account the effects of historical and continuing disadvantage by presupposing that all players have an equal starting point. The continuing unequal provision of unpaid care mean that, in the case of women and men, this is simply not true and their different starting points, as already established, have arisen, in part, due to predominant political ideologies that have determined individual and group experiences. Although the members of both sexes are ostensibly recognized as being sufficiently alike so as to be accorded equality, this has not always been the case. Women were expressly excluded from full political participation until relatively recently on the basis that they lacked the requisite level of rationality. The legacy of this exclusion continues through contemporary arrangements, such as the division of labour within families and employment-based discrimination and supporting institutional and social norms. As decades of legislation aimed at the prohibition of discrimination have proved, the conferment of formal equality has not eradicated the effects of historical, legally sanctioned inequality. Although the impact of law is limited in this respect, if its normative effects are considered greater progress might have been expected. Furthermore, even those aspects of inequality which appear, *prima facie*, to be appropriate targets for legislative intervention have been slow to change as the approach applied continually misses the target—the most obvious example being the persistence of gendered pay gaps. Ronald Dworkin's rights-based approach offers a response to the dilemma posed by the need to formulate a legal response capable of bestowing substantive equality on the one hand, whilst preserving the traditional liberal values associated with individualism and freedom of choice on the other.

Like Rawls, Dworkin can be categorized as a 'modified liberal'[57] as his work, which seeks the attainment of equality as an individual right and endorses the use of the market as a suitable means of distributing resources, recognizes the role of the State in securing that right. A central tenet of Dworkin's thesis is the distinction

[56] See Wollstonecraft, n 30 above, 21 and, in the context of the US race debate, R. Wasserstrom, 'Racism, Sexism and Preferential Treatment: an Approach to the Topics', *University of California Los Angeles Law Review*, 24 (1977), 581.

[57] See also the work of Joseph Raz, specifically *The Morality of Freedom* (Oxford: Clarendon Press, 1986).

between the right to equal treatment and the right to treatment as an equal.[58] The first entails the equal distribution of opportunities, resources, and burdens and the second is the right 'to be treated with the same respect and concern as anyone else'.[59] In recognizing the differing needs of individuals, the appropriate treatment may vary to enable all individuals to be treated as equals—this is fundamental whereas the right to equal treatment is derivative. As Dworkin notes, 'In some circumstances, the right to treatment as an equal will entail a right to equal treatment, but not, by any means in all circumstances.'[60] This is essentially a pluralist argument that recognizes and accommodates difference and which goes some way towards countering the difficulties inherent in the application of the 'equal treatment' approach in the context of the gendered conflict between unpaid care and paid work. Although 'Dworkin's theory can be categorised as individualistic to the extent that it is each individual's conception of the good that matters',[61] he argues that it is possible for individual conceptions of the good to involve work for the community.[62]

Dworkin's approach enables consideration of the relative positions of the targets of equality to be considered in the formulation of political responses and even endorses reverse discrimination or preferential treatment in certain circumstances. This builds on the conceptualization of interests as rights and is grounded in the utilitarian ideal,[63] the achievement of which, Dworkin argues, gives claims of rights a special force that will always trump policy considerations and even general utility on the grounds that resources should always be targeted at those who need them most. Explicit in Dworkin's theory is a core belief that 'conceptions of legal rights are irreducibly connected to wider precepts of political morality'.[64] As his focus on law as a moral-based construct illustrates, Dworkin's analysis is grounded in an attachment to the natural law school of thought and a rejection of legal positivism.[65] The latter's dependence on rules based on purely human phenomena as the determinants of law and legal systems cannot be reconciled with Dworkin's belief in the fundamental importance of principles which represent '. . . a standard that is to be observed, not because it will advance or secure an economic, political, or social

[58] R. Dworkin, *Taking Rights Seriously* (London: Duckworth, 1978), 227.
[59] Ibid.
[60] Ibid.
[61] Fredman, n 2 above, 19.
[62] R. Dworkin, 'Liberalism' in *A Matter of Principle* (Oxford: Clarendon Press, 1985), 203.
[63] Under a strict utilitarian approach, the concept of equality is of paramount concern in attainment of Bentham's ideal that 'each is to count for one, no-one more than one'. On this basis, the interests of all should be treated equally regardless of the nature of those interests or the individual situations out of which they arise, the overall goal being the maximization of human happiness. In the context of group or social activity, the morally correct action is the one that maximizes utility. See further, R. M. Hare, *Moral Thinking: Its Levels, Method and Point* (Oxford: Oxford University Press, 1981).
[64] Lacey, n 30 above, 20.
[65] See Dworkin, *Taking Rights Seriously,* n 58 above, in which Dworkin takes positivism in general, and H. L. A. Hart's theory in particular, to task on the basis that it is rights, underpinned by principles, and not judicial discretion which determine the outcome of difficult cases. Dworkin cannot be categorized as a strict follower of the natural law school as he has formulated his own theory which, while founded in natural law, encompasses a wider range of concepts.

situation deemed desirable, but because it is a requirement of justice or fairness or some other dimension of morality'.[66]

Dworkin views the market as a useful means of distributing resources and endorses State intervention as long as such interference in the market is predicated on an obligation to treat all individuals as being entitled to equal concern and respect. Intervention by the State is, therefore, justified in order to prevent discrimination and to ensure fair distribution of available resources. Dworkin hypothesizes that the equal distribution of resources involves an auction in which everyone can accumulate bundles of resources through equal means of payment with the value of the resources devoted to a person's life being measured by the importance of those resources to others.[67] Once the auction is complete, free market distribution depends on an individual's ambition, with post-auction inequalities attributable to personal responsibility on the basis of 'option luck'. Where unjustified inequalities arise, these should be countered by way of a differentiated insurance system.

Dworkin's form of modified liberalism with its acceptance of a tolerant State, respectful of individual difference yet proactively engaged in protecting against discrimination on moral grounds, has much to commend it as an appropriate theoretical basis for legal intervention aimed at countering inequality and, on the face of it, as a means of responding to the unpaid care/paid work conflict. Indeed his observations on the appropriate legal response to racial discrimination have been widely influential and provide a compelling justification for the use of affirmative action in certain circumstances.[68] However, his theories have not found such wide acceptance in their application in the context of gender, due largely to his unsatisfactory treatment of the family and familial relations. As Fredman has noted, 'his notions of rationality, autonomy and individualism fail to recognise, and therefore to value, relations of dependence and care, the paradigm example being that of mother and child'.[69] This lack of recognition, which stems from Dworkin's acceptance of the individual's conception of the good life as the central value attracting State protection, 'simply fails to capture a relationship whereby one person's activities are dictated by another's needs for care, particularly if the dependent could not otherwise survive'.[70] Dworkin's lack of appreciation for the existence of altruism in certain contexts[71] is symptomatic of deeper flaws in his analyses of community in general and the family in particular. The very framework within which his consideration of the family takes place is, in itself, questionable. His use of terminology is inappropriate—he consistently refers to familial

[66] Ibid, 22.
[67] Dworkin, 'What is Equality? Part II: Equality of Resources', *Philosophy and Public Affairs*, 10 (1981) 283–345, 290 (reprinted in *Sovereign Virtues. The Theory and Practice of Equality* (Cambridge MA: Harvard University Press, 2000), 65–119).
[68] See 'Reverse Discrimination' in *Taking Rights Seriously*, n 58 above.
[69] Fredman, n 2 above, 20.
[70] Ibid.
[71] Whether such altruism is exercised through choice or not—see R. Dworkin, *Law's Empire* (London: Fontana Press, 1986), 437, n 20 in which he remarks that becoming a parent is matter of 'choice' which, of course is not always the case.

obligations as 'fraternal',[72] his exposition of group obligations as always reciprocal[73] is undoubtedly flawed, and his consideration of specific family relationships reveals a particularly worrying dynamic.[74]

In common with many of the most celebrated political and social theorists, Dworkin neglects to specifically account for the life experiences of women in his consideration of the 'general politics of integrity, community, and fraternity'.[75] This omission resonates through his work which, after all, claims to 'identify and distinguish the diverse and often competitive dimensions of political value'[76] indicating that his 'grand theory' of equality does not offer a suitable theoretical framework within which to address the unpaid care/paid work conflict which, by its very nature, requires the incorporation of the causes and effects of family relations and their placement in the wider society.

Liberalism and the Feminist Challenge: Charting a Way Forward

As the preceding consideration of prominent social theory has demonstrated, Dworkin is not alone in his neglect of the family and, in particular, the position of women within it. The Greek philosophers and early social contract theorists favoured an essentialist approach attributing women's position in the family to their biological function which, although particularly ill suited to contemporary studies of society, at least offered some explanation for gender difference which is largely absent from twentieth-century expositions of the principles of justice and equality. Furthermore, in the current context, Rawls's and Dworkin's focus on the distribution of commodities[77] is difficult to reconcile with the provision of personal care which, in many respects, is non-commodifiable.[78] Although by no means a uniquely female preserve, the care relationship has rightly been accorded special significance in considerations of woman's contribution to society and this dimension is lacking in the work of Rawls and Dworkin. It is, therefore, no wonder that a body of theory has emerged specifically in defence of women's perspective in analyses of social, political, and economic life. Collectively 'feminist theory'

[72] Ibid, 198.

[73] For example, see ibid, 196.

[74] For example, in *Law's Empire* in his analysis of the concept of integrity which infers that 'each citizen must accept demands on him' and may 'make demands of others' (at 89), he uses the example of 'the dutiful daughter' asking if she has 'an obligation to defer to her father's wishes in cultures that give parents powers to choose spouses for their daughters but not sons?' (at 204) observing that, if she marries against her father's wishes she 'has something to regret. She owes him at least an accounting and perhaps an apology, and should in other ways strive to continue her standing as a member of the community she otherwise has a duty to honour' (at 205). This overlooks the daughter's right to freedom and autonomy and has been attributed to his implicit acceptance of the 'oppression of women masquerading as honour', see A. C. Hutchinson, 'The Law Emperor?' in *Reading Dworkin Critically* (Oxford: Berg, 1992), 63.

[75] Preface to *Law's Empire*, n 71 above, at vii.

[76] Ibid, viii.

[77] 'Primary goods' in Rawls's analysis and the 'equality of resources' advocated by Dworkin.

[78] See further Chapter 3.

encompasses a range of ideas so diverse that the use of a common term perhaps obscures more differences than the similarities its use purports to unite. However, central to all of these ideas is a commitment to include the hitherto excluded voices of women in accounts and explanations of the past with a view to advocating suitable political and legal reform for the future.

Whilst recognizing the important contributions of those from across the broad spectrum of liberal, socialist, radical, and difference feminism,[79] the focus of this book on the use and development of a liberal rights framework, means that particular emphasis must be placed on those feminist theorists whose work can be accommodated within the liberal tradition.[80] This is not to say that such writers have not had occasion to question that tradition's suitability to the furtherance of the feminist cause of recognizing, incorporating, and promoting women's voices in the advocacy of legal and policy reform. As the preceding discussion demonstrates, despite an underlying compatibility between the means of liberalism and the ends of reconciling the demands of unpaid care and paid employment, there is still much to be done in this respect. One of the central endeavours of this book is to contribute towards that task and, as the remaining Chapters argue, it is certainly achievable within the confines of the existing framework.

In returning to the central aim of this Chapter, there is much in the work of the liberal theorists discussed here that can be utilized in the identification of a suitable theoretical perspective from which a right to care might be positioned *as long as* such theory is viewed through a feminist lens. The work of some of the most prominent liberal feminist theorists has been referred to throughout as a means of critiquing the theories under review and further references will be made to their contributions and those of others throughout the remainder of the book. Drawing on those critiques it is possible to summarize the requirements of a theoretical perspective from which to develop a right to care that can be accommodated within European employment law in the following terms:

- It must sit comfortably within the confines of the liberal tradition and view autonomy, freedom, and equality in their broadest applications[81] as desirable goals.
- It must be 'conceptually flexible' to enable the accommodation of human diversity and all related activities.

[79] Although, as Lacey has observed (n 30 above, 20–5), the liberal and socialist schools amount to specific applications of existing political philosophies to women rather than autonomous and distinctive theories in their own right. Furthermore, it should be noted that the classifications represent models, rather than self-inclusive theories, with the work of many theorists falling between several of the categories.

[80] For examples, see the work of early feminist theorists such as Mill and Wollstonecraft. The work of liberal theorists such as Ronald Dworkin can also be aligned with this perspective insofar as it can be described as 'feminist'. Dworkin's equality theory, discussed *infra*, is distinct from the 'equal opportunities' approach generally identified with liberal feminism as it recognizes and endorses the use of reverse discrimination as necessary for achievement of the individual right to treatment as an equal.

[81] So as to enable their application to those who are cared for as well as to those who are the providers of care.

- It must be 'people-centred' in that its regulatory function must be responsive to the needs of individuals.
- It must be 'feminist' in that it must explicitly consider and take account of women's experience, whether it is the same or different from men's, and seek to eliminate unnecessary differences wherever possible.[82]

With these criteria in mind, I will now give detailed consideration to the capabilities approach (CA), starting with its application by Martha Nussbaum in her quest to reconcile traditional liberal doctrine with feminist theory.

Using the Capabilities Approach to Construct a Right to Care

Nussbaum has considered the applicability of liberalism to gender relations and feminism's response at length.[83] In her analysis, Rawls's conceptualization is flawed due to his adherence to the 'Kantian split', which distinguishes between human dignity and moral capacity (dignity's source) on the one hand and the natural world on the other, which encourages us to 'slight aspects of our lives that have worth'[84] and makes us think of the core of ourselves as self-sufficient. This distinction, which presumes that we are autonomous beings at all stages of our lives, ignores the effects of old age, disease, and accident and takes no account of the variations in levels of dependency over the life-cycle. The resulting dichotomization denies the animalism that is a central feature of the human condition and which is so apparent in relationships of dependency in which we all engage at either end of and, for those with profound disabilities, throughout the life-cycle.

Although Rawls acknowledges the need to care for dependants and builds this into the foundations of social contract theory, he vastly underestimates the level of dependency that might arise in certain situations and places reliance on reciprocity in this context, thus assuming that all contracting parties are competent adults. His analysis proceeds on the basis that 'all citizens are fully cooperating members of society over the course of a complete life'[85] and, although he recognizes that care for those who do not fit these criteria is a 'pressing practical question', he contends that if social justice can be negotiated between 'those who are full and active and morally conscientious participants in society' it can, perhaps, be extended 'to other cases

[82] As O'Donovan states, liberal feminism is 'committed to creating similarities between women and men where possible and to eliminating the differences between them', K. O'Donovan, *Sexual Divisions in Law* (London: Weidenfeld and Nicolson, 1985), 35. Pursuance of this strategy will 'lead to assimilation of women to men in the public world', the downside being a corresponding potential for 'denial of needs and responsibilities in the private'. What the proposals contained in this book aim to do is to assimilate men to women in the private sphere of the family.

[83] See, *inter alia*, Nussbaum, n 53 above, particularly Chapter 2; and in Feder Kittay and Feder (eds), n 51 above, 186–214.

[84] Nussbaum, n 51 above, 189.

[85] J. Rawls, The Dewey Lectures, 'Kantian Constructivism in Moral Theory', *The Journal of Philosophy*, 77 (1980), 515–71, 546.

later'.[86] Nussbaum contends that this approach is inadequate as it belittles the real urgency of care and underestimates the effects of dependency on the distribution of resources.[87] In order for his account of social justice to encompass all members of society regardless of levels of autonomy and independence, Rawls 'will need to find a way of measuring well-being that does not rely on income and wealth alone, but looks at the abilities of citizens to engage in a wide range of human activities'.[88]

The conception of liberalism adopted by Rawls fails to deal adequately with the issue of dependency on two crucial grounds. First, he omits to include those who give and receive care. In doing so, he replicates the approach of earlier social contract theorists by overlooking the contribution of women through their role as the main providers of care and thus excluding their participation in liberal society as well as denying the dependency which we all experience at various stages over the life-cycle. Second, his overemphasis of income and wealth as indicators of success and attainment of 'the good' inspires a particular interpretation of liberalism which neglects to take account of other less material rewards that may, nevertheless, be highly valued and of great mutual benefit to those engaged in care relationships.[89] In current economic policy, this conception of liberalism conforms to the features of what might better be characterized as 'neo-liberalism' based on the operation of the free market so that the two are mistakenly perceived as being identical in all material respects. This distinction and the impact of an overemphasis of the latter formulation of liberalism will be considered in detail in Chapter 4, in the specific context of labour market regulation.

In Nussbaum's view, social contract theory is unable to provide a full account of morality necessary 'to cope with the facts of extreme dependency'.[90] In order to give care and dependency sufficient prominence, we need to seek a full ethical theory without which any theory of justice is incomplete. Other theorists have suggested ways in which Rawls's work might be modified to incorporate this crucial aspect. Kittay[91] suggests that the need for care during periods of extreme and asymmetrical dependency could be added to the list of primary goods as it comprises one of the basic needs of citizens but this would place it in the same class as the commodities of which the list is comprised which, as noted, is conceptually problematic as, unlike wealth and income, it cannot be measured by the amount of it which citizens have. This draws attention to the fact that Rawls's list of primary goods is heterogeneous as it encompasses tangible items such as wealth and income as well as human capabilities to function in various ways such as freedom, power, and self-respect. Nussbaum contends that the entire list of primary goods might be more usefully comprised of basic capabilities which

[86] Ibid. [87] Nussbaum, n 53 above, 190. [88] Ibid, 191.

[89] See further Chapter 3.

[90] Nussbaum, n 53 above, 191, see T. Scanlon, *What We Owe to Each Other* (Cambridge: Harvard University Press, 1999) from whom Nussbaum takes this point.

[91] E. Feder Kittay, *Love's Labor, Essays on Women, Equality and Dependency* (New York: Routledge, 1999), 102–3.

would enable us to 'deal better with people's needs for various types of love and care'.[92]

This method of measuring the well-being of citizens, not by wealth and income, but by the degree to which they possess capabilities is the 'capabilities approach' (CA) expounded by Amartya Sen,[93] although Sen's formulation differs from Nussbaum's as, *inter alia*, he desists from providing an actual list of capabilities.[94] This approach has much to commend it in the current context, not least through its challenge to the paid work/unpaid care conflict by the recognition that 'one may be well-off in terms of income and wealth and yet unable to function well in the workplace, because of burdens of care-giving at home'[95] or, conversely, poorly paid at work due to an association (in either personal or professional terms or both) with care-giving and thus vulnerable in market terms but, nevertheless, in receipt of valuable contributions to personal well-being such as the love of those for whom the care is provided. Nussbaum posits that the requisite political concept of the person which recognizes both our need and capability lies outside of the contract. This is because the value attributed to care through the contract approach, even in its modified form, is related to our own independence so that our ultimate aim is to return as soon as possible to a state of autonomy.[96] Furthermore, in securing a capability to a citizen it is not enough to create a sphere of non-interference as, rather than relying on the interdependent but private relations between the parties to a contract, the public conception must provide an institutional environment which is capable of affording the 'requisite affirmative support for all the relevant capabilities'.[97]

This position, although ostensibly logical in the context of an unregulated market,[98] is disputable on the grounds that the contract approach, if modified by regulatory means, can be modelled in a way which provides a satisfactory formulation of human relations by incorporating dependency and care. In fact, when applied to the unpaid care/paid work conflict, there is no alternative *but* its incorporation into the contractual nexus due to the reliance of the regulation of

[92] Nussbaum, n 53 above, at 192 and also *Women and Human Development: The Capabilities Approach* (Cambridge: Cambridge University Press, 2000), at Chapter 1 in which she proposes an actual list of the central capabilities analogous to primary goods—see Chapter 7.

[93] See, *inter alia*, 'Personal Utilities and Public Judgments: Or What's Wrong with Welfare Economics?', *The Economic Journal*, 89 (1979), 537; *Rights and Capabilities in Resources, Values and Development* (Cambridge MA: Harvard University Press, 1984); *Commodities and Capabilities* (New Delhi: Oxford University Press, 1987); 'Well-being, Agency and Freedom', *The Journal of Philosophy*, LXXXII/4 (1987), 169; 'The Standard of Living' in *The Standard of Living*, G. Hawthorn (ed) (Cambridge: Cambridge University Press, 1987); 'Gender and Co-operative Conflicts' in *Persistent Inequalities*, I. Tinker (ed) (Oxford: Oxford University Press, 1990); *Inequality Re-examined* (Oxford: Clarendon Press, 1992); 'Capability and Well-being' in *The Quality of Life*, A. Nussbaum and A. Sen (eds) (Oxford: Clarendon Press, 1993); *Development as Freedom* (New York: Knopf, 1999); J. Dréze and A. Sen, *India: Development and Participation* (Oxford: Oxford University Press, 2002); *The Idea of Justice* (London: Allen Lane, 2009).

[94] See Chapter 7.

[95] Nussbaum, n 53 above, 192.

[96] Ibid, 193.

[97] Ibid, 195.

[98] Nussbaum's consideration takes place in the context of the US regulatory model.

paid work on that very mechanism. Not to incorporate the unpaid care aspect of the equation as part of the contractual relationship is to replicate the steps that have led to that conflict in the first place, resulting in the market-based conception of autonomous adulthood which dominates perceptions of what constitutes 'work'. Within this particular conception, those who seek, through choice or necessity, to combine unpaid care with paid work are classified as 'atypical' and, in effect, face punitive measures due to their inability to conform to the standard worker 'norm'.[99] In the legal conception of the contractual nexus,[100] the recognition of inequality between contracting parties has long served as justification for State intervention by which the parties' positions might be brought closer together in certain respects. In no other context is this more relevant than that of the employment contract by which such means are provided through the allocation of rights, for example, in terms of bargaining power or to respond to the market's inability to recognize and correct anomalies that arise due to irrational prejudices or discrimination on the grounds of specific personal characteristics such as race, sex, and disability.[101] As the remaining Chapters of this book will demonstrate, there is certainly scope for using the market-based conception of contract as a means of rationalizing the provision of social rights to redress imbalances in the relative positions of contracting parties within a capabilities framework, although it is worth stressing that the advocacy of a rights-based approach does not preclude other forms of State intervention which may also be necessary.[102]

The weakness of liberalism in the current context, it is submitted, lies not in its adherence to the contract approach but rather in the particular conceptions that have been conferred on such terms as equality, freedom, and autonomy which are, in fact, perfectly attainable according to each individual's capabilities through a modified bargaining process. This is not to say that what is proposed would require no further amendment to the social contract framework. On the contrary, it would necessitate a fundamental repositioning of the contract with greater emphasis placed on State intervention as we move from a public ethic of care to the provision of a legally recognized right to care. However, rather than engendering a radical overhaul of the current space within which employment relations are played out, what is envisaged requires a re-evaluation of the basic tenets of liberalism which, once reinterpreted to facilitate expression of their true values, would enable their relational and relative worth to be recognized. This reformulation of the contract approach is completely attuned to the notion that '[t]he liberal ideas of freedom and of the human need for various types of liberty of action are precious ideas that

[99] See Chapters 3 and 4.

[100] Which, admittedly, may vary from the broader philosophical conception, but is surely the one that really matters in the context of translating theoretical concepts into strategies which improve people's lives.

[101] Also included in the current formulation of legally protected characteristics are: sexual orientation, age, and religion or belief. This list could be extended considerably to include, *inter alia*, socio-economic background and carer status.

[102] Such as the provision of affordable good quality formal care and an accessible system of welfare support.

feminist philosophers... should cherish and further develop, creating theories that makes it possible for all citizens to have the support they need for the full development of their human capabilities'.[103]

Use of the CA as an Evaluative Framework

Although Nussbaum's work has been crucial in exploring the CA's utilization as a means of effecting gender equality, the approach as expounded in the work of both Nussbaum[104] and its main proponent Amartya Sen[105] actually provides a much broader normative framework for evaluating individual well-being and social arrangements.[106] In contrast to the utilitarian perspective and its emphasis on the relative position of an individual's mental state along the scale of human happiness, the CA focuses on what people are effectively able to do and to be, that is, on their capabilities, by achievement of a range of 'beings' and 'doings'. Sen refers to these 'beings' and 'doings' as individual 'functionings' and, once realized, they are referred to as 'achieved fuctionings' which together constitute what makes a life valuable. Although closely related, functionings and capabilities should be distinguished as, '[a] functioning is an achievement, whereas a capability is the ability to achieve'.[107] The difference between achieved functionings and capabilities, thus, lies in the distinction between what is realized and what is effectively possible, in other words, capabilities are analogous to freedom. It is society's collective responsibility to strive to ensure that each individual has the freedom (capability) to live the kind of life she wants to live, to do what she wants to do, and to be the person she wants to be. The approach is not prescriptive about how our lives should be led as, once an individual has the requisite capability, she is free to choose whether to exercise it or not.

A central feature of Sen's CA is its classification as an evaluative framework which can be used for a wide range of activities.[108] This distinguishes it from the more specified theories of, for example, Rawls and Dworkin discussed above. Sen asserts that, although its use can contribute to a theory of justice, it is incomplete in this respect as it does not specify an aggregative principle but focuses on distributive considerations by providing an 'evaluative space' within which judgements about

[103] Nussbaum, n 53 above, 196.

[104] See notes 51 and 53 above and 'Human Functioning and Social Justice: In Defense of Aristotelian Essentialism', *Political Theory*, 20/2 (1992), 202; 'Human Capabilities, Female Human Beings' in *Women, Culture and Development*, M. Nussbaum and J. Glover (eds) (Oxford: Clarendon Press, 1995); *Women and Human Development: The Capabilities Approach*, n 92 above; 'Capabilities and Social Justice', *International Studies Review*, 4/2 (2002), 123; 'Capabilities as Fundamental Entitlements: Sen and Social Justice', *Feminist Economics*, 9/3 (2003), 33.

[105] See n 93 above.

[106] Sen's approach which has been used in both empirical and theoretical studies, has made significant contributions to, *inter alia*, the human development paradigm, see S. Fukuda Parr and A. K. Shiva Kumar, *Readings in Human Development* (Delhi: Oxford University Press, 2003) and Dréze and Sen, n 93 above.

[107] *Commodities and Capabilities*, n 93 above, 36.

[108] 'Capability and Well-being', n 93 above.

individual well-being and social policies can be made. In using the CA to evaluate social arrangements and to influence policy design, the focus should be on what individuals are able to do and be and on the overall quality of their lives. Obstacles which prevent individuals from having the requisite freedom to live the kind of life they would choose should be removed where possible, as:

> The capability approach to a person's advantage is concerned with evaluating it in terms of his or her actual ability to achieve various valuable functionings as a part of living. The corresponding approach to social advantage—for aggregative appraisal as well as for the choice of institutions and policy—takes the set of individual capabilities as constituting an indispensible and central part of the relevant informational base of such evaluation.[109]

By concentrating on the potential achievements of individuals, the CA transcends the debate and lack of consensus on which specific factors, such as income and wealth or the 'fair' distribution of goods via the market, should be used as indicators of equality or inequality.[110] This enables recognition and subsequent valuing of different and diverse factors (functionings) which may be intrinsically important to the individual's well-being, yet non-commodifiable as market-based resources. The CA's potentially broad application, thus, gives it a particular appeal in the current context as it enables account to be taken of personal characteristics as well of as social institutions and arrangements which might, for various reasons, present barriers to the achievement of an individual's potential, whilst recognizing that the market alone may not always provide a viable solution to personal conflict which might arise in reconciling the degree of individual autonomy provided by participation in paid employment with the need to provide unpaid care for another. In the specific context of the unpaid care/paid employment conflict this enables full consideration to be given to the effects of gender as well as to other relevant factors such as class, race, and disability either at their intersections or as self-standing aspects of an individual's identity. Its non-prescriptive nature also enables the inclusion of male carers in considerations of work and family reconciliation and places emphasis on identifying and meeting the individual needs of those requiring care.

Conclusion

On the face of it, the CA has much to commend its use as a theoretical framework within which a right to care might be developed. It certainly complies with the qualifying criteria set out above in that it is undeniably a liberal theory which recognizes and values the principles of autonomy, freedom, and equality and, in giving full recognition to each individual's right to freedom, it also has the requisite conceptual flexibility as its central tenet is the accommodation of human diversity. Thus, the approach also places the needs of individuals at its centre, particularly in

[109] Ibid, 30.

[110] Whilst acknowledging that such indicators may be part of the information necessary to make such evaluation.

Sen's incarnation, by enabling and encouraging involvement in the selection of the very tools required for policy appraisal and design. Finally, by rejecting the use of either a single factor or a narrow set of indicators for the purposes of measuring success, the CA avoids the potential traps of both the utilitarian focus on mental state and the Rawlsian emphasis on income and wealth. This enables consideration and inclusion of a broader set of capabilities than those associated with neo-liberal conceptions of the good life and expands its potential use to enable considerations of an individual's well-being in terms of her physical and mental states and within the 'private' as well as the 'public' domain. This means that it can be used to evaluate the full range of human activities including those intrinsic to both parties to the care relationship—carer and cared for. This gives it limitless potential as an evaluative framework able to take full account of women's experiences, whether the same or different from men's, and capable of eliminating unnecessary differences. In the next Chapter the two sides of the unpaid care/paid work conflict will be considered in order to explore how they might be reconciled by the use of regulatory means.

3

Paid Work and Unpaid Care: The Unsolved Conflict

Introduction

The aim of this Chapter is to explore what has been termed the 'unsolved conflict' between paid work and unpaid care.[1] Given women's contributions to both paid and unpaid labour, the contextualization of this conflict involves consideration of the gendered organization of paid work within labour markets as well as of the unregulated division of labour within families. If the working lives of most women (and some men) can be characterized as comprising a paid work/unpaid care equation, it is apparent that much of the existing literature in this area, at least from the labour law perspective, consists of useful insights into the 'paid work' side of the equation but all too often neglects to define and consider the nature of the 'unpaid care' component. This is unsurprising as the current demarcation between social policy and law[2] dictates that the influence of labour law as a catalyst for change in this respect is confined to the regulation of the working relationship between employer and employee and is possible only through manipulation of the agreement between the parties regarding the market aspects of that relationship: that is the bargain struck over the provision of labour and resulting measurable output, and the rate of pay and associated aspects of remuneration given in return.

As Chapter 2 argued, this restricted approach has reached its limits as a means of producing effective reform and what is now required is the development of more holistic interventions that are capable of connecting disparate policy strands to take account of the full range of human activities. Such an approach calls into question the compartmentalized regulation of different aspects of a person's life as determined by the current divisions of law and policy and causes us to rethink existing conceptions of responsibility and the respective contributions of the individual, the family, employers, and the wider society. This necessitates consideration of the role

[1] M. Barbera, 'The Unsolved Conflict: Reshaping Family Work and Market Work in the EU Legal Order', in T. Hervey and J. Kenner (eds), *Economic and Social Rights under the EU Charter of Fundamental Social Rights: A Legal Perspective* (Oxford: Hart Publishing, 2003), 139–60.

[2] Manifested in political and legal systems through, for example, the organization of government into specific portfolios and departments, the composition of judicial structures with specialist courts, and the arrangement of supporting institutions such as social and welfare services. This demarcation strongly echoes the existing dichotomization between the 'private' (family) and 'public' (paid work and political participation), see Chapter 2.

of the State in regulation of the private as well as the public domains and over aspects of the uncommodifiable as well as the commodifiable contributions of individuals.

The chapter will start by considering what is meant by the term 'care relationship' in the current context. Drawing on existing empirical and theoretical literature, the diversity of relationships between carers and those cared for will be explored in relation to the levels of relevant dependency and corresponding support required and the consequently complex, finely-tuned, and often delicate nature of care arrangements into which those who combine care-giving with paid employment are compelled to enter. The aim is to highlight the need to recognize care as an essential and everyday human activity, which incorporates both mundane and life-enhancing aspects, that carries a heavy social burden which could be lessened through shared responsibility for meeting the needs of those cared for and those who do the labour of caring. The carer's burden is not always transferable due to the inalienable nature of certain aspects of care which comprise a non-negotiable component of an individual's working life. This necessitates looking beyond the contracting out of care when seeking to discharge the social obligations it imposes. Although it is often overlooked in considerations of labour market policy, the subject of unpaid care and its intersection with paid work has gained some prominence in academic analyses across disciplines in recent years and has been a particular focus of attention within the US literature.[3] In setting out the moral basis for a right to care, extensive use will be made of such analyses. The second part of the chapter comprises an overview of women's labour market position relative to that of men. The high levels of gendered segregation that occur across Europe are a product of the division of labour within families as well as being reflective of the gender stereotyping that results from the female-carer/male-breadwinner classifications. However, women's participation in paid employment is increasing and this factor, alongside other aspects of the transformation that is currently taking place in working arrangements, offers new opportunities to review the existing regulatory approach to the reconciliation of paid work and unpaid care.

The Care Relationship

In *Justice, Gender and the Family*[4] Okin considered the unjust gendered division of labour that takes place within the family and the 'mythical assumption that every worker has "someone else" at home to raise "his" children'.[5] In advocating more

[3] Eg, J. Tronto, *Moral Boundaries: A Political Argument for an Ethic of Care* (New York: Routledge, 1993); D. Bubeck, *Care, Justice and Gender* (New York: Oxford University Press, 1995); E. Feder Kittay, *Love's Labor: Essays on Women, Equality and Dependency* (New York: Routledge, 1999); M. Fineman, *The Autonomy Myth: A Theory of Dependency* (New York: The New Press, 2004); A. Alstott, *No Exit: What Parents Owe their Children and What Society Owes Parents* (New York: Oxford University Press, 2004).

[4] (New York: Basic Books, 1989).

[5] Ibid, 176.

equitable care arrangements, Okin placed special obligations on employers to make positive provision for the fact that most workers are also parents and may be required to care for children and other family members at some point in their working lives. This, she envisaged, would require greater flexibility in setting terms and conditions of employment which might be subject to adjustment over time in line with changes to the care demands placed on the individual worker-carer. Central to this vision of a more egalitarian division of responsibility for care is the notion that 'public policies and laws should generally assume no social differentiation of the sexes'.[6]

Okin's aspiration for a gender-blind society is conceptually sound and laudable in its aim, particularly when the effects of combining unpaid care and paid work on the life chances of those (women) who do both are considered. What is surprising is that her call for change was made 20 years ago and, although now apparently accepted by many mainstream commentators and policy-makers, is still far from realized. Part of the reason for such little progress, despite consensus regarding the need for change, lies in labour law's continued failure to acknowledge, except in very specific circumstances,[7] the effect of care-giving on an individual's ability to conform to the standard often demanded by pre-existing structures. This is not the same as (and cannot be remedied by) the recognition and established prohibition of sex discrimination which, in order to be more effective, should focus on outcomes rather than processes by seeking to overcome the restrictions placed on most women due to the gendering of care. Alongside strengthened sex discrimination legislation, gender-free outcomes require targeted policy which does not distinguish between men and women so that legal intervention aimed at the reconciliation of personal and professional life should be available to either sex. Only through such provisions will it be possible to give full recognition and improved status to unpaid care itself which, in turn, will facilitate a move away from its feminization towards a more equal distribution of unpaid labour between the sexes.

From a market perspective, the uneasy relationship between gender, care, and paid work might arguably be solved by the outsourcing of care, particularly as individuals become increasingly engaged in meeting the demands of globalized capitalism and commit to full-time employment's promise of individual autonomy. However, in reality the depersonalization of care is rarely desirable for either party to the type of informal arrangements with which this book is concerned. Carers, although undoubtedly time poor and in need of support and assistance, are often unwilling to hand over the care of a child, sick partner, or elder to a third party however good the quality of care might be because, setting the obvious cost implications aside, to do so would deny them and their loved one the reciprocal rewards of a caring relationship. For the recipient of care, the affective aspects of the relationship are unlikely to be provided in an institutional setting without the

[6] Ibid, 175.

[7] Namely pregnancy and the restricted 'protected period' of maternity following childbirth, see Chapter 5.

intimate connections on which ties of family and friendship are based. The inalienable nature of care is often neglected in the market-based conceptions of 'work' which underpin labour market policy.[8]

However, to dichotomize care as either commodifiable and, thus, marketable or as inalienable and therefore only appropriately provided within the context of an intimate relationship is to oversimplify its nature. By masking care's true complexities and those of the multitude of relationships within which it occurs, such polarization risks perpetuating stereotypes of carers as either cold, third party providers or as equally faceless beings who give selflessly for the well-being of others. In reality, the provision of care consists of a combination of activities and emotional properties[9] incorporating both the mundane and the profound.

Defining Care

In her study of the moral context and content of care, Tronto sought to reconceptualize care in order to 'move it from its current peripheral location to a place near the centre of human life'.[10] In attempting to capture the full range of properties intrinsic to the term, she suggested that 'caring' be defined as

> [a] species activity that includes everything that we do to maintain, continue, and repair our 'world' so that we can live in it as well as possible. That includes our bodies, ourselves, and our environment, all of which we seek to interweave in a complex, life-sustaining web.[11]

Tronto's definition is intentionally broad-based and seeks to avoid the assumption that caring is dyadic or individualistic. By placing the care relationship within a more general framework than that consisting of the interaction between two individuals, Tronto lifts it out of the romanticized paradigm of the mother and child relationship and emphasizes its social and collective dimensions. This is helpful in the current context which requires recognition of the fact that care for one person can, in certain circumstances, be provided by more than one carer, regardless of gender, and also that the diverse arrangements surrounding its provision may be culturally significant. Furthermore, it is important to capture the ongoing nature of care which forms part of everyday life, so that it is 'both a practice and a disposition'.[12] While the often mundane and perpetual nature of care-giving is undeniably important in any attempt to encapsulate its essence, its temporality must also be acknowledged as, in most circumstances, degrees of dependency lessen

[8] See K. Lynch, J. Baker, and M. Lyons, *Affective Equality: Love, Care and Injustice* (Basingstoke: Palgrave MacMillan, 2009).

[9] On the point that care is both an emotional state and an activity, see D. Bubeck, 'Justice and the Labor of Care' in E. Feder Kittay and E. Feder (eds) *The Subject of Care: Feminist Perspectives on Dependency* (New York: Rowan and Littlefield, 2002), 163.

[10] Note 3 above, 101.

[11] Ibid, 103.

[12] Ibid, 104.

or diminish as children grow up and dependants who are ill recover, develop individual coping strategies enabling a more independent existence, or die.[13]

Acknowledgment of the varying degrees of dependency and corresponding levels of care, which may vary over the life-cycle, enables consolidation of the wide variety of needs encapsulated by the term 'to care' and indicates that any related right must be broadly based in terms of scope so as to avoid an overly prescriptive approach based on a narrow perception of the parties to the relationship as well as being conceptually flexible to enable incorporation of a wide diversity of arrangements. Furthermore, a process of review and amendment must be incorporated as both carers' and care recipients' needs change over time. All of these aspects will be given consideration in the discussion of the most suitable regulatory approach in Chapters 5 and 7.

The realization that care amounts to no more or less than an aspect of everyday life challenges the belief that those who engage in it are somehow predestined on the basis of their individual characteristics to do so and the related assumption that an ability to care is predetermined by the possession of certain personality traits or an individual propensity. This is central to the development of a socially recognized ethic of care in place of the essentially-based notion that 'women's morality' makes them better suited to selfless giving than men.[14] Rather than continuing to justify the exclusion of those engaged in unpaid care from full participation in political and economic life as a natural consequence of perceived suitability, society needs to redraw its moral boundaries so as to give care its rightful place at the centre of all human activity. Only by doing so is it possible to realize the potential for the sharing of care within families and other relevant associations and across gendered and other divisions. If care remains bound to the erroneous belief that women are biologically predetermined to perform it, its categorization as instinctive or as irrevocably embedded in social or cultural practices places it outside of the realms of moral choice and renders its social arrangement incapable of change. Furthermore, the stereotypical portrayal of carers as a selfless beings, motivated only by altruistic concern denies recognition of their, all too often unmet, needs. The development of a socially recognized ethic of care does not necessitate new paradigms of care but, on the contrary, requires us to look to established models of good practice which can provide blueprints for greater participation in and responsibility for care around which other aspects of human activity can be ordered.

Like all essential human activities, care is multifaceted and consists of a range of inter-related properties which require both emotional and physical investment so that, 'It is a labor, an attitude, and a virtue.'[15] Even where care is provided under

[13] Of course this is not to deny the reality of long-term care provision for those who are chronically ill or profoundly disabled and who require high degrees of care throughout their often long lives.

[14] On the issue of different types of moral expression, see C. Gilligan, *In a Different Voice: Psychological Theory and Women's Development* (Cambridge: Harvard University Press, 1982). Although Gilligan never definitively claimed that the 'different voice' was gendered, this is how her findings have been widely interpreted.

[15] E. Feder Kittay, 'When Caring is Just and Justice is Caring', in Feder Kittay and Feder (eds), n 9 above, 257–76 at 259.

intimate conditions, the task of maintaining its provision in difficult and personally disadvantageous circumstances requires cultivation of the virtue[16] by which the care-giver must make a transition from self-interest to a focus on the situation of the one in need of care. This reliance on goodwill can leave the care-giver vulnerable to exploitation and the current informal arrangements within which care takes place can see her confined to the private sphere of the family and denied a personal identity and public voice with which to articulate her specific needs.

As noted above, a common response to the unpaid care/paid work conflict lies in the justification that it results from the exercise of choice, so that the misfortunes experienced by those who engage in paid employment and unpaid care are the result of a process of rational decision-making. Under this line of reasoning, individuals, when faced with conflict, should make alternative choices that would ease their burden and enable them to focus their time and energy on whichever aspect of their life they favour. Such reasoning underpins human capital theory[17] and the related belief espoused by followers of neo-classical economic theory[18] that the market provides the best means of resource distribution with lower wage rates and associated remuneration rationalized by selective decision-making. However, the assumption of a 'free' labour market underpinning such beliefs is highly questionable as is the accompanying assumption that carers are autonomous individuals who are in a position to exercise free choice regarding their life courses. According to Fineman, our preferences are structured by and through existing societal institutions so that choices are made in the context of 'social relations that reflect long-standing cultural and social arrangements and dominant ideologies about gender and gender roles'.[19] Furthermore, our beliefs regarding the appropriateness of such arrangements often operate at the sub-conscious level placing them beyond scrutiny so that we, apparently instinctively, know 'what constitutes the good mother, the ideal husband, and the perfect marriage'.[20]

In addition to the complexities of social conditioning, the carer often has other more tangible constraints on her freedom to make choices. In her analysis of modern parenting, Alstott posits that society's expectation that parents will provide continuity of care for their children imposes a double burden in that, as well as the long-term commitment to their children, parents are also expected to 'reshuffle their priorities: parents must strive to meet their children's material and emotional need, and they must, if need be, limit their own aspirations and forgo opportunities to do so.'[21] This reprioritization applies, to varying degrees, to all carers regardless of whom they care for and is the source of one-off dilemmas as well as of ongoing conflict and compromise. Perhaps the most obvious manifestation of the 'no exit' effect referred to by Alstott can be illustrated by way of the sick child who cannot be

[16] Ibid, 260. [17] See below at p 59.
[18] See below at p 57. Contemporary social policy is based on similar assumptions.
[19] Fineman, n 3 above, 40.
[20] Ibid, 41. [21] Alstott, n 3 above, 52.

left with her normal childcare provider to enable her primary carer (mother) to go to her paid employment despite the fact that if the carer/mother takes unauthorized leave, she risks her job security. Despite years of equality and anti-discrimination legislation, labour law has no effective response to the 'dilemma' posed for the mother in this situation.

Although the 'choice' rationalization might be applied when such dilemmas involve children on the grounds that parenthood is the end result of a decision-making process,[22] what of other care relationships? To what extent can the loss of a carer's personal autonomy be rationalized on the basis of preference or choice in the provision of elder care or in cases involving profound disability or terminal illness? In such circumstances the 'choices' available to the carer between the personal performance or outsourcing of care often involve financial constraints that serve to further limit the narrow range of available options. The classification of care-giving as a matter of individual choice enables circumvention of society's collective responsibility to provide for those who are vulnerable through their status as either dependant or carer. Furthermore, treating care-giving as a commodity risks neglecting its affective dimension which renders certain aspects of it inalienable and, thus, outside of the scope of market exchange.

The Affective Dimension

The affective dimension of the care relationship arises due to the universal human need and capacity for intimacy and attachment which is satisfied most fully through a network of caring relationships. It is these relationships that bind us together and that give us our sense of identity and belonging. The care and love that we receive over our lifetimes enable us to form stable, loving relationships of our own and to lead successful and fulfilling lives.[23] Although theoretically the needs of one individual might be satisfied by the exclusive provision of care by another, in most instances, particularly where the level of dependency is great, it will be necessary for the carer to look outside of that relationship in order to ensure that her own needs are adequately met. This can require the input of a wide range of individuals and collectives which together comprise an interdependent coalition or network of care which is based on solidarity between individuals in recognition of the fact that care cannot and should not be a solitary and isolated practice. However, as outlined above, there are also aspects of care, particularly in the context of its personal provision, which cannot effectively be provided or performed

[22] Of course this is a highly contentious assumption in itself due to the effects of social conditioning, itself subject to cultural diversity, and the fact that pregnancy is not always the result of rational decision-making. The classification of care-giving as a matter of individual choice enables circumvention of society's collective responsibility to take care of those who are vulnerable through their status as either dependant or carer.

[23] M. Nussbaum, 'Human Capabilities, Female Human Beings' in M. Nussbaum and J. Glover (eds), *Women, Culture and Development: A Study of Human Capabilities* (Oxford: Oxford University Press, 1995), 61–104.

by anyone other than the primary carer. The imposition of this burden of care on one individual emphasizes the importance of solidarity through which the involvement of others[24] can alleviate responsibilities in other respects as well as providing practical and empathetic support.

The grounding of care in personal relationships of love and obligation renders certain, although not all, aspects of it inalienable and, thus, unsuitable for market exchange. Indeed, improvements to the process of and conditions for commodification of certain care tasks would assist in the avoidance of exploitation.[25] However the emotional work incurred in loving another cannot be transferred to a third party in exchange for payment and to attempt to do so would 'undermine the premise of care and mutuality that is at the heart of intimacy and friendship'.[26] In market terms, the inalienability of love's labour renders it formless, unquantifiable, and impossible to ascribe a specific value to. It cannot be condensed into particular periods of time.[27] Furthermore, its nurturing and affective qualities do not lend themselves to the type of hierarchical structure designed, ostensibly at least, to reward effort and to record progression in market terms.

In their empirical study of relationships of love, care, and solidarity, Lynch et al[28] have argued that Western society's 'deep ambivalence about caring and loving'[29] has found expression in the academy's cross-disciplinary interpretations of the liberal and radical egalitarian traditions. In sociological, economic, legal, and political thought, this is manifested in a number of recurring features such as the focus on the public sphere, the core assumption that the 'prototypical, human being is a self-sufficient rational economic man' and the neglect of 'the reality of dependency for all human beings, both in childhood and at times of illness and infirmity'[30] leading to the unequal satisfaction of individual needs. As well as preventing us from developing and fostering vital connections with one another, such 'affective inequality' can deprive the providers of unpaid care of important human goods such as an adequate livelihood. To counter such inequality, it is necessary to challenge contemporary social arrangements such as the division of labour within families and also to change the institutions that hinder the development of such vital bonds including the arrangements surrounding the organization of paid work. This requires recognition of the needs, not just of those who depend on unpaid care, but of those who provide it so that, in the current context, the demands placed on

[24] This includes the provision of formal care to supplement rather than replace that provided informally, for example, as a form of respite.

[25] See G. Meagher, 'Is it Wrong to Pay for Housework?', *Hypatia*, 18/2 (2002), 52–66.

[26] K. Lynch and J. Walsh, 'Love, Care and Solidarity: What is and is Not Commodifiable' in Lynch *et al* (eds), n 8 above, 33–77, 51.

[27] The concept of 'quality time' as care which takes place in reduced time is illusory as its preconditions are grounded in the trust and understanding between individuals built up over a longer period, see J. Tronto, 'Time's Place', *Feminist Theory*, 4/2 (2003), 119–38, 123.

[28] K. Lynch, J. Baker, S. Cantillon, and J. Walsh, 'Which Equalities Matter? The Place of Affective Equality in Egalitarian Thinking' in Lynch *et al* (eds), n 8 above, 12–34.

[29] Ibid, 12.

[30] Ibid and see also M. V. Lee Badgett and N. Folbre, 'Assigning Care: Gender Norms and Economic Outcomes', *International Labour Review*, 138/3 (1999), 311–26.

an individual through the provision of unpaid care should be accounted for through amendment to the paid work component of her life. This, in turn, requires reassessment and realignment of the responsibilities and obligations incurred in both the private and public spheres. The issue of responsibility and legal obligation will be more fully explored in Chapter 4 but, in order to rationalize the necessary shift in social arrangements, attention will be given to the need to provide care for the carer.

Caring for the Carer

In her work on the morality of care, Kittay[31] argues that our motivation for providing care arises from our own intrinsic need for a co-dependent relationship. This cycle of care, in which an individual may be at once giver and recipient, is the source of deep and satisfying bonds which 'count among those we most cherish'.[32] At its most basic level, care is crucial for perpetuation of the species through the nurturing of infants and beyond and the provision of support to those who are or become dependent in the years between birth and death is the most fundamental expression of a decent and civilized society. The giving of care is imperative for the individual well-being of both dependents and carers and, in the collective sense, for the achievement and maintenance of a just community.

The conceptualization of the rights and obligations arising from the care relationship thus proceeds from an assertion that dependency is a fundamental component of the human condition. This factor is often overlooked in both feminist theory and in the conception of political liberalism expounded most influentially by Rawls considered in Chapter 2.[33] The assumption of autonomy underpinning Rawlsian theory presupposes that all citizens are equally free to negotiate contractual exchanges in order to achieve their particular ends. However, in the context of the care relationship, the element of 'choice' is both contested and complex and the reciprocity which emerges as a precondition for equality in Rawls's thesis must be reconfigured in the context of the interactions between dependants, their carers, and the wider society, which means 'acknowledging the importance of reciprocating the efforts of those who do the labor of caring'.[34] Due to the very nature of dependency, the return on effort expended in providing care cannot always be forthcoming from those who are dependent so other sources must be identified. This form of reciprocity is best performed through a public ethic of care which Kittay has termed '*doulia*'.[35] Although specific to the mother and child relationship, the concept of

[31] Kittay, n 3 above and 'A Feminist Public Ethic of Care Meets the New Communitarian Family Policy', *Ethics*, 111/3 (2001), 523–47.

[32] Ibid, 527.

[33] See J. Rawls, *Political Liberalism* (New York: Columbia University Press, 1993).

[34] Kittay (2001), n 31 above, 532.

[35] Ibid. Which is adopted 'from the postpartum caretaker, the *doula*, who assists the mother who has just given birth, not by caring for the infant but by caring for the mother so that the mother can herself care for the infant'.

doulia or the carer's need for care is applicable to the whole range of care relationships across the spectrum of needs. It is what is missing from the unpaid care/paid work conflict as the formal recognition of the need to care for the carer elevates the status of care-giving to its rightful place as an activity that is worthy of attracting a specific social value by commanding protection for those who engage in it. The moral imperative informing the notion of a public ethic of care is sufficiently compelling so as to justify public intervention in the form of a legal right to care and, in turn, to be cared for. Furthermore, because responsibility for the provision of such support rests with the wider society, it is logical to assume that all areas of law and policy that are in some way related to the social and economic life of the individual should be appropriated in order to give it expression. This would certainly apply to labour law, which regulates a key aspect of our lives which is intrinsically important to our psychological and physical well-being and which provides the means by which we are able to achieve full or partial economic independence.

Labour law's intervention in the unpaid care/paid work conflict has traditionally been concerned with identifying and applying specific policies which satisfy employers' requirements,[36] and it is thus generally neglectful and, in some instances, implicitly hostile to the notion of incorporating the specific needs of carers. The language of such policy is informative as to its origins and aspirations: the term 'family friendly' suggests, by implication, that alternative policies are legitimately assumed to be 'unfriendly' to families. Likewise, the phrase 'work/life balance' confers an easy separation between those activities that can be classified as 'work' (paid work) and all other aspects of 'life' (including the unpaid work of care-giving), which is meaningless to those who participate in both types of activity often with little to distinguish them in terms of time or effort. Although such terms appear, on face value, as innocuous, perhaps even comforting, they actually serve to perpetuate the dichotomization of paid work and unpaid care. Correspondingly, those who combine unpaid care with paid work through, for example, part-time arrangements are classified as 'atypical' as their working patterns differ from the 'norm' of full-time, permanent employment. The fact that such arrangements are overwhelmingly sought by women only serves to confirm that man is 'the subject' and woman is 'the other'.[37] The working mother of pre-school or school-age children, although a growing demographic, personifies this combination of the public and private in a way which appears to have confounded policy-makers.

In attempting to reorient our conception of the relationship between paid and unpaid work so that labour law might better accommodate the care aspect, it is necessary to move from an employment-centric vantage point to a care-centred approach. This throws up a whole set of interesting questions regarding responsibility and the discharge of obligations requiring consideration of economic, social, moral, and ethical dimensions. This shift in focus, if placed within the context of the labour law framework, requires a corresponding change of emphasis so that rather

[36] See Chapter 4.
[37] From S. de Beauvoir, *The Second Sex* (New York: Vintage, 1949), referred to in Chapter 2.

than conducting an exploration of the employment rights of carers, the primary investigation becomes a consideration of the caring rights of employees.

The rationalization of the moral argument presented here for shared social responsibility for care, whether realized through gender-neutral policy or compensatory provisions, lies in the fact that the nurturing and support that occur through the provision of unpaid care makes market participation possible by enabling the so called autonomy of market players. This takes place at the beginning of life and throughout childhood often by way of the mother/child relationship and also occurs through the transfer of responsibility from one individual to another in order that the former might be 'free' to participate in the market. In this configuration, we are all, to varying degrees, 'dependent'. However, the overwhelming burden and high personal cost of unpaid care falls to certain individuals whose labour market prospects are significantly reduced as a consequence. In the next section, such disadvantage will be considered and explanations advanced for its enduring nature in light of targeted legal and policy reforms intended to counter some of its contributory factors.

Unpaid Care in the European Labour Market

The post-war growth in women's employment is often heralded as being unprecedented, but it is important to interpret the relevant statistics cautiously in this context. Hakim[38] has shown that although the trend in women's participation rates over the post-war period is undoubtedly an upward one, a longitudinal analysis of women's engagement in paid employment reveals that, since the mid-nineteenth century, female employment rates have remained remarkably stable. It is the nature of work and the working arrangements that have changed, notably with the growth of paid part-time work that has taken place since the 1970s. An historical perspective reveals that the relatively high rates of female labour market participation are not necessarily a twentieth century phenomenon. The distinction between paid work outside of the home and unpaid work within it originates from the time of the industrial revolution and the concentration of labour in factories, prior to which divisions between different forms of work had been largely obscured by the prevalence of subsistence agriculture and the various forms of craft work emanating from cottage industries. In the UK, for example, the recorded participation rates of married women engaged in paid labour declined sharply from 25 per cent in 1851 to 8.7 per cent in 1921.[39] With increasing industrialization, paid work outside of the home replaced informal working arrangements and women's childcare responsibilities impacted on their labour market opportunities with a constraining effect in both the ideological and practical senses, so that they were prevented from obtaining paid work by what was believed to be appropriate for them to do and also

[38] See C. Hakim, 'The Myth of Rising Female Employment', *Work, Employment and Society*, 7 (1993), 97.

[39] S. Atkins and B. Hoggett, *Women and the Law* (Oxford: Blackwell, 1984), 18–19.

by what they could actually do. Both of these factors continue to have an influence over the labour market experiences of women.

Even if the changes to women's aggregate employment patterns are historically contextualized in order to identify the social and economic factors that have shaped them, it is nevertheless true that a transformation has taken place within the confines of twentieth century Western Europe.[40] Women's labour market participation rates have increased in all of the EU15 Member States since the end of the Second World War so that, in 2007, 59 per cent of women were economically active[41] compared with an average of below 40 per cent in 1960.[42] Closer scrutiny of the statistics reveals that the aggregate figures mask a range of diverse arrangements in relation to the types of paid work in which women are engaged. This diversity relates to hours of work and other terms and conditions of employment. In the EU27 29.4 per cent of women aged between 25 to 49 work part-time compared with 4.7 per cent[43] of men and more women than men are employed on fixed-term contracts.[44] The reasons why individuals work part-time are far more likely to relate to caring responsibilities for women[45] and a lack of alternative employment opportunities for men.[46] Furthermore, although women's aggregate participation rate has risen, it still lags 15.5 percentage points behind that of men,[47] with the mothers of small children having a significantly lower participation rate than childless women.[48] The participation rate of mothers of children aged between 0–5 years is 59.7 per cent compared with 91.2 per cent for fathers.[49]

The persistence of gendered pay gaps in all Member States means that, on average, women earn 17.8 per cent less per hour than men.[50] This is partially due to such factors as women's lower educational attainment and professional

[40] That is among EU15. Although the statistics presented in this section use EU27 wherever possible, EU15 statistics are used for time series purposes as comparative longitudinal data is not available for all of the 27 current Member States.

[41] European Commission, *Reconciliation between Work, Private and Family Life in the European Union* (Brussels: Eurostat, 2009), 9. The figures are based on the participation rates of those aged 15–64. For EU27, this figure is 58.3%.

[42] The statistics for 1960 are based on the labour market participation rates of women aged 25 to 49.

[43] European Commission, n 41 above, 20. Figures are for 2006.

[44] Ibid, 24. In 2006 in EU27, 13% of women aged 25 to 49 were on fixed-term contracts compared with 11.2% of men, although the percentage increase for both sexes from 2000–2006 was 2.4%.

[45] In the 2006 Labour Force Survey (EU27), 61.1% of women who work part-time did so due to care commitments or other personal or family reasons compared to 13.9% of men: European Commission (2009), n 41 above, 22.

[46] 43% of men who work part-time did so as they had been unable to find a full-time job compared with just 21% of women, ibid.

[47] For EU27, ibid, 18.

[48] In 2004, it was some 12.7% lower—see European Commission, *Report on Equality between Men and Women*, COM (2004) 115 final, 4.

[49] European Commission, n 41 above, 34. Based on 25 to 49 age group for EU27. The age group is significant because the average age at which women have their first child is 28 in almost all EU Member States, ibid, 17.

[50] European Commission, *Strategy for Equality between Women and Men*, COM (2010) 491 final, 6. This is the figure for EU27 in 2008. The gendered pay gap has remained fairly static in recent years and it is significantly higher in the private sector compared to the public sector.

development with further explanations lying in the highly segregated nature of labour markets which are gendered, so that women work in different employment sectors and in different jobs from men (horizontal segregation) and at different levels within occupational hierarchies (vertical segregation).[51] Although women have made some inroads into previously male-dominated areas of work, the most constant and enduring feature of women's employment in the post-war era can be said to be its comparatively low status.

The Nature of 'Women's Work'

A high level of gendered segregation still persists in the labour markets of all Member States[52] despite the fact that women have increased their share of employment and have made important inroads into some previously male-dominated sectors and jobs over the past 40 years.[53] The highly segregated nature of labour markets has led to the identification of certain types of paid employment as 'women's work'. Such work is crowded into a narrow range of occupations and, as well as its predominance within certain sectors, has other characteristics which are common to the types of paid work undertaken by large number of women across Europe.

Research indicates that there is a high concentration of women in the public sector which accounts for 32 per cent of all women employees, compared with 19 per cent of all male employees.[54] Women who work in the private sector tend to be employed in small and medium-sized companies rather than large ones.[55] Women's employment is concentrated in health care, education, and public administration, while men predominate in construction, manufacturing, transport, agriculture, and financial services.[56] Most people work in sectors in which their own sex either forms the majority or the entirety. In the occupational context, women's jobs tend to involve caring, nurturing, and service-related activities with men predominating in jobs involving managerial responsibility and manual and technical work often categorized as 'heavy' or 'complex'. Thus, men fill 80 per cent of the employed armed forces, craft, and related trades and jobs associated with plant and machine operation. Men also hold more than two-thirds of the skilled agricultural and fishery jobs with women predominating in two-thirds of clerical, service, and sales jobs.[57]

[51] Ibid.

[52] P. Paoli and D. Merllié, European Foundation for the Improvement of Living and Working Conditions, *Third European Survey on Working Conditions 2000* (Luxembourg: Office for Official Publications of the European Communities, 2001); C. Fagan and B. Burchell, European Foundation for the Improvement of Living and Working Conditions, *Gender, Jobs and Working Conditions in the European Union* (Luxembourg, Office for Official Publications of the European Communities, 2002).

[53] Eurostat, *The Life of Women and Men in Europe: A Statistical Portrait* (Luxembourg, Office for Official Publications of the European Communities, 2000).

[54] *Third European Survey on Working Conditions 2000*, n 52 above.

[55] Fagan and Burchell, n 52 above.

[56] *Third European Survey on Working Conditions 2000* and European Commission (2010), n 50 above, 6.

[57] Organisation for Economic Co-operation and Development, *Employment Outlook* (Paris: OECD, 2002).

In professional and manual occupations, there is a more even split between men and women at the aggregate level with segregation discernable at the sub-category level: men holding the vast majority of jobs within the physical, mathematical, and engineering professions and women predominating in the health and education professions.[58] Women are under-represented in self-employment and account for only 33 per cent of self-employed workers in the European labour market.[59]

Vertical segregation occurs where, in any given sector or industry, one or other sex predominates in senior, managerial, or well-paid positions and the other is correspondingly over-represented in lower paid jobs and within certain types of employment contract. Although women in Europe have increased their representation within managerial jobs in recent years, there are still clear differences in the gender composition of those filling such jobs[60]—63 per cent of European workers have a man as their immediate superior, with only 21 per cent working under the authority of a woman.[61] Women who are managers or supervisors are more likely to be in charge of other women as less than 10 per cent of male workers have a female manager or supervisor. Men occupy more than 60 per cent of the legislative and managerial occupations, rising to over 70 per cent if the sub-categories of corporate managers and senior government officials are considered.

The transformation that has taken place within the European labour market is not restricted to the composition of its workforce as the nature of employment is also changing. Dickens[62] has attributed one of the reasons for such change to a growth in 'atypical' or 'flexible' employment with the other dominant feature being the rise of 'networked, boundaryless, (sometimes virtual) organisations in which highly skilled autonomous professional individuals, with occupational or portfolio careers rather than organizational careers, link together with others to work on a non-hierarchical project basis'.[63] This highly valued and well rewarded work is generally performed by self-employed (male) individuals through contracts for services with increases in low status 'atypical' employment more commonly reflected in women's aggregate work patterns. Both of these changes to the working environment have been reflected in recent developments in policy-making at the European level and were reflected in the goal of the Lisbon Agenda[64] 'to become the most competitive and dynamic knowledge-based economy in the world capable of sustainable economic growth with more and better jobs and greater social cohesion'.[65]

[58] European Foundation for the Improvement of Living and Working Conditions, *Quality of Women's Work and Employment: Tools for Change* (Luxembourg: Office for Official Publications of the European Communities, 2002), 12.

[59] European Commission (2010), n 50 above, 5.

[60] Ibid, 13.

[61] The remainder do not have a manager.

[62] L. Dickens, 'Problems of Fit: Changing Employment and Labour Regulation', *British Journal of Industrial Relations*, 42/4 (2004), 595–616.

[63] Ibid, 595.

[64] Adopted by the Member States' representatives at the meeting of the European Council in 2000.

[65] See the Presidency Conclusions of the Lisbon European Council of 23 and 24 March 2000, available at <http://www.europarl.europa.eu/summits/lis1_en.htm> accessed 7 December 2010. The

This shift in Europe's social policy objectives, which has effected a reorientation of focus away from the programme of harmonization of social standards towards facilitation of the co-existence of national policies,[66] is likely to have a marked influence on the shape of future regulation at the supranational level. The rationale for such redesign is based on the notion that greater labour market flexibility requires a move away from State intervention towards deregulation. This, according to the industrial relations literature, is a flawed assumption based on an over-simplification of the relationship between regulation and labour market behaviour.[67] If sustained, this notion has obvious implications for the future quality and supply of women's employment, demand for which is closely intertwined with the growth in atypical work due to the gendered nature of unpaid care which is overwhelmingly provided by women. The specific responses of EU law to changes in the nature and composition of paid work will be more closely considered in Chapter 5, in which it is argued that the move away from labour market regulation places an increased emphasis on the European Court's interpretation of the constitutional or fundamental rights conferred on the citizens of the European Union by the Treaties' provisions as a means of settling employment disputes based on contested levels of protection. First it is worth exploring how those with caring responsibilities have collectively engaged with the labour market in the post-war era. The aggregate patterns of female market participation reveal that women's attachment to paid work has changed during this period and continues to move closer towards what has been termed the 'adult worker model' traditionally associated with male employment despite the fact that men's participation in unpaid care has remained static and low.[68]

Modelling Women's Labour Market Participation

Although women's employment rates have risen in all EU15 Member States since the mid-1960s, there has been considerable variation in the increases that have taken place in specific countries which can be usefully analysed with reference to the different relationships between motherhood and paid work that co-exist within the European Union. The three main categorizations which were originally used to describe patterns of female labour market participation[69] are no longer as relevant

Lisbon Agenda and its articulation through the European Employment Strategy are discussed in Chapter 4 below.

[66] See D. Ashiagbor, *The European Employment Strategy: Labour Market Regulation and New Governance* (Oxford: Oxford University Press, 2005).

[67] See G. Standing, 'Globalisation, Labour Flexibility and Insecurity: The Era of Market Regulation', *European Journal of Industrial Relations*, 3/1 (1999), 7–37; R. Hyman, 'The Europeanisation—or the Erosion—of Industrial Relations?', *Industrial Relations Journal*, 32/4 (2002), 280–94.

[68] J. Gershuny, *Changing Times: Work and Leisure in Post-Industrial Society* (Oxford: Oxford University Press, 2000).

[69] Namely the Scandinavian, Southern European, and camel's back models—see N. Le Feuvre and M. Andriocci, *Employment Opportunities for Women in Europe, A report of the EU-funded project*

as they once were, as the labour market participation rates of women in the 25 to 49 age group have increased in all Western European Member States[70] indicating that the impact of motherhood on women's participation in paid work has decreased causing their labour market behaviour to move closer to that of men.

Although a detailed analysis of the reasons behind this shift in behaviour is beyond the scope of the current text, it is important to note that it amounts to more than a mere reflection of changes to family formation and dissolution which have led to an increase in the number of lone mothers and a shift towards motherhood at a later life stage for many women. As Lewis et al[71] have noted, explanations for diversity in and changes to patterns of paid and unpaid work among Europe's women are linked to the complex relationship between economic necessity and personal choice which are, in turn, determined by opportunities and constraints so that 'it may well be that mothers' decisions/strategies for combining work and care depend on a compromise between the possible and the preferred'.[72] The role and effectiveness of policy in this respect is contested and, although it is likely that 'policy matters', it is 'remarkably hard to prove it'.[73]

At the household level, this change in patterns of paid work and unpaid care can be classified as a move away from the 'male breadwinner model family', in which men are primarily responsible for earning and women for providing unpaid care, towards the 'adult worker model family' in which all adults regardless of sex or parental status are assumed to engage in paid employment outside of the home.[74] As Giullari and Lewis[75] have noted, although the male breadwinner model made provision for care-giving within the family by its implicit acceptance of women's provision as part of the 'package', this shift in the balance of paid work/unpaid care is accompanied by no such provision. In fact, an analysis of relevant policy responses reveals an assumption on the part of governments and policy experts that care provision will increasingly move to the formal, paid sector.[76] As explored above, this assumption is problematic due to the uncommodifiable nature of certain aspects of care.[77]

'Employment and Women's Studies: The Impact of Women's Studies Training on Women's Employment in Europe' (Luxembourg: European Commission, 2003), 16.

[70] See notes 41 and 42 above.

[71] J. Lewis, M. Campbell, and C. Huerta, 'Patterns of Paid and Unpaid Work in Western Europe: Gender, Commodification, Preferences and the Implications for Policy', *Journal of European Social Policy* (2008), 18, 21.

[72] Ibid, 25. See also European Foundation for the Improvement of Living and Working Conditions, *Working Time Options over the Life Course: New Work Patterns and Company Strategies* (Dublin: Eurofound, 2006).

[73] Lewis *et al*, n 71 above, 25.

[74] R. Crompton (ed) (1999), *Restructuring Gender Relationships and Employment: The Decline of the Male Breadwinner* (Oxford: Oxford University Press, 1999); *Employment and the Family* (Cambridge: Cambridge University Press, 2006); J. Lewis, 'The Decline of the Male Breadwinner Model: Implications for Work and Care', *Social Politics*, 8/2 (2001), 152–70.

[75] S. Giullari and J. Lewis, *The Adult Worker Model Family, Gender Equality and Care: The Search for New Policy Principles, and the Possibilities and Problems of a Capabilities Approach*, United Nations Research Institute, Social Policy and Development Programme (2005) Paper No 19, at 1.

[76] Ibid.

[77] See p 47 above.

The obvious tension between caring responsibilities and labour market participation has undoubtedly been the most relevant factor in the rise of women's part-time employment in the post-war era. That such work has, until relatively recently, been detrimentally differentiated from full-time employment by Member States' legal systems reflects the State's reluctance to intervene in the operation of the labour market and the willingness of governments to trade off women's employment rights in favour of increased flexibility for employers. As the continuing rise in women's share of the paid labour market relative to men's shows, the key to improving 'women's work' lies not in increasing its quantity, but rather in enhancing its quality.[78]

Explaining the Poor Quality of 'Women's Work'

Before turning to the issue of unpaid care and its specific policy requirements, it is worth considering the various responses which are most commonly advanced as explanations for the poor quality of women's work relative to that undertaken by men. The rationalization offered by the neo-classical economic and human capital schools rely heavily on a particular neo-liberal interpretation of the core liberal values of individualism, autonomy, and freedom through which an individual's worth is assessed exclusively on the basis of his or her commodifiable contribution to the market. This overlooks the essential contribution to human well-being that is realized through the labour of unpaid care, much of which can not be commodified and is, thus, unsuitable for measurement or exchange in market terms. This restricted approach does not, therefore, provide a satisfactory explanation for the behaviour of individuals who combine care-giving with paid work as it takes account of only one aspect of their lives. Furthermore, it provides an inadequate framework within which to assess the application of the core values of individualism, autonomy, and freedom to those who require care for their survival due to their non-participation in the process of market exchange. In any case, the interrelationship between unpaid care and paid work as well as other extraneous factors, means that the categorization of the labour market as a 'free market' is conceptually flawed. The sensitivity of the 'work for pay' exchange to other factors outside of the relationship between the parties to the employment contract leaves this aspect of the unpaid care/paid work conflict susceptible to legal and policy interventions which, if specifically targeted, could have a normative effect on the division of labour within families as well as countering the current deficit in shared social responsibility for unpaid care. Finally, segmented labour market theory is offered as an alternative means of assessing labour markets by taking account of factors outside of the employment relationship which, nevertheless, have an undeniable impact on its operation.

[78] See Chapter 5.

Neo-classical Economics

Those who believe in the primacy and efficacy of the free market as the central means of distributing resources[79] argue that the jobs performed by women and the pay they receive are the result of rational decision-making based on free choice by the individuals concerned. Following this thesis, the price of labour is determined in the same way as the price of all commodities, namely by the forces of supply and demand. Wage levels settle at the lowest rate employers can pay while still being able to attract suitable applicants; discrimination appears to be irrational and unnecessary as women's apparent willingness to work for less pay than men should lead to an increase in their employment across all relevant sectors and occupations which will, in turn, break down gendered segregation and contribute to an evening out of the pay differential.[80] As the available statistics reveal, this hypothesis has not proved to be accurate within the Western European Member States, all of which continue to experience gendered segregation and pay gaps which neo-classical economists attribute to women's career choices which are made on the basis of their 'natural' capacity as carers. Following this rationale, occupations such as nursing are poorly paid because large numbers of women choose to pursue careers in such sectors on the basis of factors other than pay, such as the altruistic pleasure of 'caring' and the resulting satisfaction in community well-being.[81]

As well as the problematic assumption that such 'choices' are made freely and not as a result of social conditioning or within a narrow range of options due to social and economic constraints, the fact that this thesis is premised on the operation of a 'free' labour market has been the subject of criticism. According to Hyman, 'only in limited respects do "labour markets" actually constitute markets'[82] as they lack the key determinants such as a saleable commodity.[83] Furthermore, their sensitivity to influences other than market factors distinguishes labour markets from other, more traditional places of exchange. Such factors are manifested through the national industrial relations systems which, in the EU context, 'represent varieties of institutional structures which ensure that the employer-employee relationship is not primarily determined by market forces'.[84]

The neo-classical view that the labour market constitutes a marketplace in the economic sense is, thus, flawed due to the influence of external pressures which

[79] For the most well-known example of neo-classical economic theory applied in the context of sex discrimination, see S. W. Polachek and W. S. Siebert, *The Economics of Earnings* (Cambridge: Cambridge University Press, 1993). The authors are also proponents of human capital theory (discussed at p 59 below) as the next 'logical' step in explaining the persistence of wage anomalies within a 'free market' order.

[80] Ibid, 141.

[81] Ibid, 206.

[82] Hyman, n 67 above, 281.

[83] Marx's view was that 'labour' is not a commodity, rather the worker sells her (or his) ability to work, making it impossible to measure any quantifiable property with precision as would be the case with a commodity traded in a product marketplace.

[84] Hyman, n 67 above, 281.

serve to dilute the purity of the market so that distribution of relevant resources, through the allocation of jobs and pay rates, is not controlled by market forces. According to Craig et al, this point can be illustrated with reference to three central principles: 'the rate for the job; no money wage cuts and the right to retain jobs in relation to other potential recruits'.[85] In the valuing of labour, unlike in product markets, the worth of a particular job is not fixed by the market but is vulnerable to sectoral, regional, and organizational variation with many employers operating internal markets where increases in pay are based on such non-market factors as length of service. Public sector collective bargaining can be said to result in the closest thing to a 'going rate', but even in the public sector, wage rates are subject to wide diversity.[86] The preservation of terms and conditions under a 'live' employment contract makes wage cuts in monetary terms difficult to achieve, even where drops in productivity occur, and this factor also contributes to the protection of employment. As consideration of these principles demonstrates, social factors are more likely to provide explanations for divergence in pay levels than the economic laws of supply and demand.

This is not to say that the neo-classical perspective can be completely dismissed in analyses of the gendered nature of labour markets. On the contrary, its acceptance into mainstream ideology has informed much of the policy development in this area in recent years. Attempts to transplant market-based principles into the operation of labour markets include the increasing use of short-term contracts and of contracting-out arrangements, by which workers can be legally dismissed and re-engaged through a third party on a lower rate of pay.[87] It is, in fact, particularly important to keep the neo-classical perspective firmly in view as some observers have identified a return to the dominance of market factors in the management of industrial relations in Europe.[88] In neo-classical theory the market is assumed to be an impersonal mechanism that operates for the greater good, separate from the prejudices which might influence the thought-processes of its participants. In reality, the market is no more or less than the sum of its parts which are constituted by the behaviour of those participants as much as by any other influencing factor and which may well include a propensity to discriminate. Furthermore, the very foundations on which the market is built are vulnerable to the effects of institutional discrimination and the organizing forces of industrial relations' systems themselves, such as 'management, trade unions and the State—which appear in the literature as gender neutral are indeed profoundly gendered'.[89] Perhaps this explains why neo-classical analyses have failed to address the persistence of gendered segregation across Member States in what has otherwise become a fast-moving and

[85] C. Craig, E. Garnsey, and J. Rubery, *Payment Structures in Smaller Firms: Women's Employment in Segmented Labour Markets* (London: Department of Employment, 1984), 5.

[86] A trend which looks set to continue as many public sector employers seek a move towards localized bargaining processes.

[87] See Case C-256/01 *Allonby v Accrington and Rossendale College and Others* [2004] ECR I-873.

[88] See, eg Hyman, n 67 above.

[89] J. Wajcman, 'Feminism Facing Industrial Relations in Britain', *British Journal of Industrial Relations*, 38/2 (2000), 183, 184.

dynamic social environment. This failure has caused proponents of labour market rationalization to develop an alternative approach which, although similar to the neo-classical perspective in its foundations, develops further the justification of differences in women's labour market position relative to that of men.

Human Capital Theory

Human capital[90] theory uses the rationality of free choice as a basis for explaining the relatively low pay and diminution in other terms and conditions of employment which characterize 'women's work'. Following this view, the reasons for such divergence between the pay rates of women and men arise out of a conscious choice made by some women not to invest in their human capital. This is due to the likelihood that such investment will be wasted when, during the years of child-bearing and rearing, they will cease to participate in the public domain of paid employment and return to the private sphere of the home. 'Human capital' is measured by the investment made by an individual in his or her career in terms of such factors as education and training. Investment is translated into monetary worth on the labour market so that an individual who is highly skilled is worth more than an unskilled worker with little formal education and low levels of training. As Polachek and Siebert postulate, women's lower human capital is due to a 'rational (family wealth maximizing) division of labour in the home due to women's comparative advantage in child-bearing and rearing'.[91] This position is underpinned by an assumption that women are less productive than men in economic terms because of their child-bearing capacity.

The closure of the pay gap between men and women in respect of full-time employment, which has arisen partially on the basis of women obtaining more and better qualifications,[92] may provide some evidence to support this theory. However, this analysis presents more problems than solutions which are both empirical and conceptual in nature. First, the persistently high value afforded to some forms of qualification over others cannot be easily explained by application of human capital theory. The fact that scientific and technical tasks and appropriate qualifications are valued more highly than the socially important tasks undertaken by qualified primary school teachers indicates that their relative worth owes more to

[90] The theory presented here should be distinguished from the use of 'human capital' as a means of classifying and measuring the contribution that humans make, for example to organizations and in social and economic terms, as a tangible asset incorporating such factors as the knowledge, skills, abilities, and capacity to develop and innovate. This conception of human capital has much in common with Sen's Capabilities Approach (see Chapters 2 and 7) as both 'put humanity at the centre of attention, although the narrower view of the human capital approach fits into the more inclusive perspective of human capability', A. Sen, Editorial: Human Capital and Human Capability, *World Development*, 25/12 (1997), 1959, 1959–60.

[91] Polachek and Siebert, n 79 above. Although, as woman is the only sex capable of child-bearing, her capacity in this respect is exclusive rather than comparatively advantageous.

[92] In 2003 58% of new graduates in Europe were women, Equal Opportunities Commission, *Women: Europe's Competitive Edge* (Manchester: EOC, 2005), 1.

the sex of those who predominate within associated jobs than any other factor. Such differentiation also raises questions about whether the relevant (right) factors are rewarded when pay rates are set on the basis of qualifications and skill. Second, evidence suggests that other grounds for extended absence from work do not have the same consequences for an individual's career prospects or the same impact on loss of earnings as breaks related to child-bearing or rearing. The difficulties in obtaining employment experienced by women returning to work after extended absence on such grounds point to the conclusion that the 'choice' exercised in relation to the length and consequences of such absences may be that of employers rather than of workers. When such factors are considered together, it is apparent that the human capital perspective fails to adequately explain the persistence of gendered pay gaps.

Human capital theory's conceptual flaw rests in its assumption that all decisions regarding whether to participate in paid employment are made freely and rationally. In reality, the full information on which to base such decisions is rarely available and, even when it is, decisions are likely to be based on how best to manage the conflict between unpaid care and paid employment than the result of free choice. Furthermore, the perpetually low status afforded to 'women's work' may produce a self-fulfilling effect by which women who realize that their prospects are poor will not take the risk of making the necessary investment to improve them. However, the most fundamental problem with this particular theory as an explanation for the relatively poor labour market position of women lies in its apportionment of responsibility so that it is the women who find themselves in low paid, low status work who are responsible for their own misfortune. This approach exonerates employers and the State from any responsibility for the operation of labour markets and, by implication, any discriminatory practices. In addition, the responsibility for unpaid care is placed firmly and exclusively on women who implicitly bear the consequences of reproduction through reduced employment prospects, leaving fathers, the wider society, and the State outside of the equation. This perpetuates stereotypical views of working mothers who are perceived as unreliable and lacking in commitment to paid work which, in turn, justifies employers' low risk strategies through precarious employment arrangements, which many women have little choice but to accept, or decisions not to employ them at all.

In both the neo-classical and human capital perspectives, the focus on market rationalization mitigates against the use of legal intervention as a means of improving the quality of women's work on the basis that the market will deal effectively with discrimination where it occurs. The neo-liberal incarnation of this model has been very influential in relation to government policy-making in recent years.[93] The empirical basis on which economic theory is predicated has the effect of

[93] Although a modified version of the neo-liberal non-interventionist model has been particularly influential across Western Europe. The 'Third Way' ideology underpins much of the European Social Model and, in the UK context, New Labour's 'New Deal' policy initiatives of the last decade. For a feminist critique of this movement and its effects on women's employment, see S. Fredman, 'The Ideology of New Labour Law' in C. Barnard, S. Deakin, and G. Morris (eds), *Essays in Honour of Bob Hepple* (Oxford: Hart Publishing, 2004).

making its application appear plausible and, therefore, persuasive. However, as Fredman has observed, economics is a subjective discipline which is not scientifically objective so that, 'like law, [it] is deeply ideological'.[94] Market discourse applies the conceptual tools of liberal theory so that it engenders a focus on individualism, autonomy, and the role of the State but within the neo-liberal incarnation which applies a specific interpretation of those principles which is not conducive to the attainment of the liberal ideal for all as discussed in Chapter 2. This particular conceptualization of liberal values and their application to policy in recent years has had a particularly damaging effect on analyses of the different labour market experiences of men and women. Once apparently rationalized on the basis of the exercise of individual freedom, such differences cease to be subjected to the scrutiny necessary to effect change. The third and final economic perspective uses some of these features of market rationalization, albeit alongside deeper considerations of other socio-economic factors, and applies them from a feminist viewpoint which seeks to avoid 'blaming the victim' and thus results in a more sympathetic, enlightened, and enlightening approach.

Segmented Labour Market Theory

In seeking to explain why women are employed in certain jobs which, on average, attract lower rates of pay than those filled predominantly by men, Beechey[95] distinguished between two types of job: primary and secondary. Each type predominates within a particular section of the labour market to such an extent that there are, in effect, two separate markets operating simultaneously. Primary sector jobs have 'relatively high earnings, good fringe benefits, good working conditions, a high degree of job security and good opportunities for advancement while secondary jobs have relatively low earnings levels, poor working conditions, negligible opportunities for advancement and a low degree of job security'.[96] Primary jobs are part of a highly structured internal market within which jobs are organized hierarchically, dependent on skills level and corresponding rewards. Recruitment to all but the lowest level jobs is through promotion within the internal market. Secondary jobs are not subject to the same opportunities for advancement and the low skill levels required in performing such jobs means that training is non-existent or minimal. This detracts from the ability of secondary job holders, who are predominantly female, to make advancements in their careers.

Although dual labour market theory provides a useful starting point in analyses of men's and women's work, it does not explain gendered occupational segregation adequately but merely describes what happens on the labour market. This provides a useful insight into the causes of vertical segregation, by which occupational hierarchies are linked to reward schemes, but does not touch upon horizontal

[94] S. Fredman, *Women and the Law* (Oxford: Oxford University Press, 1997), 405.
[95] V. Beechey, *Unequal Work* (London: Verso, 1987).
[96] Ibid, 32.

segregation through which certain occupations are identified as 'women's work'.[97] Furthermore, Craig et al found that many workers in secondary jobs actually have 'considerable levels of skill and experience acquired through informal on-the-job training, and undertake work which makes heavy demands on the workers'.[98] In her later work, Beechey has asserted that the undervaluing of the requisite skills for the jobs predominantly performed by women rests on the basis of those skills, which are often learned informally in the home and, as such, are not subjected to the same forms of formal measurement applied to other skill sets. Faced with opposition from employers, trade unions have been unable (or unwilling) to establish such skills as being worthy of recognition in pay determination. Such factors have had a profound effect, illustrating that 'the concept of skill is socially constructed, and an adequate account of the exclusion of women from skilled jobs has to take account of this'.[99]

The separation of markets into distinct entities, thus, appears to be far more complex than the binary model presented by dual market theory. Craig et al posit the existence of a structured or differentiated labour supply which is 'created through the interaction of the employment system and the system of social organisation'.[100] Through the process of matching jobs with applicants, a market emerges which consists of many diverse segments with differences in the supply of labour dependent on four inter-related factors. First, even if workers enter the labour market with similar characteristics and opportunities, they will acquire different work histories, experience, and skills. These factors will limit the mobility of some workers and may even restrict their prospects. Second, the different social characteristics of individuals which are manifested through such factors as educational qualifications and family connections translate into unequal access to jobs on entry to the labour market. Third, the social and family networks through which workers pool or share income with others lead to employers' assumptions about the relative income needs of specific demographic groups in structuring pay and employment practices. Even if they are not borne out in reality, workers must adjust to those assumptions in order to gain and keep employment. Fourth, different levels of caring responsibilities simply restrict some workers' availability in the labour market. Employers are able to take advantage of workers with high levels of unpaid care commitments by paying lower rates that are not necessarily reflective of productivity levels. Through the interaction of these four factors, it is possible to reach an understanding of women's relative disadvantage in the labour market. The operation of each of the factors allows for the possibility of discrimination which may be direct or indirect and may operate at the organizational level or through more covert, institutional means.

[97] V. Beechey, 'Women's Employment in Contemporary Britain' in V. Beechey and E. Whitlegg (eds), *Women in Britain Today* (Oxford: Oxford University Press, 1986), 111.

[98] Craig *et al*, n 85 above, 92.

[99] Beechey, n 97 above, 121; see also A. Phillips and B. Taylor, 'Sex and Skill: Notes towards a Feminist Economics', *Feminist Review*, 6 (1980), 79.

[100] Craig *et al*, n 85 above, 6.

The gendering or sex-typing of jobs arises due to a combination of all of these factors so that employers' assumptions and workers' aspirations converge in a cycle of influence. Cockburn has shown how it is not only skills but the whole concept of work which is purposefully constructed on gender lines including the use of tools, machinery, and new technology.[101] Her fieldwork explored the relationship between gender and the various physical manifestations of specific jobs which in certain instances is so strongly influenced by the association of particular objects with one or other sex that 'it is impossible to get a teenage lad to wipe the floor with a mop, although he might be persuaded to sweep it with a broom'.[102] Attempts to resist such sex-typing place the dissenter outside of the established workplace norms and the resistance encountered from peers and superiors results in such high social costs that the gendering of jobs is rarely challenged. As Cockburn observed: 'The dichotomies, separations and power inequalities that occur at home and those that occur at work are related and mutually reinforcing.'[103]

Identification of the existence and persistence of segmented labour markets on gendered grounds offers a valuable insight into the nature of men's and women's paid work, with women's contribution generally undervalued through its association with the private sphere of the family in which the labour expended is unmeasured and financially unrewarded. Given the stated aims of governments and policy-makers at both national and supranational levels in relation to the furtherance of sex equality, it is notable that little attempt has been made to mount an effective challenge in relation to this factor. A cursory glance at relevant policy developments in recent years actually indicates the opposite as evidenced by the reliance that is placed on the perpetuation of the normative construct of the standard worker model in the distribution of resources and the continued polarization of different working arrangements.[104]

Dickens has identified a misfit between the changed circumstances of the working relationship and the current regulatory framework which is based on the model of a 'standard' arrangement, specifically that of full-time, permanent employment between an employee and single employer.[105] If gender is added to the mix, the 'standard' worker is male and there is an implicit assumption that he has responsibility for earning, if not all, the majority of the 'family wage'. Despite its decline and replacement with new forms of social arrangement, this model is the basis on which much employment and social policy continues to be based.[106]

Women 'choose' to work part-time, often through precarious arrangements, because they are expected to combine high levels of unpaid care with paid work. Furthermore, the targeted use of such work as a means of overcoming high unemployment rates illustrates the stubborn refusal of policy-makers to reassess the world of work with a view to uncovering a more reflective model on which to base policy initiatives. While such a refusal may result in injustices to women, it

[101] C. Cockburn, *In the Way of Women: Men's Resistance to Sex Equality in Organisations* (London: Macmillan, 1991).
[102] Ibid, 38. [103] Ibid, 41. [104] Giullari and Lewis, n 75 above.
[105] Dickens, n 62 above, 597. [106] Ibid, 611; Wajcman, n 89 above, 195.

very effectively preserves existing arrangements whilst appearing to offer an alternative. The continuing rise of women's labour market participation rates, largely within such 'atypical' employment, provides a useful antidote to critics, which, in turn, gives such initiatives 'the illusion of inclusion'. This self-serving cycle preserves the *status quo* by enabling women to perform their 'dual role' of carer and worker while the assumption of the existence of a male breadwinner within each family unit actually endorses the precariousness of such employment on the grounds that 'women's work' is actually extraneous to the family wage.

The continued undervaluing of women's work, and the subjection of the female workforce through marginalization of the forms of working arrangement with which women are predominantly associated, provide clear evidence that the forces of patriarchy continue to influence and shape the nature of employment and related policy within the Member States of the European Union. The absence of any real policy focus on care beyond its commodification further illustrates that it is the nuclear family with its distribution of roles and responsibilities that holds the attention of policy-makers despite its demographic decline. Segmented labour market theory provides the most satisfactory explanation for the continuation and perpetuation of the distinct working patterns and employment experiences of men and women. Furthermore, despite the stated aims of government at both the national and supranational levels to improve women's employment prospects, it appears that labour markets are becoming more segmented over time[107] with greater differentiation of work and associated arrangements and regulatory regimes, through their adherence to outdated models of behaviour, are failing to keep abreast of such change.

The division of labour within households, although the most significant determinant of women's labour market participation, is arguably the most difficult aspect of human activity to shape or influence by regulatory means. However, as Chapter 5 asserts, by adopting a joined up approach to policy-making aimed at reconciling the demands of unpaid care and paid work it is possible to establish a normative framework capable of influencing the organization of private as well as public relations between individuals and the State. The rationalization for such intervention rests on the recognition that the provision of care for the vulnerable members of any community, including family units, carries wider social responsibilities than those which are capable of being discharged within the confines of the care relationship itself.

Conclusions

Given the gendered nature of unpaid care, it is important to consider it alongside the commodified labour market work that (female) carers typically engage in. This enables full consideration of the two, as yet unresolved, aspects of an individual's

[107] See Dickens, n 62 above, and Hyman, n 67 above.

life which, although intrinsically valuable to our overall well-being, continue to comprise a source of personal conflict. The main source of this conflict is the inability of those engaged in the non-negotiable work of caring to conform to the practices ascribed by established and apparently unyielding structures surrounding paid work which dictate how, where, and when it should take place. This non-conformance has resulted in the exercise of 'alternative' strategies, such as the growth in part-time work, which are often accompanied by a reduction in legal protection against the vagaries of the market which is heralded as the determinant of what are deemed to be appropriate standards of behaviour. In fact, the operation of unfettered forces within labour markets is illusory as the various institutional factors that influence outcomes in this respect make their manipulation largely a matter of policy choice. As such, it is possible and desirable to seek alternative ways of conceptualizing and organizing 'work' which take account of the full range of human activities relevant to the regulation of paid work, including its intersection with unpaid care. Such approaches should necessarily challenge the dominant neo-liberal conceptualization of the traditional liberal values of independence, autonomy, and freedom in order that they might be achievable for *all* members of society. This quest for alternative approaches is in fact necessary in order to realign labour law with the substantial changes that are taking place in the context of the employment relationship and the world of paid work generally. This necessitates labour law's consideration of the full range of human activities with the ultimate social goal identified as being autonomy for all citizens regardless of personal characteristics such as gender, race, age, sexuality, degree of physical or mental ability, or caring responsibilities. This vision for the future regulation of work, although apparently at odds with the current conception of liberalism as perceived through the neo-liberal policy domain, is in fact perfectly compatible with its underlying and sustainable ethos. The rationalization for a public ethic of care to be recognized on the grounds of social morality will be further developed in Chapter 4 in which its proposed realization through an employment rights framework will be considered.

4

Situating a Right to Care in European Employment Law

Introduction

The main aim of this Chapter is to identify the appropriate form and content of the proposed right to care which, it is asserted, should be established within European employment law. Form matters because, despite the restrictions on the law-making institutions' competence to those areas and procedures provided for in the Treaties,[1] there are a number of different avenues available through which relevant initiatives could be expressed and developed. Furthermore, as will be explored in Chapter 5, there are already a range of provisions across the spectrum of EU law and policy which are related both directly and indirectly to the proposed right and which could assist or impede the current proposal. Regardless of the form of any such proposed right and its potential location within the pre-existing EU *acquis*, it is only by ensuring that it accords with current thinking within the institutions and the Member States and also that it is compatible, at least ostensibly, with the ideology underpinning the current framework that it will be possible to make progress.

The Chapter opens with a discussion of the classification of different types of rights in which the various associated claims and means of invocation will be explored for the purposes of identifying the role and significance of ideology in their formulation and interpretation and also to establish why certain rights are given prominence over others. The proposed right to care is difficult to situate within the traditional paradigm as it combines civil, political, and social claims which have generally been kept apart, largely due to the hierarchy of rights in which some are classified as 'fundamental' and, thus, deemed to have priority over others,[2] but also partly in deference to the private/public dichotomy discussed in Chapter 2. In considering the formulation of the proposed right, it is asserted that, although it is most appropriately classified as a social right within the European employment law framework in order that the reconciliation of paid and unpaid work can be accommodated, authority for such a right is clearly enshrined in the fundamental

[1] See the 'principle of conferral', Art 5(1) TFEU.

[2] The incorporation of the Charter of Fundamental Rights (CFR) into the constitutional law by the Lisbon Treaty in December 2009 signals a reclassification of rights within the EU order, see Chapter 5.

principles of EU law which are embedded in the Treaties' provisions[3] themselves and which rely for their realization on secondary legislation and on the interpretive role of the European Court. Furthermore, if the right to care is to operate effectively, for example as a means of enabling women's full participation in political life and in the development of welfare rights for those carers for whom paid work is not a viable option, related claims which have political and civil dimensions must also be legally recognized.[4]

The hybrid nature of the proposal makes it difficult to situate within the pre-existing paradigm of rights and, consequently, within the employment or labour law framework and this raises questions regarding the continuing relevance of that framework, particularly at the national level where the diversity in approaches to work and welfare add further complexity. In the second part of this Chapter, the relationship between political influence and labour rights and its effect on labour market regulation at the national level will be explored. UK labour law will be used as an example to demonstrate how neo-liberal ideology has pervaded not just the relevant policy approaches but also the conceptualization and interpretation of the principles underpinning employment relations. In place of a dominant political dogma founded on a specific strain of economic rationalization, the development of an alternative ideology is asserted which takes, as its foundations, moral and ethical considerations and an enhanced emphasis on substantive equality. It is argued that such a change in theoretical perspective is in line with the transformation that is currently taking place within labour markets by which the foundations on which traditional conceptions of employment regulation are based are shifting.[5] The composition of the labour force has changed dramatically in the post-war era and the notion of 'work' itself has been transformed due to substantial changes in the types of paid work in which we engage and the methods by which it is performed. The law has been slow to catch up with such developments and, consequently, the conceptualization of work on which traditional forms of regulation are based is contested. The legal framework, thus, requires to be updated and an important part of that process must be recognition of the contribution that unpaid care makes to market integration. In formally recognizing and accommodating unpaid care, related policy needs to take full account of its relationship to paid work and resolution of the conflict between the two.

To deal adequately with this conflict necessitates reconciliation of the conference of specific social rights with the requirements and functioning of the market in order that the dominant neo-liberal conceptions of the nature and value of work within a market-based economy can be countered and a return to the true values of

[3] See Art 3(3) TEU which provides that the EU shall 'combat social exclusion and discrimination' and 'promote social justice and protection'; Arts 151–3 and 157 TFEU and Chapter III CFR on equality; and Art 33 CFR on the reconciliation of family and professional life.

[4] Although, given the limited competence of the EU in law and policy-making, such recognition might be better accommodated as an aspect of national law-making by the Member States than at the supranational level.

[5] See Chapter 3.

liberalism established. The third and final section of this Chapter considers how this might be achieved by concluding with an assessment of the use of Sen's capabilities approach (CA).[6] The CA has much to commend it in this respect: its conceptual flexibility and holistic approach to diagnostic evaluation make it a useful tool in the formulation and monitoring of broad-based reflexive policy. Such an approach is compatible with the market order as it incorporates traditional liberal values in the achievement of its primary goal which, rather than seeking to guarantee that all individuals possess a given set of resources, is to enable individuals to develop the capacity to be free to make effective choices through which they are able to interact with the market. As well as effecting a transformation in the 'private' lives of Europe's citizens, the reconciliation of paid work and unpaid care which will flow from the establishment of a right to provide care alongside labour market participation will also contribute towards a more efficient operation of the market itself. However, this is not the principal rationale for advocating such a right which is primarily based on the moral case and which is intended to enable reconciliation of the current paid work/unpaid care conflict and, thus, contribute towards the EU's stated objectives of 'improved living and working conditions' and 'proper social protection'.[7]

A Hierarchy of Rights?

In his classic exposition of the nature and role of different rights in the construction of citizenship,[8] Marshall distinguished social rights from civil and political rights. Civil rights were 'necessary for the individual freedom – liberty of the person, freedom of speech, thought and faith, the right to own property and to conclude valid contracts, and the right to justice', whereas political rights were classified as providing 'the right to participate in the exercise of political power, as a member of a body invested with political authority or as an elector of the members of such a body'.[9] Social rights, in contrast, incorporated a series of diverse general claims 'from the right to a modicum of economic welfare and security to the right to share to the full in the social heritage and to live the life of a civilised being according to the standards prevailing in society'.[10]

The individual nature of civil rights as envisaged by Marshall meant that they 'harmonised with the individualistic phase of capitalism'[11] and were, thus, compatible with the market. However, according to this classification, social rights provided a 'basic conflict'[12] with the market as their recognition would engender the creation of 'a universal right to real income which is not proportionate to the market value of the claimant'.[13] As Deakin and Browne have noted, despite his

[6] See Chapter 2. [7] Art 151 TFEU.

[8] T. H. Marshall, *Citizenship and Social Class and other Essays* (Cambridge: Cambridge University Press, 1950, reprinted 1992).

[9] Ibid, 8. [10] Ibid. [11] Ibid, 26. [12] Ibid, 42. [13] Ibid, 28.

reservations relating to the perceived mismatch between the aspirational nature of social rights and the operation of the market, Marshall 'was also aware that social rights can be viewed in a different sense, as part of the market order'.[14] This is because, although the declaration of such rights implies 'an invasion of contract by status'[15] which interferes with the notion of a 'free bargain', they are, nonetheless, 'entrenched within the contract system itself'.[16] The impact of collective bargaining on the UK's national industrial relations system was immense at the time that Marshall made his observations and, even in the current individualized employment relations environment, the sensitivity of labour markets to outside influences ensures that the conditions on which the employer/employee relationship are predicated are not primarily determined by market forces.[17] On the contrary, the emergence of new forms of boundaryless working in some segments of the labour market means that the prevalence of status over contract is in fact more marked than in Marshall's day for, on the one hand, a relatively small and privileged elite and, on the other, due to a process of deregulation and subsequent casualization, in the form of low paid, precarious work for those (largely female) workers classified as self employed as a means of ensuring labour market flexibility on the part of employing organizations.[18]

Alongside his observations relating to the incompatibility of social rights with the efficient functioning of the market, Marshall also concluded that, in contrast to the clear legal status afforded to civil and political rights, social rights were not necessarily amenable to juridical enforcement and judicial interpretation due to their aspirational nature which made it difficult for them to be 'precisely defined'. Marshall suggested that the associated rights of citizenship would be better served by the 'superstructure of legitimate expectations',[19] a view which appears to have held fast as, according to Deakin and Wilkinson, a notable feature of British social legislation during the golden era of the welfare state was 'how few justiciable legal rights it conferred upon individuals, either as workers or recipients of social security'.[20] This is, in part, explained by the fact that the problematic legal status of social rights is likely to be most pronounced in common law liberal democracies because of their reliance on the exercise of political power for the authority and legitimacy of such rights.[21]

[14] S. Deakin and J. Browne, 'Social Rights and Market Order: Adapting the Capability Approach' in T. Hervey and J. Kenner (eds), *Economic and Social Rights under the EU Charter of Fundamental Rights* (Oxford: Hart Publishing, 2003), 27–44, 29.

[15] Marshall, n 8 above, 40.

[16] Ibid.

[17] See Chapter 3 at p 57.

[18] See S. Fredman, 'Labour Law in Flux: The Changing Composition of the Workforce', *Industrial Law Journal*, 26/4 (1997), 337; and 'Women at Work: The Broken Promise of Flexicurity', *Industrial Law Journal*, 33/4 (2004), 299.

[19] Marshall, n 8 above, 34.

[20] S. Deakin and F. Wilkinson, *The Law of the Labour Market: Industrialisation, Employment and Legal Evolution* (Oxford: Oxford University Press, 2005).

[21] See J. Fudge, 'The New Discourse of Labor Rights: From Social to Fundamental Rights?', *Comparative Labour Law and Policy Journal*, 30 (2007), 29, 34–5.

At the time that Marshall was constructing his theory on the evolutionary development of social rights, Britain, on which his observations were largely based, was experiencing economic growth and an expansion in social welfare. Furthermore, the sovereignty of the nation state which has traditionally been the 'main author'[22] of social welfare and labour legislation was unquestionable. However, as Hepple proclaims in his call for a new approach to labour market regulation, 'The world in which Marshall's theory was conceived has disappeared.'[23] The internationalization of rights has tracked developments in global trade with the opening-up of ever greater markets and resulting challenges to the welfare state and to collectivism in industrial relations. Against this contemporary backdrop, Hepple counsels against viewing social rights as an 'immanent development within capitalist society' which will emerge as a natural consequence of citizenship, instead appealing for their categorization as human rights—'those moral rights which one has simply because one is a human being'[24]—as a more appropriate classification in the new global economy.

In his influential observations regarding the nature of the rights that have emerged with internationalization under the 'new dawn of social and labour rights'[25] and their differences from those that followed the introduction of the welfare state, Hepple identifies four central features. The first signals a departure from Marshall's traditional conception of social rights as being incompatible with the market so that they are now seen as being an integral feature of efficient and competitive markets. Rather than providing a source of conflict, such rights can now be interpreted as a viable means of enabling participation in the labour market.[26] Second, rather than imposing positive obligations on State intervention, such rights provide normative standards and serve as a useful means of embedding specific principles in institutional design. Third, the nature of the new generation of rights has led to a redefinition of the role of law in their achievement, with a move away from the imposition of sanction-enforced standards to the conferment of procedural rights which enable individuals to participate in the setting of appropriate standards and compliance monitoring.[27] Finally, the emerging structure of rights does not (and should not) presuppose a contract of employment.

The significance of these changes to the environment within which employment-related rights operate and their effect on the European regulatory framework will be explored further in Chapter 5 but, as well as establishing the vocational impact of such change, it is also important to consider its effects on the theorization

[22] Ibid, 38.

[23] B. Hepple, 'The Future of Labour Law', *Industrial Law Journal*, 24/4 (1995), 317.

[24] Ibid. This is the very basis on which the right to care advocated in this book is based—see Chapter 2.

[25] B. Hepple, 'Introduction' to *Social and Labour Rights in a Global Context: International and Comparative Perspectives* (ed B. Hepple) (Cambridge: Cambridge University Press, 2002), 1, 15.

[26] See Deakin and Browne, n 14 above.

[27] Known as 'responsive' or 'reflexive' regulation, see B. Hepple, M. Coussey, and T. Choudhury, *Equality: A New Framework* (Oxford: Hart Publishing, 2000).

of employment law at the national level. Only by undertaking such analysis are we able to ascertain the particular lens through which such developments are interpreted and ultimately presented, not merely in the context of academic discourse, but also to and by policy-makers. In the next section, the UK example is used to demonstrate how a particular neo-liberal interpretation of the conditions required for further market integration has been incorporated within the existing labour law framework so that its impact on employment relations is apparently rationalized on the basis of the spontaneous effect of the market itself. Rather than acknowledging the effects of particular policy choices, the resulting adherence to an increasingly outdated framework is presented as an unavoidable consequence of increased globalization. This process, it is contended, has been subject to a high degree of manipulation by those concerned with the promotion of neo-liberal economic rationalization as the dominant political ideology.

The Role of Ideology in the Construction of Employment Law

Collectively, the four features of the new generation of employment rights identified by Hepple[28] signify a movement towards the internalization of employment relations so that any resulting new rights are likely to be developed through workplace strategies designed to respond to the changes to working relationships brought about by enhanced market integration. In the UK, this approach replaces the traditional system of industrial relations by which differences between workers and employers were externalized, sometimes resulting in conflict, but ultimately the subject of collectively agreed settlements reached through a process of negotiation by which the parties traded priorities until acceptable accommodations could be made, often by way of mutual compromise. Through this process, regulation, where it existed, tracked the developments in working relationships between the two sides rather than, as is now increasingly the case, setting the agenda by which individual relationships are managed. The benefits of this new approach lie in its potential for reflexive regulation by which appropriate standards can be set and achieved through a process of agreement between all of those who are directly affected. However, the individualization of the worker side of the relationship and the lack of either mandatory procedures for collective consultation and negotiation[29] or legislative sanctions for non-compliance through the replacement of regulation with systems of local governance[30] leaves the process open to neglect or manipulation by powerful employing organizations, particularly in times of market instability.[31] In order to avoid the resulting exploitation of already vulnerable

[28] See n 23 above.

[29] See Chapter 5 at p 117 *et seq* for a discussion of the role of the social partners in agreeing supranational labour standards.

[30] Or, in the case of the EU, national compliance with supranational standards—see Chapter 5.

[31] See H. Collins, 'The Productive Disintegration of Labour Law', *Industrial Law Journal*, 26/4 (1997), 295; K. Ewing, 'Democratic Socialism and Labour Law', *Industrial Law Journal*, 24/2 (1995), 103.

workers, it is imperative that such an approach is underpinned by a clear commitment to core principles such as equality and non-discrimination, compliance with which should be supported by juridical means.

As Ewing has noted the need to ensure the democratic functioning of the relationship between worker and employer and compliance with the rule of law 'suggests the need for external regulation of the employment relationship'.[32] The process of regulation has traditionally been managed through realization of the two distinct yet interrelated purposes of labour law, one of which results from the private law relationship between employer and worker and the other which recognizes the public law function of that relationship through which the appropriate principles are applied.[33] By combining the two distinct aspects of law-making in this way, labour law was traditionally able to achieve both its wider social justice purpose as well as serving a more fundamental democratic end. As summarized by Kahn-Freund, the principal purpose of labour law was 'to regulate, to support and to restrain the power of management and the power of organised labour'.[34] Despite changes to the way in which labour is organized and to the predominating structures within which it operates, '[t]he case for labour law remains essentially a political one',[35] with future progress still likely to result from disputes between the parties, albeit in a different guise from that traditionally associated with collective bargaining, a view echoed by Hepple's recognition of the fact that '[t]he labour legislation of the future, like that of the past, will be the outcome of processes of conflict between different social groups and competing ideologies'.[36]

Form or Content?

If labour law's primary role is acknowledged as being to redress the imbalance of power in the relationship between workers and employing organizations, albeit in a very different world to that in which Kahn-Freund made his observations, it is the nature and source of that power which is important. In the current context, identification of the source involves the positioning of workplace relations in their wider social context so that, as discussed in Chapter 3, the effect of employment practices on the lives of carers and those for whom they care is considered in relation to the full range of their activities. Such repositioning enables account to be taken of what Conaghan has called 'multiple standpoints'[37] in order to 'illustrate how a focus on work and family can contribute to a better understanding of labour law by reassessing it from the standpoint of those who engage in large amounts of

[32] Ewing, n 31 above, 119.
[33] Ibid, 111.
[34] P. Davies and M. Freedland, *Khan-Freund's Labour and the Law* (London: Stevens and Sons, 1983), 15.
[35] Ewing, n 31 above, 131.
[36] Hepple, n 23 above, 305.
[37] J. Conaghan, 'Work, Family, and the Discipline of Labour Law' in J. Conaghan and K. Rittich (eds) *Labour Law, Work and Family* (Oxford: Oxford University Press, 2005), 25.

unpaid, care-giving work'.[38] Adoption of this perspective reveals the power deficit that exists between those who combine paid work with unpaid care and employing organizations[39] which arises, not due to some novel desire on the part of the carer to choose a particular lifestyle, but rather due to the traditional separation of the particular conceptions of 'work' and 'family' which has informed the development and provision of labour law. In reality, the link between productive and reproductive work has always existed,[40] it is the law's failure to take account of this link which has caused and perpetuated the current conflict in the paid work/unpaid care context. This distinction between the 'official narrative' and the 'hidden reality'[41] and its concealment of the gendered nature of unpaid care/paid work can only be bridged by recognition of paid work's place within its wider socio-economic environment.

In seeking to identify the political nature of the relationship between worker and employer and how best to regulate its observance of what are essentially civil and political rights based on the recognition of core principles, it is necessary to distinguish between the form of law and its content, that is, to consider whether it is the positioning of the relevant legal intervention, for example at the constitutional level, or its underlying ideology that is more likely to be instrumental in achievement of its aims. In respect of the form that might be appropriate, the proposed right to care is difficult to situate within the traditional paradigm as it combines civil, political, and social claims which must all be recognized in order to give it full effect. Furthermore, the wide diversity in the systems of law and corresponding classifications that operate across the range of Member States make this a complex exercise at the supranational level which may, in any case, be futile as, according to Kenner, the hierarchical categorization of rights is largely illusory because '[c]ategories of rights cannot logically or practically be separated or compartmentalised and indeed are mutually dependent'.[42]

The traditional separation between civil and political rights on the one hand, and economic and social rights on the other has been reinforced by their cost implications, with the former generally perceived as being relatively cost free, whereas realization of the latter 'requires a substantial investment of resources, the establishment of an effective infrastructure and progressive taxation over a sustained period'.[43] This justification for the compartmentalization of rights is both 'oversimplified and fallacious',[44] a point which can be illustrated by the example of the State's role in ensuring the right to equality which would, under the traditional

[38] Ibid, 26.

[39] See Fredman (2004), n 18 above, for examples of how this power deficit manifests itself in the context of EU regulation.

[40] See J. Conaghan, 'Contesting the Terrain' in A. Morris and T. O'Donnell (eds), *Feminist Perspectives on Employment Law* (London: Cavendish, 1999), 13.

[41] Conaghan, n 37 above, 29.

[42] J. Kenner, 'Economic and Social Rights in the EU Legal Order' in T. Hervey and J. Kenner (eds), *Economic and Social Rights under the EU Charter of Fundamental Rights: A Legal Perspective* (Oxford: Hart Publishing, 2003), 1, 3.

[43] Ibid.

[44] Ibid.

classification, be categorized as 'fundamental' and, thus, require non-interference on the part of the State in order to ensure its observance in relation to the individual. However, as the preceding considerations of equality between men and women and between carers and non-carers illustrate, realization of equality as an individual right requires positive steps on the part of government in order to ensure 'meaningful participation in society and equal opportunities for all'.[45] As well as its apparent implausibility, the notion that a hierarchy of rights exists as a natural phenomenon places it beyond question and serves as justification for the entrenchment of existing inequalities through the preservation of the public/private dichotomy and the corresponding role of State intervention in the former but not in the latter.[46]

The emphasis on the importance of policy rather than form as a means of developing and ensuring social rights is confirmed by Hepple's scepticism regarding claims that a focus on 'positive rights' and their constitutionalization will right the wrongs of the neo-liberal shift towards the individualization of labour law.[47] In noting his own reservations in this respect, Hepple draws on the observations of Wedderburn[48] and Kahn-Freund, the latter unconvinced by the 'magic belief in the efficacy of the law in shaping human conduct and social relations' which he contended was 'a superstition which is itself a fact of political importance but a superstition all the same'.[49] Hepple argues that the correlation of causal links between a 'legal superstructure and an economic base' is problematic as it is difficult to prove that '[l]egal institutions that came into being before relevant changes in technology or property and employment relations are the cause of those changes, or that legal rules made after those changes are their consequences'.[50] However, the lack of clear evidence regarding the nature of the relationship between law and what are often claimed as its consequences should not result in a denial of the importance of law which, in the current context, has 'legitimated an ideology of individualistic self interest' so that 'a different strategy needs a clear ideology'.[51] Thus, it is law's power as an ideological tool rather than its form which is important in shaping and influencing social relations through its normative effects. If this is accepted, using the law effectively to achieve particular outcomes appears largely a matter of policy choice rather than as the result of a somewhat mysterious process by which

45 Ibid. See also Hepple's contention (n 23 above, 318) that '[w]ithout such policies [as those advocated by Tom Paine's Rights of Man], social rights are bound to be ineffective'. The type of policies envisaged by Hepple in this context include the use of fiscal policy as a means of wealth redistribution.

46 See Chapter 2.

47 Hepple, n 23 above, 311.

48 In *Labour Law and Freedom: Further Essays in Labour Law* (London: Lawrence & Wishart, 1995), Lord Wedderburn states (at 408) that an emphasis on the form of law over its content 'undervalues the determination and unified resolve of the authors of the 1980s [UK] legislation, and of the class forces sustaining them to attack the already weak legal protections of workers' organisations in Britain'.

49 O. Kahn-Freund, 'Industrial Relations and the Law—Retrospect and Prospect', *British Journal of Industrial Relations*, 7 (1969), 301, 311.

50 Hepple, n 23 above, 312.

51 Ibid, 312.

outcomes are predetermined by the place of various unspecified components within an unyielding and self-perpetuating superstructure.

What Choices are the 'Right' Choices?

In recognizing the importance of choice in the development of an alternative ideology it is 'necessary to distinguish those principles (from which rights flow), which are fundamental to democratic societies, from particular economic and social policies which, by their very nature, are conditioned by the level of socio-economic development of a particular country'.[52] This is particularly important in the contemplation of policy development at the supranational level. Further, the constitutionalization of rights does not place them beyond the reaches of political choice but merely replaces one set of policy actors with another as '[b]y classifying a particular right as "fundamental" and making it constitutionally enforceable, we shift the resolution of disputes from the political and industrial spheres to the sphere of public lawyers and the judiciary'.[53]

The potential for political manipulation of what are perceived as 'fundamental rights' and those rights which are, by implication, deemed to be merely derivative is obvious. The architects of neo-liberal economic policy have used this distinction to great effect in the carefully crafted development of law and policy in selected areas and its complete denial in others. One effect of such re-orchestration of the law and its constituent parts is that policy and principle have become assimilated to such an extent that it is difficult to distinguish between them, making the identification of what amounts to political ideology and its separation from long-standing legal principles in the context of resulting law and policy a complex task. When aligned with accompanying claims regarding the primacy of the market as an unfettered force in the determination of social relations it is apparent that the dominant ideology which underpins current political structures and decision-making mitigates against the application of specific legal protections in response to claims by socially and economically vulnerable groups. It is asserted that this situation, if unchecked, at the very least threatens the independence of the legal institutions themselves and could herald a breakdown in observance of the rule of law.

It has traditionally been the role of labour lawyers to critique the relevant legal provisions through participation in their practical application and also as interested observers of the developments taking place within the discipline itself in both its vocational and theoretical contexts. However, perhaps as a result of what has been described as 'a theoretical lacuna lying at the heart of labour law itself?'[54] there appears to have been a disengagement among labour lawyers from participation in

[52] Ibid, 318.

[53] Ibid, 320. As Kahn-Freund noted in his consideration of the German and American experiences, 'it is very easy for judges to read their own notions of policy into the bill of rights', see O. Kahn-Freund, 'The Impact of Constitutions of Labour Law', *Cambridge Law Journal* (1976), 240, 270.

[54] Conaghan, n 40 above, 15.

analyses of the deeper ideological issues which have informed the transformation in the organization of work outlined in Chapter 3. This is not, by any means, intended to imply that there has not been much rigorous research undertaken by which specific policies have been critically scrutinized, but rather that the wide-ranging analyses of the ideological foundations of labour law of old appear to have largely disappeared from the academic literature at both the national and supranational levels.[55] The reasons for this are unclear but its coincidence with the growth of neo-liberalism as the dominant political ideology and the resulting 'collapse of the traditional analytical framework within which labour law had long been understood and interpreted'[56] make it a likely consequence of that very transformation.

Collins has attributed the failure of those engaged with the discipline to adequately examine such changes in its ideological fibre to a preoccupation with the sociological aspects of the employment relationship by which its characterization as a system of 'collective laissez faire' meant that, at the time of its fall, 'the labour law analysis was almost deaf to the discourses which brought about its demise, so that when the fall came, and the analysis no longer made sense of the environment, there was a sense of shock and aimlessness in the legal analysis'.[57] Under Collins's thesis, the discipline itself, at least in its British incarnation, amounts more to a contextual field of legal study rather than a doctrinal category in itself and this fact has rendered labour law 'unusually open compared to many legal subjects to the influence of other disciplines and discourses'.[58] This fact enabled labour lawyers to 'make some selections from the offerings of sociology, economics and politics'.[59] It was the emergence of three distinct interpretations of the industrial relations system in the 1980s that displaced the sociological rationale and which were all subjected to the 'types of deafness' that left their plausibility untested and unquestioned within the labour law paradigm.[60] The first was the fledgling but steady development of macro-economic policy which, through its focus on the reconciliation of full employment with low inflation, soon emerged as the dominant agenda. Taking root at the same time was the prevalence of individual rights as the predominant means of legal intervention in the workplace. The opportunity to consider whether such rights had an intrinsic value unrelated to the collective system of workplace governance was, however, largely missed as this 'was not a principle which the labour law discourse could easily grasp'.[61] The third and final of Collin's 'types of deafness' arose in relation to the failure to incorporate notions of distributive justice

[55] For support for this claim, see Conaghan, n 40 above, and Collins, n 31 above.

[56] Conaghan, n 40 above, 15.

[57] Collins, n 31 above, 301, but see also Wedderburn's strong rebuttal of Collins's views, particularly the latter's assertion that labour law's associations with 'the sociological method and industrial relations perspectives made scholars "deaf" to social justice, social rights or the macroeconomic background', L. Wedderburn, 'Labour Law 2008: 40 Years On', *Industrial Law Journal*, 36/4 (2007), 397, 403.

[58] Collins, n 31 above, 295.

[59] Ibid, 296.

[60] Ibid, 302.

[61] Ibid, 305.

within labour law analyses.[62] This oversight on the part of labour lawyers, based on an over-reliance on the role of collective agreements as a means of ensuring fair and equal distribution of resources, failed to acknowledge the existence of segmented labour markets[63] by which many vulnerable workers were denied access to the means of collective representation and, thus, largely excluded from the fruits of effective bargaining. On this last point, Collins does acknowledge the role of EU social policy which, through initiatives such as its promotion of Works Councils,[64] was at least receptive to the idea that more inclusive policy with social justice and integration as its foundations might result from means other than those traditionally associated with collective bargaining.[65]

Collins concludes by positing that the unravelling of the 'close bond between the labour law discourse and the sociological conception of the system of industrial relations'[66] and the subsequent spread of attention by those concerned with the analysis of labour law over the three discourses he identifies has placed a 'subtle disintegrative pressure on the labour law discourse itself'. This leads to us to question whether there is a single subject left and, if so, to seek to identify what brings it cohesion as 'the resulting productive engagement between discourses oriented towards the different contexts'[67] will require more sophisticated frameworks within which to 'map, analyse, and criticise the law'. This multiplicity of discourses has one distinct advantage in that 'we no longer fall into the trap of thinking that reflexive law requires abstentionism, that law must always be destined to be the midwife rather than the mother', although he rightly cautions against the replacement of one dominating context or 'type of deafness' with another.

Implanting a Feminist Perspective in an Alternative Strategy

In seeking to develop a suitable framework within which analyses of this multiplicity of discourses can take place, it is important to identify the specific analytical tools which are necessary to navigate the extended boundaries mapped out by Collins. To adequately capture the full range of relevant factors, the resulting process of theoretical reconstruction must be undertaken along lines which are parallel to the transformation in work which has signalled its necessity. The process,

[62] See Chapter 2.
[63] See Chapter 3.
[64] Council Directive 94/45/EC on the establishment of a European Works Council, OJ 1994 L 254/64. The framework directives on part-time work, fixed-term work, and parental leave also illustrate EU law's recognition of the need to develop more inclusive forms of policy-making, see Chapter 5.
[65] This is not to say that Collins (or the current author) is necessarily satisfied with the *results* of the EU's social policy in this respect as a means of achieving their original objectives, rather that he acknowledges that the objectives of the policy themselves arose from 'a measure of democratisation of the workplace for the sake of softening the hierarchies in the distribution of power in the workplace and other sites of subordination', Collins, n 31 above, 307.
[66] Ibid, 308.
[67] Ibid.

therefore, requires the input of those whose concerns echo the interests of previously excluded or marginalized actors in the provision and development of labour law and related policy. In this endeavour, according to Conaghan, 'Feminism clearly forms part of the narrative that needs to be told'[68] as, if the provision and operation of labour law are viewed through the lens of women's needs and aspirations, 'equality issues emerge not as a discrete specialism within the field of labour law but, rather, as a pervasive theme which penetrates both its inner core and outer reaches'.[69] Such an approach further elucidates the 'deep ideological crisis at the heart of traditional labour law' which has come about through the collapse of the standard (male) worker and the collective framework which 'purports to serve him'.[70]

In developing a clear ideology on which to base an alternative strategy[71] to that expounded by the disciples of neo-liberal economic theory, feminist analysis is able to make a particularly valuable contribution. This is because the very foundations on which its engagement with labour law is based directly challenge many of the established neo-liberal preconceptions and assumptions regarding the interaction between law, the State, and social and economic organization. By seeking recognition of the role of women within all areas of society, feminist discourses of labour law pose some challenging questions which cannot be answered by reference to what is, in many respects, a single-principle dogma. For example, the emphasis placed by free market ideology on the factors of supply and demand as the key determinants of wage levels and corresponding labour conditions overlooks the important role of social factors in influencing conditions within the labour market. Through its belief that discrimination arises as a consequence of irrational decision-making, '[n]eo liberalism legitimises market generated inequality'[72] because the supporting ideology preaches non-intervention in response to labour market inequality so that legislation which is aimed at correcting the excesses of the market is viewed as an unnecessary infringement on market freedom.[73] However, the very different social conditions under which men and women interact with paid work, which are best expressed through segmented labour market theory, illustrate that the market is not a spontaneous mechanism which provides a neutral framework but, rather, the sum total of its various components which can be shaped depending on the dominant ideology of the time. The displacement of political and moral responsibility which is enabled by the neo-liberal belief in the primacy of the market is unsustainable if the role of social relations in determining market outcomes is recognized, so that 'Once it is accepted that the market is deeply and deliberately distributive, a political concern with inequality becomes not only legitimate but, indeed, morally imperative.'[74]

[68] Conaghan, n 40 above, 21.
[69] Ibid.
[70] Ibid. See Chapter 3.
[71] Hepple, n 23 above, 14.
[72] Conaghan, n 40 above, 32.
[73] See F. Hayek, *Law, Legislation and Liberty, Vol. II* (London: Routledge and Keegan, 1982), 3.
[74] Conaghan, n 40 above, 33.

The principles of equality and non-discrimination are particularly salient in this context as they inspire and enable considerations of the productive/reproductive dichotomy, and question the apparent distinction between justice in the public and private domains.[75] After all, the market view of the traditional organization of the family as the most efficient means of providing care is only plausible if the work necessary for it to function continues to be provided on an unpaid basis. The assumption that women's participation in such provision will continue overlooks individual aspirations and ambitions for personal development[76] and enables circumvention of responsibility for the distribution of resources on the part of the State. These, as yet, unresolved issues have their solutions in the import of the principles of social justice as a predominating factor in the development, interpretation, and application of labour law.

It is likely that, were we to try hard enough, it would be possible to construct a competing set of economics-based justifications capable of challenging the neo-classical economist's exposition of market structures and behaviour on which to base an argument for legal intervention in the labour market along the lines proposed in this book. We should, however, desist from replacing one set of economics-based rationalizations with another[77] but instead seek to base arguments in support of social justice on ethical, moral foundations as it is only by doing so that the political manipulation to which all disciplines, including economics, are susceptible can be avoided. The ideological choices made by economists in the development of neo-liberal theory have influenced and shaped current conceptions of 'work', 'labour', and 'time' as well as employing specific interpretations of traditional liberal values.[78] Such choices and their assimilation into political dogma and subsequent general acceptance as maxims for how to live have tended to privilege productive activity and undervalue or neglect reproductive activity. By this process the market imperative has become paramount in all that we do and strive for with no consideration for the value of other, non-commodifiable, but crucial factors such as empathy or altruism.

Legal Intervention in the Employment Relationship

The acceptance that labour law is in need of recasting provides the opportunity to reconsider its basic tenets in order to determine where it should go from here. Hepple has called for modernization of its 'auxiliary function' by which participative methods can be developed and employed which are appropriate for the

[75] See Chapters 2 and 3.
[76] On the part of men such aspirations may relate to the desire to spend more time caring for their children and others.
[77] Conaghan, n 40 above, 35. This echoes Collins's reservation, see n 31 above. As Conaghan argues (at 36), 'The orientation of traditional economics is revealed as ideological, and its application to labour law thus yields conclusions which, while claiming validity as 'science' are morally and politically contestable.'
[78] See Chapter 2.

contemporary decentralized system of employment relations. Alongside this, a broadening of its empirical base would extend its regulatory function to provide 'an adequate floor of rights for non-standard workers'[79] and a new 'integrative function'[80] could incorporate innovative welfare measures aimed at combating social exclusion such as enhanced opportunities for personal development and supportive measures to make it easier to combine work and family responsibilities.[81] The whole system would require to be underpinned by an ideology capable of legitimizing and reinforcing this vision of labour law's future 'radical pluralism' which 'would abandon the misleading claims of traditional pluralism to "abstention" of the law or "neutrality" of the State'[82] and replace them with the overriding value of equality alongside reassertion of the principle that labour is not a commodity.

Hepple's vision is a fitting one which corresponds with the current proposal for a right to care. The participation of workers and employers in partnerships aimed at developing and utilizing law which is fit for purpose is central to the idea of reflexive regulation. The extension of the regulatory function to accommodate adequate protections for non-standard workers is a crucial aspect of the proposed right as the case analysis in Chapter 6 demonstrates. Finally the integrative function has particular resonance within the confines of the current proposal as it offers an opportunity by which the traditional—and outdated—demarcations both within labour law[83] and between it and related fields such as social policy can be reworked in order to produce a more cohesive and coherent policy approach to tackling the various forms of inequality that are characteristic of the current system. In seeking to recognize the functional and conceptual relationship between the realms of work and family,[84] which has hitherto been largely neglected in mainstream policy, the success of such an endeavour will depend on the use of a new and appropriate evaluative framework by which the potential achievements of each individual are recognized and facilitated and Sen's capabilities approach has much to offer in this respect.[85]

Before considering how Hepple's vision of the future of labour law and its application in the current context might be housed within the European Union's regulatory framework, it is worth dwelling on the ideological aspiration for the reassertion of labour's non-commodification. Although it is, at first sight, beyond question that labour should not be subjected to the same treatment as other units of market exchange on the grounds of its human dimension, a consideration of the current manifestation of labour relations and the regulatory system within which

[79] Hepple, n 23 above, 321. Although there has been considerable progress in this area in the EU context since Hepple's paper was published in the late 1990s, the regulatory response to the growth of 'atypical' work arrangements remains unsatisfactory, see Chapter 5.

[80] Ibid, 322.

[81] Such as childcare and improved parental rights.

[82] Ibid.

[83] For example, the separation between public and private law, both of which labour law has a foot in as noted above in the context of Ewing's work (at n 31) and which currently legitimizes the distinction between the private sphere of home and the public sphere of work discussed in Chapter 2.

[84] Conaghan, n 37 above, 31.

[85] See Chapters 2 and 7.

they operate reveals a worrying trend towards its increasing commodification. Connected to this and of direct relevance in the current context, is the question of how labour is defined for regulatory purposes. Is the 'labour' in labour law capable of denoting only that which is the subject of market exchange, or could its expansion incorporate unpaid work into the appropriate framework?

The Commodification of Labour

If the economic relationship between worker and employing organization lies at the heart of labour law's primary function which is to regulate that relationship,[86] labour law can be characterized as being almost exclusively concerned with paid work. As Conaghan has noted, 'labour law is not primarily or even predominantly about the world of work. It is about *paid* work and, indeed, about particular forms of paid work.'[87] This poses a particular challenge for the current proposal for a right to care which requires that labour law's scope should be expanded so as to take account of the full range of an individual's activities to incorporate unpaid as well as paid work in its widest incarnation. Only by doing so can the important interception between the two, which is of crucial importance in the enhancement of an individual's life chances, be incorporated. In support of such a radical redrawing of labour law's boundaries is its normative assumption that labour is non-commodifiable[88] so that, in this respect, paid work corresponds with its unpaid counterpart.[89] This implies, at least ostensibly, that there may be scope for their closer association by way of labour law's regulatory function which, through its protective role, is well placed to recognize and counter exploitation of an individual's market vulnerability arising due to her caring responsibilities. However, the threats posed by labour law's focus on a narrowly constructed conception of paid work are crystallized in its functional need to locate a contractual nexus in order to assign responsibility for specific individual protections surrounding job security.

Although this can be attributed to labour law's private law categorization, its contractual basis has acquired a particular resonance through the predominance of neo-liberalism as the central and pervasive ideology within which individualized employment rights have found favour. In fact, if labour law's wider purpose and

[86] Referred to by Kahn-Freund as the 'cornerstone of the edifice', O. Kahn-Freund, 'Blackstone's Neglected Child: the Contract of Employment', *Law Quarterly Review*, 93 (1978), 508.

[87] Conaghan, n 37 above, 34. In the UK context, labour law's scope is even further restricted so that the full range of rights is only available to those who work under a contract of employment. See also P. Davies and M. Freedland, 'Employees, Workers and the Autonomy of Labour Law' in H. Collins, P. Davies, and R. Rideout (eds), *Legal Regulation of the Employment Relation* (London: Kluwer Law International, 2000), 267, where the authors assert that 'work contracts' are not the exclusive domain of labour law as many are regulated by commercial or consumer law.

[88] As Fudge states: 'A central feature of social rights is the decommodification of labor through the existence of a social safety net and labor standards that ameliorate the harshness of the market', see n 21 above, 34.

[89] See Chapter 3.

consequent public law function are considered,[90] this in itself appears to be the result of political manoeuvring through a process of policy choice which has promoted the private law dimension of the law's engagement with work above all other concerns.[91] One consequence of the individualization of labour law has been the emphasis on personal scope which has had a delimiting effect on the reach of the law by restricting its provision on the grounds of occupational or employment status in contrast to more broadly available citizenship rights.[92] The exclusion of large groups of workers from the scope of labour law through increased casualization[93] and the use of tripartite contractual arrangements,[94] coupled with the strategic paring back of collective rights, has had a commodifying effect on labour. Hepple's proposal that labour law's regulatory function should be extended to provide rights for non-standard workers[95] recognizes the need to alleviate this trend but, at a more fundamental level, it is necessary to refocus on the protective purpose of labour law which can only be achieved through recognition of its public law function by which the appropriate principles are applied to achieve democratic outcomes.[96]

The worrying trend towards the commodification of dependent labour, which is implicitly rationalized by the neo-liberal preoccupation with the need for increased labour market flexibility, requires to be countered as a matter of urgency. This depends on recognition of the vulnerability of labour law to political manipulation and, subsequently, on a strategic separation of policy from principle only possible at the macro-level.[97] Achievement of such separation requires a reconsideration of the current delineation of labour so that the dichotomous distinctions between public and private, paid and unpaid, and formal and informal are removed in order to make way for a new 'boundaryless' approach to labour market regulation which echoes the reformulation of working practices occurring within the labour market itself.[98] The provision of a right to care within the labour law framework would represent a

[90] See Ewing, n 31 above.

[91] The effect of this on the operation of the specific protections offered, although still limited, is partially mitigated by the potential for judicial review which, at least in some circumstances, offers an opportunity for the scrutiny of governments' responses to specific labour-related issues. See, for example in the UK context, *R v Secretary of State for Employment ex parte Seymour-Smith and Perez (No 2)* [2000] IRLR 263, HL.

[92] Although, as Standing has noted, citizenship rights based on welfare state provisions have traditionally omitted to take account of the need to give and receive care and 'thus, like employment, have tended to be biased against recognising women's contribution through unpaid labour and granting them full citizenship status', G. Standing, *Global Labour Flexibility: Seeking Distributive Justice* (Basingstoke: MacMillan, 1999), 349.

[93] Manifested at the national and supranational levels by the various methods of 'outsourcing' which also occur across national boundaries so that the commodification of labour is a global phenomenon.

[94] EU law has introduced regulation in this respect, see Council Directive 1999/70/EC of 28 June 1999 concerning the framework agreement on fixed-term work concluded by ETUC, UNICE and CEEP, OJ 1999 L 244/64 and Directive 2008/104/EC of the European Parliament and Council of 19 November 2008 on temporary agency work, OJ 2008 L 327/9.

[95] Hepple, n 23 above, 321.

[96] Ewing, n 31 above, 111.

[97] Be it through national or supranational regulatory means.

[98] See Conaghan, n 37 above, 38.

substantial contribution towards the achievement of this aim by its necessary re-evaluation of the boundaries between paid and unpaid work. Such demarcation is, after all, a feature of the politically and socially constructed separation between the private and public aspects of an individual's life currently legitimized by law's adherence to outdated notions of work and family which are reinforced by a misguided acceptance of the autonomy of market forces. The exclusion of unpaid care from the dominant definitions of 'work' on which current law and policy are based is due to the particular conceptions that have for too long been utilized, and not for any other reason.

The need to develop a more suitable framework within which to regulate work beyond the narrowly constructed standard employment relationship is recognized in the ILO's concept of 'decent work' which is based on a much broader conception intended to capture the 'aspirations of people in their working lives' and which incorporates 'opportunity and income; rights; voice and recognition; family stability and personal development; and fairness and gender equality'.[99] In attempting to accommodate this broadening of the regulatory focus brought about by the shift in working arrangements and recognition of the relationship between paid and unpaid work, the Supiot Report called for European labour law to move 'beyond employment'.[100]

In the preceding discussion it has been asserted that, although of obvious importance, the form of law necessary to give effect to a right to care is secondary to its content which is largely determined by its ideological basis. The impact of the neo-liberal conceptualization of the changes taking place within labour markets and their corresponding deregulation has led to the commodification of labour in certain respects. Although at odds with labour law's normative stance, the particular ideology that has informed this trend has had a politicizing effect on the key principles of labour law so that, for example, the realization of equality is subject to a specific interpretation which is, at once, formal and restrictive. The influence of regulation at the national level is limited in this regard due, in part, to party political affiliations but also because of the impact of globalization on labour markets which lifts control over certain aspects of their operation out of the grasp of policy-makers at the national level. EU law offers a viable alternative in this respect due to its operation at the supranational level which is further enhanced by its reputation in the field of social policy innovation. However, the restricted competency of the EU's law-making institutions means that careful consideration must be given to the form of legal intervention and its placement within the pre-existing structure of EU law so that, in this context, form really matters. This aspect will be considered in the final section of this Chapter.

[99] ILO website at <http://www.ilo.org/global/about-the-ilo/decent-work-agenda/lang-en/index.htm> accessed 7 December 2010.

[100] A. Supiot, *Beyond Employment: Changes in Work and the Future of Labour Law in Europe* (Oxford: Oxford University Press, 2001). See the discussion of the possible impact of the EU Charter of Fundamental Social Rights in this respect in Chapter 5.

Situating a Right to Care within the European Employment Law Framework

In seeking to situate a right to care within the existing European regulatory framework it is necessary to identify the status currently afforded to unpaid work by the appropriate legal institutions. In the EU context, such matters fall largely in the 'social policy' domain through which the relevant legal interventions have traditionally been made by a combination of hard law[101] and the judicial interpretation of the European Court. Given that the European Union's overriding objective is the establishment of an internal market with economic and monetary union,[102] the related social goals have been largely subordinated to the operation of a 'free' market resulting in a difficult conceptual relationship between social rights and the market order. In recent years social policy at the supranational level has undergone a shift from a system of hard law regulation aimed at the harmonization of relevant standards to a process of soft law governance by which the Member States' national policies are subjected to measurement against common indicators and benchmarks though the 'open method of co-ordination' (OMC) which, in the employment domain, has found expression by way of the European Employment Strategy (EES). Alongside these amendments to the EU regulatory model, fundamental changes to the environment within which the European labour market operates have led to a dislocation of the ideological foundations of labour law as discussed above. The accommodation of these changes and those relating to the composition of the labour force and the organization of work itself requires a rethink of the rules which regulate the employment relationship so that social rights can be reconciled with the operation of the market.[103]

In contrast to the significant obstacles that are likely to be encountered in attempts to revise individual national legal systems, the realization of such change at supranational level is expedited by the fact that many of the existing features of the relevant regulatory framework can be usefully harnessed in this respect. For example, the process of 'normalization' of 'atypical' working arrangements such as part-time work through legal intervention[104] is already an accepted feature of the current supranational regulatory framework. This is not to say that the methods currently utilized in this respect are without fault,[105] but merely to acknowledge their acceptance within the EU *acquis*. The existing method of 'soft law' governance[106] which has largely replaced 'hard law' regulation as a means of fostering

[101] Mainly in the form of directives, see Chapter 5.
[102] Art 3 TEU.
[103] See the discussion of Marshall's traditional classification of rights, this Chapter at p 68, and in Chapter 5.
[104] This is an important strategy because, as well as improving the life chances of many (women) workers, enhancement of the legal status of such arrangements would assist in overcoming the current boundaries between paid work and unpaid work by enabling more men to participate in both.
[105] See the critique provided in Chapter 5.
[106] By way of the Open Method of Co-ordination (OMC) discussed in Chapter 5.

common social standards across Member States provides a potentially useful mechanism for enforcement of social norms which rely heavily on the participation of the relevant actors through micro-level compliance measures. Furthermore, the enhanced role of the judiciary—already a feature of European social law—is a crucial device in the interpretation and application of general rules to specific circumstances.[107]

Despite its apparent acceptance of the proposed right, it is not assumed that the EU regulatory structure's accommodation of a specific right to care would be without difficulty. On the contrary, although some of the necessary components might already be in place, their utilization in this regard would require cohesion through explicit legal recognition of the right itself—a process likely to meet with some substantial hurdles. As well as the obvious difficulties inherent in the EU law-making process itself, its inclusion on the agenda would depend on gaining the specified level of consensus among Member States and the implementation of such a right would necessitate a flexible approach to regulation somewhat at odds with the top-down compliance monitoring with which EU law is more generally associated. Furthermore, the provision of a specific protective right would, under the traditional EU classification, amount to a social right to be given effect by the bringing forward of a directive whose provisions Member States would be required to implement within a specified time period. This is precisely the type of legislative activity that is no longer favoured and which has been largely replaced by the system of soft law governance under the OMC outlined above.

Such hurdles may prove insurmountable in the longer term, particularly in the context of an enlarged Europe, within which political consensus is likely to prove elusive across a range of issues. Although its recognition as a specified ground attracting a guaranteed prohibition of discrimination remains the preferred foundation on which to base a right to care, such considerations make it both prudent and pragmatic to look beyond the utilization of hard law means, at least as a preliminary step, for progression of the current proposal.

Pre-existing Authority for a Right to Care?

As outlined above, the current system of governance under the OMC offers, at least potentially, an opportunity to develop a framework incorporating carers' rights to participate in paid employment through the provision of soft law instruments with compliance based on the performance measurements which are usually applied in respect of Member States' achievement of the explicit goals identified. However, the utilization of existing mechanisms in this way would still require political will and, as a pre-curser to that, the establishment of competent authority. As Chapter 5 asserts, the authority for such development is in fact already present within the EU's

[107] See Chapter 6.

constitutional law as articulated by certain Treaty provisions[108] with further elucidation through secondary legislation and policy instruments. Furthermore, the relevant provisions of EU law, far from having lain dormant since their inception, have been the subject of long and lively debate played out, not by those institutions generally charged with EU law-making, but by way of judicial interpretation as part of the ongoing dialogue between the Court of Justice and the national courts of the Member States. Chapter 6 will explore the context and nature of that dialogue by way of a detailed analysis of some of the salient cases and their relationship with the fundamental principles of EU law as applied by national courts and interpreted by the Court of Justice.

Of course, while the placement of a right to care within the pre-existing EU framework has obvious attractions, it is not without its own challenges. Chief among these must be the concern that transference of responsibility to the supranational level for what is, at least in terms of its explicit recognition, a legal innovation will not necessarily overcome some of the more fundamental ideological issues outlined above. Whilst the circumvention of a specific legislative proposal might alleviate some of the more tricky technical hurdles offered by the European law-making process, the promotion and development of such a right as a consequence of the application of pre-existing constitutional provisions to what were previously seen as unrelated circumstances is likely to bring its own challenges. The need to reach political consensus among Member States will be necessary at whatever level the proposal is pitched—the goals and guidelines identified under the EES rightly require broad agreement—and the EU's competence in soft law 'policy' areas is similarly limited. The opportunities and threats posed by the internal relations of the EU and its wider environment will be considered in the next Chapter, but first the issue of ideology within the context of EU policy-making will be addressed.

Market Integration and the Right to Care

The main ideological hurdle to the development of a right to care within EU employment law lies in the reconciliation of what is essentially a social right with the Union's overriding goal of market integration. The pervading neo-liberal doctrine is that State-initiated protective action through the provision of market regulation imposes unnecessary burdens on employers through increased costs and loss of flexibility which can be effectively overcome by non-interventionist means as, left to its own devices, the market will regulate itself. Useful in this respect has been Marshall's triple classification of rights as civil, political, or social, wherein the latter were seen to provide a 'basic conflict' with the market order through their ambiguous legal status and resulting non-justiciability.[109] However, Marshall

[108] See the general provisions in Art 3 TEU and Arts 151–3 and 157 TFEU, and Chapter III CFR on equality, and Art 33 CFR on the reconciliation of family and professional life.

[109] See above at p 69.

recognized the value of such rights in an increasingly market-led economy and his suggested solution to this conflict was reliance on the 'superstructure of legitimate expectations' for expression of the redistributive role of social provision, with its realization dependent on a system of public provision and collective financing rather than on legal entitlement. The world is a different place from that in which Marshall's thesis was formulated,[110] with the main change in this respect presented by the disintegration of collectivism as a means of negotiating acceptable standards of redistribution. This aspect, along with the increased internationalization of markets, has meant that 'legal and constitutional mechanisms are increasingly being used to assert social claims.'[111] The dual forces of globalization and neo-liberalism have led to an intertwining of the discourses of human and social rights within which the courts have assumed an increased prominence[112] at odds with Marshall's expectations regarding their role in this respect. Perhaps, given the preceding discussion regarding the need to develop a regulatory framework more attuned with its wider social and economic environment, it is time that the juridical status of social rights within the EU legal order was reviewed.[113]

As well as questioning the continued relevance of the classification of social rights as inherently non-justiciable, renewed consideration of Marshall's thesis in the contemporary EU context reveals the potential value of the current system of EU policy-making through the OMC. As outlined above, this process offers an alternative to the hard law regulation of the type that Marshall eschewed as incompatible with the market. The soft law focus of the OMC and its emphasis on policy co-ordination at the national level may well represent a viable alternative to the collective laissez faire of a previous era in line with what Marshall envisaged as the most effective means of realizing 'the superstructure of legitimate expectations' which can no longer be met by other means.[114] Supiot has summarized the effect of this shift in the governance of EU employment law thus: 'the law is relinquishing the job of establishing substantive rules, but is instead concentrating on affirming principles and laying down procedures'.[115]

Reflexive Law and the Capabilities Approach

The form of regulation facilitated by the OMC, with its enhanced focus on procedure and self-regulation in favour of direct interference with private actions,

110 See Hepple, n 23 above, and J. Browne, S. Deakin, and F. Wilkinson, 'Capabilities, Social Rights and European Market Integration' in R. Salais and R. Villeneuve (eds), *Europe and the Politics of Capabilities* (Cambridge: Cambridge University Press, 2004), 205, 206.

111 S. Deakin, 'Social Rights in a Globalised Economy' in P. Alston (ed), *Labour Rights as Human Rights* (Oxford: Oxford University Press, 2005), 52.

112 Fudge, n 21 above, 43.

113 Ibid, 31.

114 Deakin and Browne, n 14 above, 27.

115 A. Supiot, 'Governing Work and Welfare in a Global Economy' in J. Zeitlin and D. Trubeck (eds), *Governing Work and Welfare in New Economy: European and American Experiments* (Oxford: Oxford University Press, 2003), 388.

can be characterized as 'reflexive'.[116] As a concept, reflexive law is 'both descriptive and normative' enabling, at least theoretically, a linkage of the legal system with other sub-systems such as the economy and the industrial relations system.[117] Through its descriptive incarnation, reflexive law identifies and emphasizes the need for legal intervention 'to underpin and encourage autonomous processes of adjustment, in particular by supporting mechanisms of group representation and participation'.[118] In its normative guise, reflexive law utilizes 'legal norms, procedures and sanctions to 'frame' or 'steer' the process of self-regulation'.[119] In the EU context, the appropriate normative content is provided by the European Charter of Fundamental Rights[120] which combines labour and social rights as well as by the social standards in operation within the Member States themselves through an inclusive process managed by the EU institutions in place of 'a stark dichotomy between justiciable rights and untrammelled policy'.[121]

The flexibility and hybridity of the soft law approach encapsulated by the EES and OMC certainly appears to hold some attraction for its use as an effective means of advancing the proposed right to care which will rely for the establishment of its scope as well as for its legitimacy on Members States' pre-existing employment and welfare provisions. However, it would be foolish to place too much emphasis on the likelihood of this particular development providing a coherent response to the unpaid care/paid work conflict. After all, its operation to date has gleaned disappointingly little evidence of progress in this respect. Furthermore, any suggestion that the OMC might provide a suitable means of developing such a response should not assume that the exclusive operation of soft law and policy will be enough to challenge entrenched social norms and to overcome the effects of the deregulation of labour markets associated with neo-liberal economic policy. These issues will be further explored in the next Chapter in the context of a critical analysis of EU policy initiatives aimed at reconciling personal and professional life. What is worth noting at this stage is the *potential* offered by the OMC and its ability to overcome the difficulties traditionally associated with the supposed conflict between social rights and market integration in the specific context of paid and unpaid work.

This potential can be categorized as arising in respect of two distinct features, both of which result from its soft law approach. The first of these relates to the differing ideological perceptions engendered in the use of hard law regulation and soft law

[116] See G. Teubner, 'Juridification: Concepts, Aspects, Limits, Solutions' in G. Teubner (ed), *Juridification of Social Spheres: A Comparative Analysis in the Areas of Labor, Corporate, Antittrust and Social Welfare Law* (Berlin: Walter de Gruyter, 1987), 22; D. Ashiagbor, *The European Employment Strategy: Labour Market Regulation and New Governance* (Oxford: Oxford University Press, 2005), 217–20.

[117] Fudge, n 21 above, 54.

[118] C. Barnard and S. Deakin, '"Negative" and "Positive" Harmonisation of Labour Law in the European Union', *Columbia Journal of European Law*, 8 (2002), 389.

[119] C. Barnard, S. Deakin, and R. Hobbs, 'Fog in the Channel, Continent Isolated: Britain as a Model for EU Social and Economic Policy?', *Industrial Law Journal*, 34 (2002), 35.

[120] See S. Fredman, 'Transformation or Dilution: Fundamental Rights in the EU Social Space', *European Law Journal*, 12/41 (2006), 60 and Chapter 5 below.

[121] Ibid, 51. See also N. Barnard, '"A New Governance" Approach to Economic, Social and Cultural Rights in the EU' in Hervey and Kenner (eds), n 14 above, 247, 257.

governance. Use of the former, particularly at the supranational level, has long been viewed as a threat to national sovereignty and to enhanced market integration and both of these factors would provide substantial barriers to progression through their expression as Member State's rationalizations for non-activity in this area. Furthermore, the new regulatory environment within which the EU institutions now operate, make it unlikely that a proposal for labour market regulation in areas which, under current classifications, cannot be directly categorized as 'employment policy', will be adopted as a priority for legislative action. Under the policy domain, however, there is already strong evidence of a commitment to the reconciliation of paid work and unpaid care and it is on this foundation that the proposed right could be based and further developed. The second attribute which can be claimed by the OMC in the current context lies in the process which it offers as an alternative to the complaint-based enforcement of individual rights through the courts. As the previous discussion of the unpaid care/paid work conflict has shown, at the heart of the conflict between the two competing aspects of a person's life lie certain institutional flaws which can only be remedied by collective means. Such systemic failings cannot be overcome by the provision of justiciable individual rights as their resolution depends, at least as a starting point, on the facilitation of broad-based dialogue involving appropriate stakeholders.[122]

These two features combine to make exploration of the OMC's potential use in the development and furtherance of a right to care a worthwhile exercise. However, what they do not offer is the basis on which to directly reconcile the provision of such a right with the market order and, it is in this respect that Sen's capabilities approach (CA)[123] could make a valuable contribution. As Browne et al have asserted, the procedural orientation of social law which is implicit in its reflexive stance 'forms a bridge to the idea of a social choice procedure of the kind which Sen sees as providing the most appropriate basis for the achievement of equality of capability'.[124] In the context of European integration, such a procedure is required 'to address the need to locate social rights within the logic of market integration'[125] and the CA offers certain possibilities in this respect by enabling the redistribution of resources through collective means, as well as by providing a basis on which individual goals can be achieved.[126] The application of the CA in its wider context enables a binary categorization of social rights as either immediate claims to resources in the traditional sense[127] or as 'particular forms of *procedural* or institutionalized interaction (such as rules governing workplace relations, collective bargaining and corporate governance)'[128] which are capable of operating as social

[122] Fredman, n 120 above, 48; Barnard, n 121 above, 266–7.

[123] See Chapter 2.

[124] Browne *et al*, n 110 above, 211.

[125] Ibid.

[126] For discussion of the various ways in which Sen's CA might be useful in this context, particularly at the supranational level, see Supiot, n 100 above, and the various contributions in Salais and Villeneuve (eds), n 110 above.

[127] Which result in the provision of sick pay, maternity pay, and other welfare benefits.

[128] Browne *et al*, n 110 above.

conversion factors. This latter category provides the means by which individuals are able to convert their assets (such as skills or capital) into positive outcomes through what they are able to be and do, that is through their 'functionings'.[129]

The CA's explicit recognition that social and institutional settings are capable of shaping the opportunities for individuals to achieve their goals has potential positive effects which are both direct and indirect. Direct forms of intervention would encompass the provision of anti-discrimination laws, with indirect benefits achievable through the provision of supportive measures aimed at enhancing the ability of those with children to combine paid work with unpaid care. More indirectly, the existence of social rights can contribute to the development of a social ethos or set of norms which may enhance individuals' functionings or potential functionings, as '[a] society which recognises a wide range of social rights is unlikely to be a society which possesses norms and expectations which create obstacles for particular groups of individuals to engage in lives that they have reason to value'.[130] The objective of such State intervention through legal and political means is to 'seed' social conventions so that they are taken for granted in the same way as conventions of property and contract already are. The suitability of Sen's CA in this context is further enhanced by its flexibility and non-prescriptive nature, so that the particular rights that an individual should possess at any given time in order to achieve equality of capability is left undetermined but, depending on the precise context, could encompass 'direct state provision of resources, compulsory reshaping of institutions, or voluntary action to refashion widely held norms'. This form of market intervention encourages and facilitates an ongoing debate regarding the precise meaning and nature of capabilities in different circumstances and its reflexive approach, in turn, enables consideration of a full range of relevant factors including the social and economic circumstances that prevail. Through its non-dogmatic approach, the CA can be more easily rendered compatible with the market order than other forms of social rights theory so that it 'should not be seen as replacing or stifling market mechanisms but rather offering a framework for market-steering which results in better and fairer market transactions'.[131]

Conclusions

The proposed right to care, although compatible with the constitutional provisions of EU law, is difficult to situate within the traditional hierarchy of rights because of its hybrid nature by which its full realization will depend on the satisfaction of a range of claims across the civil, economic, social, and political spectrum. Furthermore, the division between broad-based labour rights and narrowly constructed

[129] See A. Sen, *Commodities and Capabilities* (New Delhi: Oxford University Press, 1987); *Development as Freedom* (New York: Knopf, 1999), discussed in Chapter 2.

[130] Browne *et al*, n 110 above, 212.

[131] Ibid.

individual employment rights, which has been bolstered by the neo-liberal ideology that has dominated Western European politics in recent years, is unhelpful in reconciling the legal intervention necessary to provide a right to care with the operation of what is perceived to be a free labour market. However, the foundations on which the classification of rights by which some are deemed fundamental and others derivative are shifting and the notion of a free market in labour is highly contested due to the resulting commodification of labour and recognition of the need for the reinstatement of labour law's democratic function by which the private relations between workers and employers become matters of public concern. The necessary reorientation of employment relations is possible through a return to the traditional liberal values of equality, autonomy, and freedom in their essential states unfettered by the political conceptualization of neo-liberalism. In Chapter 5, EU law's implicit acceptance of this shift in approach will be explored by way of a detailed consideration of its provisions.

If we accept, as has been asserted in this Chapter, that markets are the result of a range of interrelated factors including human decision-making, rather than the products of a spontaneous and mysterious process over which the only means of influence is through the application of blunt regulatory instruments aimed at stifling integration, the CA has much to commend it. Rather than catering to the neo-liberal conception that the market will remedy itself so that any resulting injustices are the natural consequence of rational decision-making, the CA acknowledges the need for proportionate and effective legal intervention aimed at facilitating individual opportunity and decommodifying labour. It is, thus, perfectly compatible with the traditional liberal values and its overall goal is inherently sympathetic to a market order as its focus is not on guaranteeing the availability of a given set of resources for all individuals regardless of need or aspiration, but rather on enabling individuals to develop the capacity to be free to make effective choices and thus participate in 'genuine and dynamic interaction in the market'.[132]

Of course, the policy choices inherent in the management of this process remain vulnerable to political hijacking of the type that has occurred in relation to the core liberal values under the neo-liberal ideology that has dominated Western politics and, by association, labour law over the past four decades. Furthermore, the danger in accepting too readily the compatibility of capabilities as a normative ground for social rights with market efficiency interpreted as a welfare goal is that it 'cedes a great deal of the moral terrain to the market'.[133] Collins, considering the basis on which Sen's CA is used to rationalize social rights as conducive to efficient market functioning in this context, questions whether such an instrumental view of social rights 'inevitably creates a greater risk that such rights might be traded off against other welfare values and interests, since in the welfare calculus rights become valued not in themselves but for their net effects'.[134] The potential pervasion of political

[132] Ibid, 213. [133] Fudge, n 21 above, 65.
[134] H. Collins, Review of S. Deakin and F. Wilkinson, 'The Law of the Labour Market: Industrialisation, Employment and Legal Evolution', *Industrial Law Journal*, 35 (2006), 105, 109.

dogma and the ideological appropriation of even those rights deemed fundamental pose significant threats, particularly as the subtle forces used for such purposes mean that their effects may not become apparent for some time. That this threat is exacerbated by the current lack of a normative framework within which to evaluate developments in labour law in both its vocational and theoretical forms, emphasizes the urgent need to identify such a framework which is capable of encompassing both the democratic function of labour law through its public law incarnation as well as its role in the private law regulation of the rights of the individual. Distinct from this requirement but related to it, is the need to ensure the separation of policy and principle, the latter relying for its observance on the protection of certain core values. In this respect, Sen's CA is capable of making a substantial contribution. By placing the values by which individuals are able to reach their potential at its centre and by focusing on outcomes rather than the means by which such achievement might be possible, the CA protects itself against such manipulation through the infiltration of political dogma to a large extent. The reflexive nature of such an approach makes it particularly well suited to the current proposal as, in order to be effective, a right to care must take full account of the full range of needs which result from attempts to combine unpaid care with paid work which will vary depending on the individual circumstances of both the carer and the recipient of care.[135] The potential of EU law to provide a suitable framework within which such a right might be placed will form the basis of the next Chapter.

[135] See Chapter 3.

5

European Union Law and Policy: Balancing Paid Employment and Unpaid Care within a Market Order

Introduction

This Chapter will consider the 'fit' of the proposed right to care within the pre-existing EU legal and policy framework. It is asserted that what is proposed is not merely compatible with many of the current provisions of that framework but is in fact necessary to provide cohesion between the various strands that, together, constitute the relevant body of law and, in doing so, to give them effect. Of course, this is not to suggest that any alteration to the current system of labour law will be without difficulty but, as stated in Chapter 1, to continue along its current path without review and appropriate amendment is likely to lead to further uncertainty and, potentially, to a loss of confidence in the ability of EU law to deliver on its constitutional promises of 'full employment and social progress', to 'combat social exclusion and discrimination', and to 'promote social justice and protection, equality between women and men, solidarity between generations and protection of the rights of the child'.[1] Furthermore, these provisions must now be read alongside the newly enshrined fundamental right to 'reconcile family and professional life' by which 'everyone shall have the right to protection from dismissal for a reason connected with maternity and the right to paid maternity leave and to parental leave following the birth or adoption of a child'.[2]

Central to these aims, and at the forefront of debates about the appropriate regulatory stance to be adopted, is the need to increase the quantity of jobs within the European Union whilst preserving and improving the quality of those jobs through protected and enhanced labour and social standards. As discussed in Chapter 3, due to its close association with unpaid care which acts as a constraint

[1] Art 3(3) TEU.

[2] Art 33(2) of the EU Charter of Fundamental Rights (CFR) which was given binding legal effect equal in status to the Treaties by the Lisbon Treaty in December 2009. McGlynn has commented that the phrasing of Art 33(2) 'simply restates existing entitlements' rather than adding anything new, and, although this assertion is entirely correct, it is in the future interpretation of the provision that its potential lies. See C. McGlynn, 'Work, Family and Parenthood: the European Union Agenda' in J. Conaghan and K. Rittich (eds), *Labour Law, Work and Family* (Oxford: Oxford University Press, 2005), 217, 228.

(real and perceived) on labour market participation, women's employment tends to be over-concentrated in a narrow range of jobs and sectors and is often characterized by its precarious nature through distinct applications of the various forms of employment protection. Placed in its wider environmental context, globalization poses further threats to notions of protected labour with regulation deemed unsustainable due to increased competition.

The European Union, for a long time heralded as the caretaker of Member States' social standards, has faced specific challenges in this respect in recent years, not least from its own expansion into the former Eastern European states. Furthermore, the demise of collectivism as a vehicle for enhanced standards through self-regulation has placed a greater emphasis on the role of individualized labour rights, many of which are dependent for their application on the existence of a contract of employment and the satisfaction of other qualifying conditions, at the same time that external competitive pressures have led to an increasingly deregulated labour market.[3] The combination of these factors, coupled with the EU's well-documented difficulties in reconciling its economic goals with its social obligations, has recently culminated in the Court of Justice's (CoJ) restrictive interpretations of the right of trade unions to organize freely against threats to their members' job security in a line of cases on the legitimate use of industrial action as a means of protecting previously agreed employment standards.[4] The danger posed to the future of Social Europe by these and related cases remains to be seen[5] but what is clear is the need for greater clarification of the relationship between the EU's social aims, as articulated *inter alia* by Article 3 TEU, and its economic goals and their relative placement within its constitutional law as provided by the Treaties.

This Chapter consists of a consideration of the body of EU social law and policy relevant to the reconciliation of unpaid care and paid work. This incorporates an exploration of the wider social and employment policy contexts within which the specific provisions are based and, as will become evident, the relevant *acquis* has not been the subject of a particularly smooth transition from closer economic co-operation to greater social integration. Nevertheless, as the identification of specific provisions indicates, there is now a substantial body of law and related policy which is intended to regulate social relations between individuals and in their dealings with the State, much of which is directly relevant to the issues under consideration. As will become apparent, the relevant law and policy has evolved in a reactive fashion, often as a means of responding to external factors, and, thus, lacks the cohesion that might have resulted from a more comprehensive overarching strategy. However, the combination of constitutional, legislative, and policy instruments provides a more than adequate foundation for the progression of a right to care

[3] See Chapter 4 above.

[4] See Case C-438/05 *Viking Line ABP v The International Transport Workers' Federation, the Finnish Seaman's Union* [2007] ECR I-10779; Case C-341/05 *Laval un Partneri Ltd v Svenska Byggnadsarbetareförbundet* [2007] ECR I-11767; Case C-346/06 *Dirk Rüffert v Land Niedersachsen* [2008] ECR I-1989; Case C-39/06 *European Commission v Luxembourg* [2009] ECR I-4323.

[5] See A. C. L. Davies, 'One Step Forward, Two Steps Back? The Viking and Laval Cases in the ECJ', *Industrial Law Journal*, 37/2 (2008), 126.

within European employment law. Interlaced with the analysis of the specific provisions of EU law, is a consideration of the Court of Justice's immense contribution in this respect. The Court has been a constant presence in both the development of Europe's social dimension and in the provision and interpretation of specific instruments related to the reconciliation of unpaid care and paid work, giving it an undoubted influence over both the content of the provisions themselves and the processes by which they have developed and are enforced.

The Development of Social Europe

The accumulated power of capital in the global era, with its mobility now unfettered through the use of assistive technologies, has resulted in 'work choice' laws[6] by which employers are able to use their enhanced powers to invest and disinvest across borders dependent on identification of the most favourable (ie profitable) market conditions. As a result, the subordination of employees to an increasingly faceless employer is gaining in prominence with contributory factors being the diminishing public sector and the growth of private sector organizations or 'units of capital' which operate across borders, are controlled by a new class of professional financial managers, and whose investors enjoy the benefits of limited liability through registered company structures. In this reconstituted world of work, '[t]he new dynamics of capital in the labour market [have] demanded that labour be sold in more precarious packages than the traditional standard employment contract'[7] thus leaving workers' rights vulnerable to the vagaries of the market. The perceived merits of both sides of the 'regulation versus flexicurity' debate will be considered below[8] in the context of the type of work more often than not performed by worker-carers. First, it is worth exploring the development of the EU's social provisions against this backdrop and in the context of the future effects of globalization before providing closer scrutiny of the specific law and policy provisions aimed at the reconciliation of paid and unpaid work within European employment law. This exploration sheds light on the underlying intentions of the EU legislature as well as enabling some assessment of the relative value attributed to the various strands of Europe's social dimension and their subsequent placement in, what appears at first glance to be, a cohesive body of law but which is ultimately revealed to suffer from the lack of a unifying philosophy and an overarching strategy.

European law has been described as an 'ideal vehicle for upholding the principle of sex equality'[9] due to its 'undoubted potential for growth',[10] and it is certainly true that the EU institutions have been at the forefront of developments in law and policy

[6] Lord Wedderburn, 'Labour Law 40 years on', *Industrial Law Journal*, 36/4 (2007), 397, 399.
[7] Ibid, 210.
[8] This Chapter at pp 106–7.
[9] E. Ellis, *EU Anti-Discrimination Law* (Oxford: Oxford University Press, 2005), 7.
[10] Ibid. This potential encompasses institutional and geographical growth as well as the extension of relevant concepts, for example, the inclusion of consideration for human rights in developing and interpreting relevant provisions of EU law.

aimed at improving women's labour market opportunities and associated terms and conditions. However, sex equality law forms part of the wider social policy area in which progress has not always been steady. The relevant substantial body consists of a collection of legal and policy instruments scattered across the full range of activities. These provisions are held together by a fledgling constitutional commitment whose development, notwithstanding the dynamic period of social action which took place during the 1970s, has occurred at a slow and incremental pace characterized by intermittent phases of activity followed by intervals of consolidation and 'bedding in' during which law-making has been sparse.

Placed in its broader context, Europe's so-called 'social dimension', which has never been the focus of proactive and cohesive planning, has emerged as the result of a combination of oversight and political opportunism. The inclusion of any explicit social provision in the original Treaty of Rome was permitted at the insistence of France as a pro-competition measure intended to protect against the market distortion that, it was claimed, would ensue due to the disparate social protection measures which were to be found in the constitutional law of the founding Member States.[11] Thus, the goal of gender equality in the EU context owes as much for its justification to the pursuit of market-making as to the realization of social justice.[12] Given such unpromising beginnings, it is perhaps not surprising that the current body of law is both complex and uneven. However, the early acknowledgment of the link between market inefficiency and worker exploitation was at least implicit in the realization that uneven social protection would result in distortion of competition. This interrelationship appears to have been forgotten in the current context within which the attainment of profit has emerged as the dominant goal of market integration even where it results directly from such inefficiency and has a widespread and damaging effect on the distribution of resources.

The main reason for the omission of an express desire for greater social protection alongside the industrial co-operation and enhanced political unity accepted by the Schuman Declaration signatories in 1950 has been attributed to a lack of political will to intervene in labour market regulation based on an assumption that the Member States' national labour law and industrial relations systems would continue to provide the requisite protection without unnecessary interference. However, the omission from the founding Treaty of a specific social objective based on enhanced worker protection has been a long lasting impediment to the development of European labour law.[13] The 'assumption that the functioning of the Common Market would bring about a raised standard of living of workers in the EC'[14] is clearly illustrated by the original wording of the Preamble to the Treaty

[11] See C. Barnard, 'The Economic Objectives of Article 119' in T. Hervey and D. O'Keeffe (eds), *Sex Equality Law in the European Union* (Chichester: John Wiley, 1996), 321, 322–4; C. Hoskyns, *Integrating Gender: Women, Law and Politics in the European Union* (London: Verso, 1996), Ch 3.

[12] J. Lewis, 'Work/Family Reconciliation, Equal Opportunities and Social Policies: The Interpretation of Policy Trajectories at the EU Level and the Meaning of Gender Equality', *Journal of European Public Policy*, 13/3 (2006), 420, 421.

[13] E. Szyszczak, *EC Labour Law* (Harlow: Longman, 2000), 6.

[14] Ibid.

which declared the Member States' resolve 'to ensure the economic and social progress of their countries by common action to eliminate the barriers which divide Europe'. The original Article 2 set out the aims of the Common Market as being, *inter alia*, to promote 'a harmonious development of economic activities' accompanied by 'an accelerated raising of the standard of living'. This vague objective was further articulated by Article 117 EC, which provided the aims and principles of the limited Social Policy Chapter of the Treaty of Rome 1957 as being 'to promote improved working conditions and an improved standard of living for workers'.[15]

The underlying lack of political interest and resulting restricted legal base meant that the early years of European integration saw little progress in the area of employment law with no specific attention paid to the promotion of measures aimed at the reconciliation of personal and professional life despite the steady increase in women's labour market participation. This situation was substantially improved by the instigation of the social action programmes under the Council's resolution in 1974 which brought together four main areas of activity under a broad employment theme.[16] The first Programme's focus on employment protection and industrial democracy[17] laid the foundations for legislative activity in the area of sex equality. The reason for this sudden emphasis on social policy has been attributed to changes in the dominant political ideologies[18] resulting from an increased international focus on civil rights which had been gaining momentum since the 1960s. Trade unions, which had hitherto organized at the national level, started to recognize the potential benefits of increased co-operation at European level. Perhaps of most significance were the converging ideologies of the social democratic governments of key Member States which, in recognizing the importance of social goals in furthering European integration, began to question the pervasive neo-liberal ideology which, although highly influential in matters of economic decision-making, had been ineffective in staving off the approaching recession.[19]

Alongside this new emphasis on social affairs in Europe's political objectives, was the Court's prominent recognition of social justice as a driver of European integration. Despite the initial lack of political appetite for a European social policy and subsequent fragile legal base, the Court from its inception was aware of its own potential for development across the full range of Community activities as

[15] Art 117 EC. To appreciate how far the development of European engagement in this area has come from these indeterminate beginnings, it is worth comparing the wording of these provisions with that of the current Article 151 TFEU, which defines the Union's objectives as including 'the promotion of employment, improved living and working conditions, so as to make possible their harmonisation while the improvement is being maintained, proper social protection, dialogue between management and labour, the development of human resources with a view to lasting high employment and the combating of exclusion'.

[16] Namely, the equal treatment of men and women at work; harmonization of labour law; the development of common standards for working conditions; and supranational employment and regional policy

[17] Bulletin of the European Communities, Supplement 2/74, at 8.

[18] M. Shanks, 'The Social Policy of the European Communities', *Common Market Law Review*, 14 (1977), 375.

[19] T. Hervey, *European Social Law and Policy* (London: Longman, 1998), 17.

evidenced by its early case law concerning the significance of certain Treaty provisions. In *Defrenne II*,[20] the Court declared that the equal pay provisions of Article 119 *were* directly effective as they:

> Form part of the social objectives of the Community, which is not merely an economic union, but at the same time intended, by common action, to ensure social progress and seek the constant improvement of the living and working conditions [of Europe's citizens][21]

The Court's activity notwithstanding, the enthusiasm for the development of a specific social policy was short-lived and by the end of the 1970s a range of factors—economic, political, and social—combined to stall further expansion of Community competence in the area of labour law. Widespread recession caused by high unemployment rates and rising inflation, as well as competition from the deregulated labour markets of the Far East and the United States, caused national governments to reconsider labour market policy and existing industrial structures. Throughout most of the following decade national governments would be prepared to commit only to 'soft law' measures in all areas of labour law, so that action was 'minimal and ad hoc'.[22] During the first half of the 1980s, the Member States' governments responded to the pressures of increased competition by protectionist strategies aimed at blocking the development of European social policy such as the watering down of Commission proposals[23] and exercise of the right of veto[24] made possible by the requirement of unanimity at Council level. A period of deregulation aimed at enhancing national labour market flexibility ensued and Member States' resistance to further European integration in the social policy area saw the enactment of limited legislation with the emphasis on 'soft law' measures[25] and policy initiatives such as the Commission-proposed programme on positive action for women.[26]

In contrast to the lack of legislative activity, the Court's engagement with social integration continued through its involvement with the Article 177 procedure.[27] Although characterized as its activist phase,[28] the interplay that the Court enjoyed

[20] Case 43/75 [1976] ECR 455 in which the Court also held that, although not directly effective, Art 117 could be used as a teleological tool for interpreting other provisions. The impact of this judgment is considered further in Chapter 6 below.

[21] Ibid, para 10.

[22] Szyszczak, n 13 above, 8. See also B. Hepple, 'The Crisis in EEC Labour Law', *Industrial Law Journal*, 18 (1987), 129.

[23] Eg the agreed text of Directive 86/378/EEC on equal treatment in occupational social security differed considerably from the original proposal.

[24] Eg COM (83) 686 final OJ 1983 C 333/6 on parental leave and leave for family reasons, an initiative that was eventually resurrected in a substantially amended form and concluded as a social partner framework agreement and enacted as Directive 96/34/EC, discussed below at p 116.

[25] It was during this period that the regulation of working time was first proposed, albeit through a 'soft law' measure, by the draft Council recommendation on the reduction and reorganisation of working time, OJ 1983 C 290/4.

[26] Which culminated in Council Recommendation 84/635/EEC of 13 December 1984 on the promotion of positive action for women, OJ 1984 L 331/34–5.

[27] Now Art 267 TFEU. This was the period in which the pivotal cases concerning the Court's conceptualization of indirect discrimination originate—see Chapter 6.

[28] See Chapter 6.

with the national courts during this period was in fact instigated by the latter's references for interpretation of Community provisions. While the Community's law-making institutions were experiencing a phase of political inertia, the Court's 'crucial role in keeping labour law issues alive'[29] was attributable to two interrelated factors. First, its judgment in *Defrenne II*[30] had undoubtedly raised claimants' and their legal advisors' expectations as to what could be achieved by the application of Community law, particularly through the direct effect of Article 119.[31] Secondly, the national courts, aware of Community law's supremacy, were increasingly willing to engage in dialogues with the European Court.[32]

In the policy context, the need to develop the internal market was used as an effective means of reigniting the institutions' engagement with social law in the second half of the decade. The French socialist administration's support for the notion of a 'European social area' gained momentum following the appointment of a new Commission under Jacques Delors's presidency in 1984. The new regime's commitment to the articulation and furtherance of Europe's social aims is illustrated by the Commission's famous White Paper of 1985[33] in which it made clear its commitment to the equivalence of social laws in the fight against 'social dumping'. The resulting Single European Act led to developments in three significant respects: the promotion of the social dialogue; the breaking of deadlock made possible by the requirement of unanimity in respect of social provisions; and the reform and realignment of the structural funds.[34] A longer view enables the development of a catalogue of social rights in the form of certain guaranteed minimum standards encapsulated by the EU Charter of Fundamental Rights (CFR) to be added to the list of positive outcomes in the social policy field emanating from this period of the EU's history.[35]

What Ellis has referred to as a scheme for 'rolling interdependence'[36] was taken a step further when the Member States pledged to make greater use of majority voting, thereby relinquishing a significant portion of national sovereignty. Article 118A EC granted power to the Community to enact legislation using qualified majority voting (QMV) and introduced the co-operation procedure with the Parliament for use in areas concerning 'the work environment'. This latter 'ingenious device',[37] based on the wide Nordic concept of 'working environment' incorporating employment protection, the organization of work, and associated

[29] Szyszczak, n 13 above, 8.

[30] See n 20 above.

[31] See A. Lester, 'The Uncertain Trumpet. References to the European Court of Justice from the United Kingdom: Equal Pay and Equal Treatment without Sex Discrimination' in H. G. Schermers (ed), *Article 177 EEC: Experiences and Problems* (The Hague: TMV Asser Instituut, 1987), 164.

[32] See C. Kilpatrick, 'Community or Communities of Courts in European Integration? Sex Equality Dialogues Between UK Courts and the ECJ', *European Law Journal*, 4/2 (1998), 121.

[33] COM (85) 310 final.

[34] Szyszczak, n 13 above, 9–12. See Arts 130 a–e/EEC (now 174–8 TFEU) which identified economic and social cohesion as one of the six priority areas in completion of the Internal Market.

[35] See below at p 123.

[36] Ellis, n 9 above, 8.

[37] Szyszczak, n 13 above, 10.

rights, offered the use of Article 118A as a legal base. Coupled with the simplified procedures, this laid the foundations for greater legislative activity, such as the adoption of directives aimed at harmonizing employment protection for pregnant workers and those who have recently given birth and at regulating working time.[38]

The 1992 Treaty on European Union contained references to federalism which attracted some dissent from among the Member States' governments (notably the UK) but was, nevertheless, ultimately accepted. The creation of the European Union, following ratification of the TEU, changed the nature of the Community, with attention focused on a wider set of issues such as the development of a Common Foreign and Security Policy and Justice and Home Affairs and the laying of the foundations for economic and monetary union. However, this apparently enhanced cohesion was accompanied by, what has been described as, the institutionalization of the Member States' differences in approach to European social policy.[39] These differences are most clearly illustrated by the contention surrounding the Social Policy Agreement (SPA) from which the UK effected an 'opt-out' and, following a change of government in 1997, an 'opt-in'.[40]

The provisions introduced by the Amsterdam Treaty[41] made technical amendments intended to reinforce the economic, social, and political links between Member States. In the social policy area, the Protocol, which had been annexed to the EC Treaty by the TEU, was incorporated into the main body,[42] replacing the existing social policy provisions. This act and the inclusion of a new Title on Employment,[43] aimed primarily at countering unemployment, were indicative of a move away from a purely economic conception of the EU towards a more overtly political organization. The prohibition of discrimination on the grounds of nationality[44] was supplemented by the insertion of a new Article 13[45] authorizing the Council 'to take appropriate action to combat discrimination based on sex, racial or ethnic origin, religion or belief, disability, age or sexual orientation'. The introduction of Article 13 is significant in that it reinforced non-discrimination as a fundamental principle and it extended the EU's legal competence by enabling

[38] Council Directive 92/85/EEC of 19 October 1992 on the introduction of measures to encourage improvements in the safety and health at work of pregnant workers and workers who have recently given birth or who are breastfeeding (tenth individual directive within the meaning of article 16(1) of Directive 89/391/EEC), OJ 1992 L 348/1, and Council Directive 93/104 of 23 November 1993 concerning certain aspects of the organisation of working time, OJ 1993 L 307/18.

[39] Hervey, n 19 above, 25.

[40] The complex and questionable constitutional arrangements supporting the opt-out saw the 12 Member States agreeing, by way of a Social Policy Protocol annexed to the Treaty, that the remaining 11 states should be enabled to utilize the EU institutions for the purposes of enacting measures provided for in the SPA. On this issue and the equally complex arrangements facilitating the 'opt-in', see N. Burrows, 'Opting in to the Opt-out: The UK and European Social Policy', *Web Journal of Current Legal Issues* 4, (1997) available at <http://webjcli.ncl.ac.uk/1997/issue4/burrows4.html>. On the general issue of varying levels of social development within the EU, see J. Shaw, 'Twin-Track Social Europe—The Inside Track' in D. O'Keefe and P. Twomey (eds), *Legal Issues of the Maastricht Treaty* (London: Wiley, 1994), 295.

[41] Which came into force on 1 May 1999 and, *inter alia*, renumbered the Treaty.

[42] In Title XI, Chapter 1, now Title X TFEU.

[43] Title VIII, now Title IX TFEU.

[44] Contained in Art 12, now Art 18 TFEU.

[45] Now Art 19 TFEU.

legislation prohibiting discrimination on a far wider range of grounds.[46] Following the Amsterdam Treaty's adoption, the promotion of equality between men and women was expressly identified as a task of the Community[47] and an increased emphasis was placed on the need to embed gender equality into all fields of policy development through a process of mainstreaming.[48] Together, these changes were significant as they enabled commitment to 'work/family reconciliation' to be more clearly integrated into employment policies than ever before as European social integration entered a new and distinctive phase in its development with a move away from the 'top-down' implementation of hard law directives towards a softer 'bottom-up' approach based on self-regulation and peer review.[49]

From Social Law to Employment Policy

Despite the amendments to the law-making process initiated by the Maastricht and Amsterdam Treaties, the anticipated development of legislative initiatives in the social area had failed to materialize as the twentieth century drew to a close due to Member States' reluctance to engage in the further harmonization of social standards at the national level. This led to the introduction of the European Employment Strategy (EES), a new way of implementing such standards at the supranational level, through the open method of co-ordination (OMC).[50] Relations between the Member States in the social law field have always been characterized by 'unresolved contradictions and tensions'[51] caused by an uneasy co-existence of conflicting social policy models. This is clearly illustrated by the

[46] Two directives have already been implemented which take Art 13 as their legal base: Council Directive 2000/43/EC implementing the principle of equal treatment between persons irrespective of racial or ethnic origin and Council Directive 2000/78/EC establishing a general framework for equal treatment in employment and occupation, which provides specifically for protection against discrimination on the grounds of religion or belief, disability, age and sexual orientation. Council and Parliament Directive 2002/73 amended the Equal Treatment Directive 76/207/EEC in order to apply the same definitions of direct and indirect discrimination to sex as those contained in the Art 13 directives which are now contained in Directive 2006/54/EC of the European Parliament and of the Council on the implementation of the principle of equal opportunities and equal treatment of men and women in matters of employment and occupation (recast), OJ 2006 L 204/23. For an assessment of the Recast Directive, see below at p 109.

[47] By Art 2 EC, now Art 3 TEU. The Amsterdam amendments also enabled an enhanced emphasis on the protection of human rights by the amendments made to Articles 6 and 7 of the TEU (retained).

[48] See T. Rees, *Mainstreaming Equality in the European Union: Education, Training and Labour Market Policies* (London: Routledge, 1998).

[49] But see Lewis's assertion (at 425) that, although the approach to social policy adopted in the late 1990s can be seen as 'something new in respect of content and method, the larger ambition—to reform social policy in order to make it a more effective complement to economic policy—was not new', J. Lewis, 'Work/Family Reconciliation, Equal Opportunities and Social Policies: The Interpretation of Policy Trajectories at the EU Level and the Meaning of Gender Equality', *Journal of European Public Policy*, 13/3 (2006), 420.

[50] The seminal text on the development and implementation of the EES and the OMC as a system of governance is D. Ashiagbor, *The European Employment Strategy: Labour Market Regulation and the New Governance* (Oxford: Oxford University Press, 2005).

[51] Hervey, n 19 above, 24.

disagreements over the harmonization of maternity provisions and the regulation of working time with the UK government taking a non-interventionist stance in accordance with the national tradition of legal abstentionism. By contrast, Germany's reliance on State regulation made such initiatives more readily acceptable, whereas the Nordic States' employee relations systems, based largely on self-regulation underpinned by collective agreements, already incorporated the broad concept of 'working environment' on the non-contentious ground of workers' well-being.

Such conceptual differences presented the Commission with a particular challenge in its attempts to make progress in the harmonization of social standards. The legislative programmes of the 1970s and early 1980s had been largely concerned with the introduction of basic rights, many of which complemented or improved those already available within the Member States' own regulatory systems, so that, with a few notable exceptions, the Commission's proposals in this respect posed no real threat to sovereignty. However, in the aftermath of Maastricht, the programme for reform had simply reached saturation point so that any new proposals in the social law area were viewed with suspicion by national governments and were, thus, unable to attract the initial agreement necessary in order to instigate the legislative process. Furthermore, and perhaps more pressingly, the economic climate across Europe meant that Member States were not particularly receptive to further labour market regulation. High unemployment rates caused by structural factors such as skills shortages and a lack of inward investment led to a loss of appetite for further intervention at the supranational level. Global economic development and corresponding changes in commercial and industrial practices led by advancements in information technology gave rise to greater competitive threats. The trend in Western welfare states was unsurprisingly towards a 'reworking of the relationship between social provision and employment'[52] with a greater emphasis on 'active' rather than 'passive' welfare reform.[53] These factors instigated a reconsideration of the policy process by the EU institutions culminating in the introduction of a system of co-ordination of the Member States' national social policy by way of the EES.[54]

The EES is based on the Employment Title[55] inserted into the EC Treaty by the Treaty of Amsterdam, but its origins date from the 1993 White Paper[56] which expressly linked growth, competitiveness, and employment for the first time by concluding that the creation of fifteen million new jobs would be necessary to address the key issues of growing unemployment and global competition. The overriding objective was to develop a joined up approach to policy-making by which employment would be integrated with other relevant areas such as fiscal policy. Structural unemployment, a feature of many Member States, was attributed

52 Lewis, n 49 above, 425.

53 See D. Wincott, 'Beyond Social Regulation? New Instruments and/or a New Agenda for Social Policy at Lisbon?', *Public Administration*, 81/3 (2003), 533.

54 See Chapter 5 of Ashiagbor, n 50 above.

55 Title VIII, now Title XI TFEU.

56 European Commission, *Growth, Competitiveness and Employment*, COM (1993) 700 final.

to a combination of social and economic exclusion requiring Keynsian and supply-side measures, specifically a mix of proactive policy designed to promote a more inclusive environment and the deregulation of certain aspects of national labour markets.[57]

The social policy amendments introduced by the Amsterdam Treaty[58] provided an opportunity to formalize the new approach. The new Title on employment enabled an extension of competence in the social policy arena[59] with its key provisions: Article 125, which established the objective of a 'co-ordinated strategy', Article 127(2) which placed 'high employment' on the EC policy agenda, and Article 128 which provided the framework for developing and monitoring the 'guidelines for employment'.[60] Despite the emphasis on the development of an overarching employment policy, the soft law nature of the strategy has led to criticism from some quarters.[61] It can be argued, however, that the new approach does enable more activity at the European level in areas of social policy previously the exclusive domain of national governments as the policy areas previously encompassed by Social Europe 'tended to lie outside the core of national social policies, so as not to upset sensitivities concerning national sovereignty'.[62] The EES, perhaps because of its soft law basis rather than despite it, is arguably a useful means of tackling central issues of concern regardless of the national industrial relations systems in place.

The new prominence given to employment policy was further developed at the Luxembourg summit in 1997 through the adoption of the first employment guidelines by the Heads of State and Government. The approved guidelines incorporated the original four pillars of the EES: employability; entrepreneurship; adaptability; and equal opportunities, which were all viewed as crucial factors in the development of sustainable job creation. At the European Council meeting in Lisbon in 2000, the Member States' representatives reiterated their commitment to a new economic and social agenda by the adoption of a strategic goal for the next decade: 'to become the most competitive and dynamic knowledge-based economy in the world capable of sustainable economic growth with more and better jobs and greater social cohesion'.[63] Achievement of this goal is through co-ordination of the

[57] European Commission, *European Employment and Social Policy: A Policy for People* (D-G for Education and Culture, 2000).

[58] The focus on employment at the Amsterdam summit has been attributed to a combination of the promotion of European monetary union (EMU) and the need for a unifying project, see J. Goetschy, 'The European Employment Strategy: Genesis and Development', *European Journal of Industrial Relations*, 5/2 (1999), 117.

[59] Which, alongside the accompanying Title XI on Social Policy, Education, Vocational Training and Youth, has been described by Burrows as 'merely part of the routine service, an oil change rather than a new engine'. N. Burrows, 'The New Employment Chapter and Social Policy Provisions of the Amsterdam Treaty' in J. Usher (ed), *The State of the European Union* (Harlow: Longman, 2000), 92.

[60] Now Arts 145, 147, and 148 TFEU.

[61] See, for example, S. Ball, 'The European Employment Strategy: The Will but not the Way?', *Industrial Law Journal*, 30/4 (2001), 353.

[62] Goetschy, n 58 above, 133.

[63] See the Presidency Conclusions of the Lisbon European Council of 23rd and 24th March 2000, available at <http://www.europarl.europa.eu/summits/lis1_en.htm> accessed 7 December 2010.

labour market policies of Member States in an annual cycle. This process, known as the open method of co-ordination (OMC), has been defined by Frank Vandenbroucke[64] as 'a mutual feedback process of planning, examination, comparison and adjustment of the policies of Member States, all of this on the basis of common objectives'.[65] At the start of each year, the Council approves the Commission's objectives which have, until now, been drawn up as guidelines based on the four pillars. Member States' national action plans (NAPs) are then submitted for approval by the Commission and the Council.

Whether the co-ordination of national employment policy represents the most effective response to the labour market manifestations of the paid work/unpaid care conflict such as persistent gendered pay gaps and increases in precarious work remains to be seen as it is debatable whether soft law instruments will provide an adequate means of responding to systemic inequalities and discriminatory practices within national labour markets in place of hard law measures aimed at the harmonization of standards. Criticism has focused on the competing objectives pursued within the framework of the EES, namely the requirement for enhanced competitive efficiency within enterprises and resulting needs on the part of employers for greater labour market flexibility, most easily achieved through the use of non-standard work which also serves as a means of increasing the employment rate but which, in the longer term, produces a tension with the dual aim of enhanced protection of and improvements in workers' quality of life and 'work-life balance'.[66] As Ashiagbor has noted, the EES's strategic aim to promote 'a skilled, trained and adaptable workforce and labour markets responsive to economic change' has resulted in employment policy which is dominated by supply-side rhetoric with the spread of precarious work seen 'as instrumental to the modernisation of European labour markets so that they can better match the changing demands of goods and services markets'.[67] In the current context the EU's trade-off for maintaining its labour market position in the increasingly competitive global environment has been the further commodification of paid work and the *de facto* neglect of its unpaid counterpart.

This retrograde step in the reconciliation of professional and personal life is, perhaps, partially curtailed by the supplementary strategic goal added by the Lisbon Agenda.[68] The co-ordinated approach advocated by the Lisbon goal which links economic aspirations with employment and social policy is a welcome development marking a change of approach by indicating, at least in rhetorical terms, 'a political willingness to prioritise the "European social model", by means of

[64] Belgian Minister of Pensions and Social Affairs and one of the main architects of the process.

[65] Cited by J. Zeitlin, *The Open Method of Co-ordination and the Future of the European Employment Strategy*, Presentation to the Employment and Social Affairs Committee of the European Parliament on the first five-year evaluation of the Employment Guidelines, 8 July 2000.

[66] See D. Ashiagbor, 'Promoting Precariousness? The Responses of EU Employment Policies to Precarious Work' in J. Fudge and R. Owens (eds), *Precarious Work, Women and the New Economy: The Challenge to Legal Norms* (Oxford: Hart Publishing, 2006), 77.

[67] Ibid.

[68] See n 63 above.

"activating" the welfare state and modernising social protection'.[69] Read alongside the EES's annual objectives, Lisbon's overarching theme in the social context appears to point to an investment in human capital as a means of improving employability and enabling individuals to become more self-sufficient. Furthermore, the institutions concerned have acknowledged the importance of the need for 'better' jobs rather than merely viewing the goal as one of job creation at the cost of social standards. The Commission's recognition of quality as a 'relative and multi-dimensional concept', the assessment of which will involve taking account of, *inter alia,* the characteristics the employee brings to the job and their subjective evaluation by the individual worker,[70] is, on the face of it, compatible with the capability approach advocated in this book as an appropriate conceptual and evaluative framework for the advancement of a right to care.[71] However, a closer consideration of the EES and Lisbon strategies and their incarnation within the pre-existing law and policy framework reveals inconsistencies in the, sometimes competing, objectives of further economic integration as well as an underlying philosophical foundation which, without clearer normative guidance, could pose a serious threat to the future application and expansion of Europe's social protection standards.

Some solace in this respect is provided by the attempt to expressly incorporate social and economic rights alongside their civil and political counterparts within the constitutional law of the EU through the CFR which is discussed in detail towards the end of this Chapter. However, the Charter does not introduce any new rights but rather articulates a range of fundamental principles or values, the application of which is likely to place a continued emphasis on the CoJ's interpretation of existing instruments, making it necessary to consider those which have direct application in the current context. As well as detailing the wide range of provisions that already exist, this analysis highlights the lack of coherence in both their underlying philosophy and practical application which further reiterates the need for the development of a unifying ideology and normalization process which is at least possible through the combined operation of the current constitutional arrangements, soft law regulatory methods, and the justiciability of certain rights through the Court's interpretive function.

The Legislative Provisions: The Policy Context

Following the early promise of a programme of harmonization of social standards aimed at a 'levelling up' of provisions intended to enhance the reconciliation of work and family life, the impact of legislative activity in this respect has been rather disappointing. This is not to say that there has been a dearth of activity: on the

[69] Ashiagbor, n 66 above, at 85.
[70] European Commission, *Employment and Social Policies: A Framework for Investing in Quality* (Luxembourg: Office for Official Publications of the European Communities, 2001), 7.
[71] See Chapters 2, 4, and 7.

contrary, there now exists a complex range of provisions arising from secondary legislation which, together, comprise the relevant *acquis*, some of which have undoubtedly had a significant impact on the area under consideration. However, as detailed above,[72] the Member States have not always shared a common vision for Europe's so-called 'social dimension' and its perceived incompatibility with the overriding goal of economic integration has meant that social objectives have often been subordinated or traded-off in favour of their economic counterparts.

Furthermore, and of particular relevance in the current context, the EU's restricted competence has resulted in a reluctance to progress measures perceived as overly prescriptive in relation to the arrangements surrounding the personal lives of Europe's citizens so that the 'private' arrangements pertaining to the division of labour within families have been largely untouched by EU provision. This reluctance to disturb the *status quo,* coupled with the explicit goal of increasing women's employment rates, have resulted in the further commodification of paid work and the *de facto* neglect of its unpaid counterpart which has been bolstered by the policy focus on what has been termed labour market flexibility, itself a contested concept.[73] In the current context, the shortcomings of the EU legal and policy regime are crystallized by the model of the 'flexible worker', a manifestation of the increasing supply of worker-carers and the assumption that flexibility enables a better work-life balance. In reality, rather than enhanced flexibility in individual workplace arrangements, it is the market that has become amorphous through deregulation, leaving such vulnerable workers with little choice over how and when they work.

As outlined above, the challenge for the EU in its attempts to promote 'more and better' jobs within a flexible labour market lies in its ability to respond to what Ashiagbor has termed the 'disincentive discourse' prevalent in European economic policy.[74] In the dichotomization of regulation or flexibility, the promotion of worker protection on grounds other than the business needs of the enterprise[75] is often viewed as an unnecessary obstacle to job creation with deregulation the preferred option. This depends on the belief that increased regulation produces a negative effect on the operation of the market with a fusion of the requisite level of flexibility and adequate security ('flexicurity') deemed to be the most effective antidote to the threat of business failure posed by regulatory hindrances. However, when the precarious employment performed by worker-carers is considered, this duality of alternatives emerges as seriously deficient on a number of counts.

Firstly, such workers have never been afforded the high levels of regulatory protection alluded to which, if they ever did exist, were largely confined to those

[72] At p 101.

[73] As Sandra Fredman has noted, 'Flexibility itself is a flexible term, and its users are often not precise as to which meaning is being referred to.' See 'Precarious Norms for Precarious Workers' in Fudge and Owens (eds), n 66 above, 177.

[74] Ashiagbor, n 66 above, 78.

[75] For example, to achieve a level paying field across the Member States or the avoidance of bad publicity though sub-standard enforcement of basic health and safety measures.

more easily able to conform to the standard worker model. In the case of worker-carers, there are surely sound foundations for arguing that enhanced protection would assist in, rather than hamper, the efficient operation of the labour market by connecting its social and economic dimensions in order to overcome the distortions which, although capable of producing profitable financial outcomes in the short term, are nonetheless the result of exploitation of certain groups of workers through unjustified discrimination.[76] Secondly, the assertion that increased regulation will inevitably result in a loss of market flexibility is rarely challenged but often relies on an outdated notion of the concept of regulation which fails to take account of the myriad of models incorporating 'light touch' approaches aimed at facilitating self-regulation as well as the more recognizable legislative controls and everything in between. Such a narrow and negative view risks overlooking the positive improvements in efficiency and cohesion and resulting increases in production which can result from the introduction of pay structures and targeted legislation so that perhaps, 'neoclassical writers have failed to grasp the point that regulation actually creates and secures employment'.[77] Finally, the rationalization of flexicurity presupposes that the labour market is like any other space in which the exchange of goods and services takes place. This is contested due to the non-commodified status of labour which has traditionally been the subject of special protection, at least in respect of paid work, through labour law's democratic function which is aimed at striking a balance between the interests of workers and the power of employing organizations.[78] This may be achieved through the use of legislative means which guarantee workers the freedom necessary to organize themselves collectively and, in relation to individual contracts, by providing a basic floor of employment protection.[79] It is with the latter that EU law has been most concerned and the resulting provisions appear, at first glance, to provide a range of protections to worker-carers on the grounds of their gender, as well as in respect of the type of working arrangements they are likely to engage in due to the need to organize caring commitments around the demands of paid work. Furthermore, EU law has been instrumental in providing positive rights for workers in respect of pregnancy and maternity and in their ongoing role as parents. However, as further scrutiny reveals, the individual provisions are deficient in certain respects and, as a body of law, lack cohesion which restricts their overall effectiveness. In the following section, each will be considered in the context of their contribution to EU law's quest for an effective solution to the paid work/unpaid care conflict.

[76] See S. Deakin and J. Browne, 'Social Rights and Market Order: Adapting the Capability Approach' in T. Hervey and J. Kenner (eds), *Economic and Social Rights under the EU Charter of Fundamental Rights* (Oxford: Hart Publishing, 2003), 27.

[77] U. Mückenberger and S. Deakin, 'From Deregulation to a European Floor of Rights: Labour Law, Flexibilisation and the European Single Market', *Zeitschrift für ausländisches und internationales Arbeits- und Sozialrecht* 3 (1989) 53, 190.

[78] See Chapter 4.

[79] See Lord Wedderburn, *The Worker and the Law* (London: Sweet & Maxwell, 1986), 6.

The EU's Anti-Discrimination Law and the Conception of Equality: Shifting or 'Slippery'?

It is almost 20 years since Fredman observed European anti-discrimination law's failure 'to address the underlying structural obstacles to women's progress'[80] by identifying a number of flawed characteristics, including the particular conception of equality on which the provisions are based.[81] Although Fredman's critique relies on an analysis of Community law made nearly two decades ago, many of the central tenets on which her objections are founded still hold true despite the substantial amendments that have been made to this area in the intervening period. In black letter terms, the particular conception of equality on which the European approach is built remains essentially unchanged as confirmed by the current definitions of the types of discrimination at which the provision of equal treatment is aimed.

Article 2(1)[82] of Directive 2006/54/EC[83] defines direct discrimination as arising 'where one person is treated less favourably on grounds of sex than another is, has been or would be treated in a comparable situation', and indirect 'where an apparently neutral provision, criterion or practice would put persons of one sex at a particular disadvantage compared with persons of the other sex'. This conception of equality as 'equal treatment',[84] which continues to be central to EU Law's provision in this respect, is 'crucially limited by its dependence on a norm of comparison, which is generally the existing male norm'.[85] Echoing a well-versed, cross-national discontent with this approach to anti-discrimination law,[86] Fredman posits that its application 'is particularly pertinent in explaining the persistence of labour market disadvantage'[87] as an inability to conform to a male norm will leave women, particularly those with caring responsibilities, unable to access certain jobs and employment-related benefits. The need for male-type conformance was particularly problematic in the CoJ's early case law concerning pregnancy and childbirth,[88]

[80] S. Fredman, 'European Community Discrimination Law: A Critique', *Industrial Law Journal*, 21/2 (1992), 119, 133.

[81] The other flaws were identified as the reliance on a dichotomy between equality and difference; the assumption of neutrality; the subordination of anti-discrimination legislation to the market order; and the individualistic nature of the provisions and their enforcement.

[82] Originally inserted into Directive 76/207/EEC by Directive 2002/73/EC. These relatively 'new' definitions of direct and indirect discrimination incorporate the interpretation given to the concepts by the ECJ in its jurisprudence on sex discrimination—see Chapter 6.

[83] See n 46 above.

[84] See Chapter 2.

[85] Fredman, n 80 above, 120.

[86] For example, from the US literature, see C. A. MacKinnon, *Feminism Unmodified: Discourses on Life and Law* (Cambridge: Harvard University Press, 1987).

[87] Fredman, n 80 above, 120.

[88] See Case C-179/88 *Handels-og Kontorfunktionaerernes Forbund i Danmark v Dansk Arbejdgiverforening (Hertz)* [1990] ECR I-3979. See also the Court's restricted rulings in Case C-32/93 *Webb v EMO Air Cargo (UK) Ltd* [1994] ECR I-3567 and Case C-394/96 *Brown v Rentokil* [1998] ECR I-4185 in which it was held that a woman absent on the grounds of pregnancy- or birth-related illness is only protected for a specified period and will then be subject to comparisons with a sick male, regardless

and can still be identified in the Court's decision-making surrounding justifications for indirect discrimination.[89]

Lewis has asserted that the policy meanings adopted in the European domain have been subject to 'slipperiness' over time due to the dominance of the overarching strategic objective of market-making which has had a negative effect on the reshaping of policy priorities linked to the attainment of gender equality.[90] However, recent amendments to the EU *acquis* have led some commentators to conclude that, subject to the appropriate interpretation by the Court, the relevant conception of equality might be shifting so as to incorporate a more substantive approach to gender equality.[91] The Court's influence in this area has already been acknowledged in respect of its early activism in interpreting the meaning and scope[92] of the principle of equality and the most recent substantive amendment to the regulatory regime incorporates, *inter alia*, codification of much of the Court's jurisprudence over the past 30 years in the form of Directive 2006/54/EC[93] (hereinafter referred to as the 'Recast Directive') which has repealed and replaced the earlier Directives on equal pay and equal treatment.

The Recast Directive

Although the scope of Article 157 TFEU[94] has been broadened significantly since its inception to provide for equal treatment as well as equal pay and has recently been extended to permit some forms of 'positive action',[95] it is worth recalling that, rather than being motivated by a concern for women's labour market inequality,[96] it was originally intended as an pro-competition measure. Despite this negligible beginning, Article 157 TFEU has grown in prominence so that, alongside Article 153,[97] it serves as a cornerstone for legislative activity in the field of gender relations providing a legal base for a range of provisions aimed at the elimination

of the nature of her illness. The provisions of Directive 92/85 have assisted in certain respects in this context by providing specific rights on the grounds of pregnancy and childbirth (see below) but comparisons with a sick male still persist if the woman's illness lasts for longer than the 'protected period' which consists of the duration of the pregnancy and the appropriate period of maternity leave which will be subject to differing national standards.

[89] See Chapter 6.

[90] See Lewis, n 12 above.

[91] See N. Burrow and M. Robison, 'An Assessment of the Recast of Community Equality Laws', *European Law Journal*, 13/2 (2007), 186.

[92] See *Defrenne II*, n 20 above.

[93] See n 46 above.

[94] Ex Art 119/EEC, 141/EC.

[95] Following its amendment by the Treaty of Amsterdam to include Art 141(4), now Art 157(4) TFEU.

[96] See n 11 above.

[97] (Ex Art 118/EEC, 137/EC) which gives the EU competence to support and complement Member States' activities relating to the equal treatment of men and women with regard to labour market opportunities and equal treatment at work, giving the Parliament and the Council the power to adopt directives.

of discrimination between the sexes. These provisions were originally divided into three parts: pay,[98] equal treatment,[99] and social security,[100] with the relevant instruments sharing a common premise, namely that the identical treatment of men and women will rectify anomalies in the market by enabling women to achieve parity with men through application of the merit principle. This particular conception relies on a symmetrical provision of equal treatment for both sexes with positive action, where permitted, arising largely as a means of ensuring that women are provided with assistance to improve their access to labour market opportunities in areas where they are underrepresented, thus enabling them to compete directly with men, for example, through the targeted provision of training. However, recent amendments have opened up the possibility of a move away from this formal application of the non-discrimination principle towards a broader and more proactive approach aimed at the realization of equality.

In 2006 the areas of equal pay and equal treatment were brought together and 'recast for modernization' under the text of the Recast Directive which also incorporates provisions on the burden of proof in sex discrimination cases.[101] When read alongside other associated amendments such as the provision of Article 157(4) TFEU and the Court's interpretation in cases concerning positive action, this consolidation and reorientation has been broadly welcomed by commentators as being indicative of 'a shift in the underlying conception of equality law . . . away from a symmetrical and formal model towards one which accommodates measures that are aimed at remedying disadvantage and achieving substantive equality'.[102] Relevant to this observation is the expansion of the Directive's title to incorporate 'equal *opportunities*' alongside 'equal *treatment*' indicating recognition of the substantial disadvantages that women face in the labour market.[103] Although falling short of any new innovations in this regard, the Directive articulates in its recitals

[98] Which was governed by Art 141 and Council Directive 75/117/EEC of 10 February 1975 on the approximation of the laws of the Member States relating to the application of the principle of equal pay for men and women, OJ 1975 L 45/19.

[99] By Art 141 and Council Directives 76/207/EEC of 9 February 1976 on the implementation of the principle of equal treatment for men and women as regards access to employment, vocational training and promotion and working conditions, OJ 1976 L 39/40, amended by Council and Parliament Directive No 2002/73 of 23 September 2003, OJ 2002 L 269/15; 86/613/EEC of 11 December 1986 on the application of the principle of equal treatment between men and women engaged in an activity, including agriculture, in a self-employed capacity, and on the protection of self-employed women during pregnancy and motherhood, OJ 1986 L 225/40; and 96/34/EC of 3 June 1996 on the framework agreement on parental leave concluded by UNICE, CEEP and the ETUC, OJ 1996 L 145/4–9.

[100] By Council Directive 79/7/EEC of 19 December 1978 on the progressive implementation of the principle of equal treatment for men and women in matters of social security, OJ 1979 L 6/24; 86/378/EEC of 24 July 1986 on the implementation of the principle of equal treatment for men and women in occupational social security schemes, OJ 1986 L 225/40, amended by Council Directive 96/97/EC of 20 December 1996, OJ 1997 L 46/20.

[101] Previously contained in Council Directive 97/80/EC of 15 December 1997 on the burden of proof in cases of discrimination based on sex, OJ 1998 L 14/6, which, in practice, straddle both equal pay and equal treatment.

[102] Burrow and Robison, n 91 above, 197.

[103] Ibid.

the need for enhanced family leave, improved childcare facilities and care for dependant persons, and flexible working for both men and women as appropriate means of promoting sex equality[104] placing responsibility for further action onto the Member States and social partners.[105] This signifies a welcome change in focus from the symmetrical model towards a commitment to address the structural barriers to women's labour market integration and the elimination of systemic discrimination through a reorientation of paid and unpaid work. In adopting the specific language of the Directive, its architects have sent a clear message to the Court and the Member States 'that Community law now requires a gear change towards achieving substantive rather than formal equality'.[106]

Alongside this important development, the Directive also displays certain significant weaknesses, some of which arise from what it omits[107] rather than what it provides. In seeking to set down a 'clear, complete and precise text on the principle of equal treatment including equal pay which reflects and integrates the case law of the Court',[108] the Commission might have been expected to extend its sights beyond the relatively narrow confines of equal pay and treatment in the workplace to incorporate the related fields of pregnancy, maternity, and parental leave. This would have provided the opportunity to remedy the uneven application of certain principles resulting from the co-existence of disparate legal regimes, as well as to formally acknowledge that inequality often results when women, because of their sex, find themselves in different situations from men—a form of direct discrimination that cannot be addressed through the provision of equal treatment.[109] However, the omission of Directive 92/85/EEC[110] from the Recast Directive's scope means that, for the time being at least,[111] the interrelationship between pregnancy and equal pay and treatment will not be formally acknowledged but will

[104] See Recital 11.

[105] See Article 21(2) which provides, 'Where consistent with national traditions and practice, Member States shall encourage the social partners, without prejudice to their autonomy, to promote equality between women and men and flexible working arrangements, with the aim of facilitating the reconciliation of work and family life.'

[106] Burrows and Robison, n 91 above, 198.

[107] In addition to the exclusion of the Directives on pregnancy and maternity (92/85/EEC, see n 38 above) and parental leave (96/34/EC, see n 99 above) which are discussed in detail below, the recast did not extend to Directive 86/613 (see n 99 above), despite a request by ECOSOC to review the Directive immediately. However, Directive 2010/41/EU (which will repeal and replace 86/613 in 2012) came into force on 4 August 2010. The amendments include the introduction of maternity benefits for self-employed workers.

[108] COM (2004) 27 final, at 4.

[109] Because it is simply not captured by the definition of direct discrimination provided by Article 2(2) is that 'one person is treated less favourably on grounds of sex than another is, has been or would be treated in a comparable situation'.

[110] See n 38 above.

[111] At the time of writing, a proposal for a directive to amend Directive 92/85 is working its way through the legislative process. See *Proposal for a directive of the European Parliament and the Council amending Council Directive 92/85/EEC on the introduction of measures to encourage improvements in the safety and health at work of pregnant workers and those who have recently given birth or are breastfeeding*, COM (2008) 600/4, discussed below at p [178].

continue to be subjected to the somewhat uneven application of related principles by the Court.[112]

In relation to family-related leave, the only other explicit references in the Recast Directive come in Recital 11, which refers to transferable parental leave as part of a possible package of measures intended to address inequalities on the labour market, and in Recital 26 which refers to the Council Resolution on the balanced participation of women and men in family and working life,[113] which encourages Members States 'to consider examining the scope for their respective legal systems to grant working men an individual and non-transferable right to paternity leave, while maintaining their rights relating to employment'.[114] In failing to consolidate the range of relevant provisions through a streamlined and simplified approach, the Commission has missed a valuable opportunity to align the conciliation of personal and professional life directly with the pursuit of gender equality and, thus, to bridge the gap between these two distinct platforms for discrimination.

The legal base selected for the recast was Article 141 (now 157 TFEU) which provides for measures relating to equal treatment for men and women in employment and which required the co-decision procedure, whereas the appropriate legal base for the inclusion of pregnancy, maternity, and parental leave would have been Article 137 (now 153 TFEU) under which preference was given to the social partners to adopt framework agreements with co-decision only applicable in the event of a failure to agree.[115] The difficulty presented by this distinction reveals a general weakness in EU law's demarcation of specific policy areas which is not amenable to the need to consolidate in the current context. However, achievement of the overriding aim of the recast exercise 'to update and simplify the Community *acquis*'[116] and the modernization's primary purpose, 'to ensure the implementation of the principle of equal opportunities and equal treatment of men and women in matters of employment and occupation'[117] would surely have provided adequate justification for a combined legal base enabling the necessary consolidation in this context.[118] By freeing the employment protection provisions surrounding pregnancy from their conceptually restrictive health and safety origins and

[112] See further, p 114 below and, for an assessment of the Court's jurisprudence on these related areas, see Chapter 6. The Court's task has been further complicated by the provision of Art 28 of the Recast Directive that it shall be without prejudice to 'provisions concerning the protection of women, particularly as regards pregnancy and maternity' and to Directive 92/85/EEC and Directive 96/34/EC on parental leave.

[113] The Resolution of the Council and the Ministers for Employment and Social Policy, meeting within the Council, of 29 June 2000, on the balanced participation of women and men in family and working life, OJ C 218, 31.7.2000.

[114] Given the wide disparity and relatively low levels of current legislative provision in this respect, a harder measure requiring a minimum period of paid leave might have been more effective.

[115] Post-Lisbon, the co-decision procedure is renamed the ordinary legislative procedure—see Art 294 TFEU.

[116] See COM (2003) 71 final, *Communication from the Commission to the Council, the European Parliament, The European Economic and Social Committee and the Committee of the Regions updating and simplifying the Community acquis.*

[117] Art 1, Directive 2006/54/EC.

[118] Now part of the proposed amendments to Directive 92/85, see n 111 above.

incorporating them within an overarching regime providing, *inter alia*, transferable family leave provisions for men *and* women, the Commission could have taken a very significant step towards the conciliation of unpaid care and paid work. This would have made a far richer contribution towards achievement of substantive equality than the preservation of a distinct rights regime based primarily on a temporal acknowledgment of the biological differences between the sexes.

Although the Recast Directive and its predecessor Directive 2002/73[119] were intended to simplify and also maintain the Community *acquis*, some commentators have cast doubt over whether this has, in fact, been achieved. Koukoulis-Spiliotopoulos[120] has contended that the new articulation of the equal treatment principle should retain the express extension of its application to 'marital or family status' contained in the original Equal Treatment Directive.[121] However, this reference was not included in the revised definitions of direct and indirect discrimination and has now disappeared from the text altogether so that the omission of an explicit reference to protection on family grounds could result in digression of the equality principle in this respect. However the emphasis placed on the Court's future interpretation enables reliance on the references in the Recitals to the need for 'both men and women to combine family and work more successfully'[122] and the 'balanced participation of women and men in family and working life'.[123] This means that the omission of a specific reference in the text does not appear to amount to a significant failure to maintain the *acquis* in this respect. Of more serious concern is the omission of any reference to the non-discrimination principle as articulated by the various human rights instruments such as the Convention on the Elimination of all Forms of Discrimination against Women (CEDAW). As Burrows and Robison note, the Recast Directive is the only recent equality instrument to omit such a reference 'perhaps leading to a more restrictive interpretation of its terms'.[124] In this context, the reliance placed on the Court's interpretation could work against maintenance of the *acquis* due to the Court's dependency on the relationships between legislative and policy provisions and the Treaties which, in respect of appropriate international standards, are established through their specific reference in EU instruments. CEDAW, along with a range of human rights instruments, was expressly cited in the Preamble to Directive 2002/73/EC[125] so that inclusion of its provisions in relation to the concept of gender equality law potentially enabled a substantive rather than formal approach to be taken. Its subsequent omission from and the lack of any replacement reference in the Recast

[119] See n 99 above.

[120] S. Koukoulis-Spiliotopoulos, 'The Amended Equal Treatment Directive 2002/73: An Expression of Constitutional Principles/Fundamental Rights', *Maastricht Journal*, 12 (2005), 327, 357.

[121] Art 2(1) of Directive 76/207/EEC provided that 'the principle of equal treatment shall mean that there shall be no discrimination whatsoever on grounds of sex either directly or indirectly by reference in particular to marital or family status'.

[122] Recital 11.

[123] Recital 26.

[124] Burrows and Robison, n 91 above, 197.

[125] See Recital 2.

Directive does, therefore, represent a diminution from the previous position which should be corrected at the earliest opportunity.

Family-based Rights

The Pregnant Workers' Directive

As discussed above, the instruments aimed at providing equality between men and women share a common approach in their reliance on a symmetrical application of the equal treatment principle. Directive 92/85/EEC[126] (The Pregnant Workers' Directive, 'PWD') which sets down rights in respect of pregnancy and maternity provides an alternative application of what is essentially the same approach and is based on the same essential premise—that women merit protection in respect of their 'otherness' in certain restricted circumstances.[127] As discussed in Chapter 3, the relationship between child-bearing and rearing has a profound effect on women's labour market activity resulting in a predominance of female workers in so-called 'atypical employment' which is often of a precarious nature. On its introduction, the Directive undoubtedly made a progressive contribution in this respect by establishing rights to minimum levels of protection which were justified on the basis of greater social integration and on the smooth operation of the market through the retention of skilled workers. However, economic imperative soon trumped the social benefits as illustrated by the Court's interpretation of the Directive in *Gillespie*[128] in which it held that maternity pay did not constitute 'pay' for the purposes of applying the equality principle and could, thus, be paid at a lower rate than the recipient's usual salary. This decision reversed the Court's record of using the equality principle to advance the rights of women in relation to pregnancy[129] and, by challenging the apparent compatibility of the dual goals of women's labour market integration and gender equality which had, hitherto, appeared to be a priority for EU provision in this respect, cast a long shadow over the proclaimed commitment to the introduction of measures designed to enable women 'to reconcile their occupational and family obligations'.[130] However, if the Directive's legal base is recalled, the judgment is not so surprising. The choice of the former Article 118A,[131] which allowed for the adoption of directives aimed at encouraging improvements and harmonizing conditions 'especially in the working environment, as regards the health and safety of workers', means that the PWD is not primarily concerned with the introduction of social measures but rather with

[126] See n 38 above.

[127] From de Beauvoir, see Chapter 2.

[128] Case C-342/93 *Gillespie and Others v Northern Health and Social Services Board and others* [1996] ECR I-475.

[129] S. Fredman, 'Transformation or Dilution: Fundamental Right in the EU Social Space', *European Law Journal*, 12/1 (2006), 41, 47.

[130] See para 16 of the Community Charter of the Fundamental Social Rights of Workers, which was cited in the original proposal for the Directive.

[131] Ex Art 137/EC, now Art 153 TFEU.

the introduction of minimum levels of protection in respect of health and safety. Part of Article 118A's appeal undoubtedly lay in its requirement of qualified majority voting rather than unanimity so that the text which did emerge in the guise of the PWD was perhaps the best that could be achieved at the time given the reluctance of national governments to engage in the legislative process in the social field.[132] Thus, the text represents a compromise with its contents the subject of considerable dilution before its final adoption in October 1992 and as a result, as *Gillespie* illustrates, the equality principle was subordinated to the basic protection of health and safety so that workplace rights in respect of pregnancy and maternity are conceptualized as arising out of a biological need based on an essentialist formulation of the differences between the sexes.

In 2008 the Commission brought forward a proposal for a directive to amend the PWD.[133] As well as extending the minimum level of maternity leave from 14 to 18 weeks,[134] revising the current provisions on dismissal during maternity leave to take account of the Court's case law,[135] and clarifying the contractual status of women returning to work following maternity leave,[136] the proposed directive also addresses the issue of legal base by adding Article 157 to the current provision of Article 153(2). This is in recognition of the fact that maternity rights straddle the areas of health and safety at work and equal opportunities and treatment between men and women as established in Article 157(3).[137] The proposal states that the use of a combined legal base is intended to assist in 'protecting the health and safety of the women concerned[138] at work... [and] will also have a beneficial effect on these women's ability to reconcile private, family and professional obligations'.[139] However, the proposal is disappointing on the issue of maternity pay, providing merely for the 'principle of the payment of the full monthly salary' during maternity leave. This is not mandatory and it is left to individual Member States to decide at what rate the payment should be set as long as it exceeds the rate for sick pay.[140] This adds nothing of substance to the current provision of Article 11(3) of the PWD which provides that maternity pay 'shall be deemed adequate if it guarantees income at least equivalent to that which the worker concerned would

[132] See p 101 above. Notably, the UK whose Government did argue that the Directive was a misuse of Art 118A in that its provisions extended beyond the boundaries of health and safety.

[133] See n 111 above.

[134] Art 8. At the time of writing, the European Parliament had submitted a proposal to amend the period of maternity leave to 20 weeks.

[135] Art 10.

[136] Art 11(2)(c).

[137] As well as Arts 21 and 23 of the CFR and Art 3 TEU, the proposed directive's preamble also refers (in Recital 7) to the fact that the achievement of a better balance between work and private and family life comprises one of the six priorities laid down in the *Roadmap for Equality between Men and Women 2006–2010*, see *Communication from the Commission to the Council, the European Parliament and the Social Committee and Committee of the Regions, A Roadmap for Equality between Men and Women*, COM (2006) 92.

[138] Ie those who are pregnant workers or workers who have recently given birth or who are breastfeeding.

[139] See n 111 above, 6.

[140] Art 11(3).

receive in the event of a break in her activities on grounds connected with her state of health'. As with all minimum standards provided under EU law, it has always been possible to improve upon this through national measures, so the proposed amendment does little to further reconcile the dual goals of women's integration into the workforce with the achievement of sex equality.

In a similar vein, the proposal for flexible working following a return from maternity leave[141] amounts to little more than an acknowledgement of the equality principle unmatched by the provision of any substantive right. The proposal is for a woman on or returning from maternity leave to have a 'right to ask her employer to adapt her working patterns or hours to the new family situation' with the employer being 'obliged to consider such a requests taking employers' and workers' needs into account' but not to 'accept or follow-up on it'.[142] The lack of any legal enforcement makes this a somewhat hollow provision and the restriction of the 'right to request' to such a narrow pool of claimants excludes mothers of older children, fathers of children of any age, and all others with caring commitments. Given the Directive's focus on pregnancy and maternity, this is perhaps unsurprising. However, its restriction merely reinforces the message that the balancing of unpaid care and paid work is confined to women on the grounds of their biological difference from men. It is, therefore, of some comfort to learn of a parallel development that has been taking place alongside the PWD's amendment culminating in an agreement between the social partners to amend the original framework agreement on which Directive 96/34/EC[143] on the provision of parental leave is based.

The Parental Leave Directive

The approach adopted by Directive 96/34/EC is to equalize the protection of employment for parents of young children who require time away from work for family-related reasons. The Directive explicitly recognizes that such duties need not be the exclusive responsibility of women by giving equal rights to both parents. The targeting of legislative activity at the alleviation of assumptions based on gender stereotyping is welcome as is the attempt to encourage men to 'assume an equal share of family responsibility'.[144] The central weakness of this particular legislation is its reliance on pre-existing arrangements within Member States' national welfare systems for its execution which leaves the *status quo* firmly intact and prevents it from being a policy-leader.[145] The fact that such leave may

[141] Art 1(5).

[142] See n 111 above, 9. This appears to be similar to the right to request a flexible work arrangement under UK law whose relative success is indicative of the dire need for such a provision rather than an endorsement of the particularly weak means by which it was provided. For an assessment of the associated package of measures, see G. James, 'The Work and Families Act 2006: Legislation to Improve Choice and Flexibility?', *Industrial Law Journal*, 35/3 (2006), 272.

[143] See n 99 above.

[144] Framework Agreement on Parental Leave annexed to Directive 96/34 at para 1(8).

[145] For a critique of the directive's provisions, see E. Caracciolo Di Torella, 'A Critical Assessment of the EC Legislation Aiming at Reconciling Work and Family Life: Lessons from the Scandinavian

be unpaid[146] adds further to the entrenchment of gendered roles as decisions regarding who should take parental leave are likely to be influenced by the fact that, for many families, loss of the women's (lower) wage for an extended period will have less financial impact than the loss of her male partner's wage.

In their renegotiated agreement on parental leave,[147] the social partners have made some significant improvements to the existing Directive, which are incorporated in Council Directive 2010/18/EU.[148] As well as extending its provisions to adoptive parents,[149] the new Directive increases the length of leave available from the current three months to four months. To encourage fathers to take parental leave, the Directive provides that at least one month's leave must be non-transferable[150] and will be lost if not taken. Echoing the proposed introduction of a right to request a flexible work arrangement on returning from maternity leave, the Directive provides a similar right to be exercised when returning from parental leave, although, in contrast to the former which would presumably be of unlimited duration, the flexible arrangements following parental leave need only be for a 'set period of time'.[151] Furthermore, the agreement calls on Member States to establish the periods of notice that workers should give in exercising the right to parental leave.[152] However, the potentially wide scope of the new rights to all workers irrespective of their type of contract[153] is severely weakened by the option given to Member States to maintain a qualification period of a maximum of one year before an employee can apply for leave.[154]

This is the first time that the European social partners have undertaken such an exercise and perhaps the most significant aspect relates more to process than to provision in that it recognizes that such agreements carry with them an ongoing commitment to monitor implementation and to improve provision as appropriate. The social partners' ready engagement in the renegotiation process and agreement on the revisions is also indicative of a willingness to participate actively in the development of normative instruments making this process a potentially useful means of developing an effective system of responsive regulation which may be of particular use in the current context.

Of course the nature of the revised Parental Leave Directive, which is based on a framework agreement which requires the Member States to provide much of the detail in accordance with national laws and practices, cannot be expected to result

Model' in H. Collins, P. Davies, and P. Ridout (eds), *Legal Regulation of the Employment Relation* (London: Kluwer Law International, 2000).

146 Clause 2(8) of the framework agreement specifies that matters relating to social security are to be determined by the Member States in accordance with national law.

147 Of 18 June 2009, see <http://www.etuc.org/IMG/pdf_Framework_agreement_parental_leave_revised__18062009.pdf> accessed 7 December 2010.

148 Which will replace Directive 96/34 when the latter is repealed in March 2012.

149 Clauses 2(1) and 5.

150 Clause 2(2).

151 Clause 6(1).

152 Clause 3(2).

153 Clause 1(2) and (3).

154 Clause 3(1)(b).

in the attainment of hard law provisions. In this respect, it varies significantly from the type of direct intervention that might be achieved if the proposed amendments to the PWD progress further. However, in the context of both sets of provisions, it is disappointing not to see the imposition of clearer and, in the case of payments for family-related leave, more generous minimum standards. The non-negotiable component of parental leave entitlement may provide a much needed 'stick' by which fathers will be encouraged to spend time with their children but what is still missing is the more important 'carrot' by way of some form of payment. With no substantive improvement in mandatory levels of pay for either maternity or parental leave, it is difficult to see how the dual goals of equality between men and women[155] and the achievement of a better balance between work and private and family life[156] can be reconciled.

Despite the fact that both sets of revisions were identified as priority initiatives at the same time,[157] the legislative procedure relevant in the case of the amended PWD[158] necessarily involves a far more lengthy and detailed procedure than that relating to the parental leave negotiations which were completed in a six-month period[159] with a revised directive published a year later in March 2010. Of course the relative merits and demerits of lengthy deliberations and more readily reactive procedures are subject to differing interpretations[160] and the distinct procedures are not the only hurdle to the development of a cohesive approach to law and policy-making in the context of family-related rights. What the existing provisions and proposed and future amendments demonstrate in both substantive and procedural terms is that the overall scheme of EU provision in this area is rife with inconsistencies due to the absence of a unifying ideology. In this respect, at least, it shares a common ground with the other aspects of the legislative provision under review, all of which lack cohesion in strategic terms.

Ideological Incoherence

The assumed dichotomy of equality and difference which informs the EU's provision in the current context owes much to the Aristotelian formula[161] which, although useful in certain respects as a starting point in the development of strategies intended to eliminate discrimination, is severely limited in its application to the unpaid care/paid work conflict. This is because the relevant conceptualization of 'difference' tends to focus on an essentialist notion based on biological

155 See Art 3 TEU, Art 157 TEU, and Arts 21 and 23 of the CFR.

156 See *A Roadmap for Equality between Men and Women* (n 137 above) which specifies this as one of the EU's priorities for 2006–2010.

157 In the Commission's work programme for 2008, see COM (2007) 640.

158 Which is ongoing at the time of writing.

159 Spanning the period from September 2008 until March 2009.

160 See the analysis of the atypical work directives which were derived from framework agreements—this Chapter, below at p 119.

161 That 'likes should be treated alike', discussed at Chapter 2.

distinction rather than on an informed gender-based interpretation that because of socially constructed phenomena[162] women, rather than being situated differently on physical grounds, often find themselves in *different situations* from men. Rather than alleviating the direct discrimination that can result from established practices and procedures, an over-reliance on protective legislation aimed at countering the physical differences between the sexes can, itself, perpetuate the use of gender stereotyping leaving women consigned as the 'weaker sex', inferior to men both physically and psychologically. Rights related to maternity and unpaid care requirements must, therefore, tread a careful path between recognition of the very real need to provide workplace support for pregnant workers' well-being and that of their unborn children on the one hand and over-protective provisions based on assumptions that pregnancy and motherhood (or their very possibility) make all women vulnerable and dependent on legal interventions which restrict their participation in public and professional life and thus their personal autonomy. Measurement against a male norm and the resulting classification of women's physical characteristics and physiological functions as 'different' colours the development and interpretation of related provisions. Finally, and perhaps most crucially, the consignment of all things care-related as 'women's work' perpetuates women's labour market disadvantage through employer assumptions about the likely effects on career aspirations and workplace commitment.

The effective targeting of legislation aimed at enhancing women's labour market security requires consideration to be given to a wide range of factors in order for it to avoid being overly prescriptive and, thus, prohibitive of the exercise of individual freedom. There is also a need to reconceptualize care responsibilities which potentially impose obligations on both men and women which might, in turn, impact on the arrangements surrounding paid work. It is only by recognizing that women's association with unpaid care arises largely due to socially constructed gender differences and not on the basis of a physical or psychological propensity that stereotyping can effectively be challenged. Admittedly, there is some recognition of such potential pitfalls within the European provisions but the overall scheme of law and policy, which has developed incrementally and in a reactive fashion as a result of differing tensions and changing priorities, is inconsistent in this respect.

Protection from Discrimination on the Grounds of Working Arrangements

The need to reconcile market forces with the operation of the equality principle has manifested itself in EU law in the context of two specific developments: first, through the use of the objective justification defence in cases of indirect discrimination[163] and, second, in respect of the targeted protection of atypical workers

[162] See G. James, *The Legal Regulation of Pregnancy and Parenting in the Labour Market* (London: Routledge Cavendish, 2009), in particular ch 1.

[163] Considered in detail in Chapter 6.

encapsulated by Directives 97/81/EC[164] and 1999/70/EC[165] which provide rights for part-time and fixed-term workers respectively.[166] In seeking to regulate so-called atypical work, the EU has been confronted with a familiar dilemma—how to reconcile EU law's social objectives ('better jobs') with its economic imperative which, due to enhanced global competition manifested in the form of comparatively cheap labour due to lower social standards, has demanded ever more creative ways of utilizing the available workforce effectively.

The original intention, in the 1980s, to jointly regulate all aspects of atypical work foundered due to lack of political consensus[167] and led to the development of separate regulatory regimes in the form of directives on part-time and fixed-term work. The resulting framework directives, agreed through a process of negotiation between the social partners, were not aimed at harmonization but rather at joint goal setting in social standards, thereby leaving a space for national diversity through self-regulation. As Ashiagbor has noted, this approach has potentially damaging implications for the resulting regulation, since, 'by eschewing binding norms and decentralising decision-making, such regulatory techniques risk privileging economic policy imperatives and job creation over social protection'.[168]

Although similar in their reliance on the comparative approach as a means of countering discrimination, there are notable differences in the aims and objectives of the directives. For example, the Part-Time Work Directive is aimed at improving the quality of such work and at facilitating its development on a voluntary basis. It also aims to contribute to the flexible organization of working time, taking account of the needs of workers and employers. In contrast, the Fixed-Term Work Directive which is reflective of the position adopted by ETUC and the Commission—that fixed-term work is low quality and its use should be limited—aims to prevent the use of successive fixed-term contracts. The direct transposition of this mutually agreed objective illustrates a departure from the classic Community method of law-making by which the Commission retains the sole right of initiative and, notwithstanding the European Parliament's increasing influence, exercises joint responsibility with the Council for final decision-making regarding the nature and scope of legislation with enforcement by the Court. In contrast, the process of agreement between the social partners which underpins these directives results in a hybrid of soft and hard law which is less interventionist and more reliant on self-regulation.

It is not only the process that differs from traditional EU law-making; the resulting content is also distinct from that which results from the more prescriptive approach. In contrast to the more traditional methods, the social partners'

164 Council Directive 97/81/EC of 15 December 1997 concerning the framework agreement on part-time work concluded by UNICE, CEEP, and the ETUC, OJ 1997 L 14/9.

165 Council Directive 1999/70/EC of 28 June 1999 concerning the framework agreement on fixed-term work concluded by ETUC, UNICE, and CEEP, OJ 1999 L 244/64.

166 At the time of writing the controversial directive on temporary agency work (2008/104/EC of the European Parliament and of the Council of 19 November 2008, OJ 2008 L 327/9) has yet to be implemented in Member States which have until December 2011 to do so. For this reason, its provisions are not specifically considered here.

167 Ashiagbor, n 66 above, 77.

168 Ibid.

agreements are given legal effect by the resulting directives which have not been subjected to the usual drafting and subsequent scrutiny and amendment. The end results are vaguely worded principles whose means of achievement are left to the Member States.[169] For example, the Fixed-Term Directive provides that Member States should determine the 'conditions under which fixed-term contracts shall be regarded as successive' and Article 5(3) of the Part-Time Directive's social partners' agreement states that employers should 'give consideration to requests' by workers to transfer between full-time and part-time work. The apportionment of such wide and amorphous discretion to the socially diverse Members States has led commentators to question the likelihood of achievement of the EU's declared commitment to improving the quality of jobs.[170] Running counter to this concern is the assertion that the setting of minimum standards is, in fact, better suited to the development and ultimate effectiveness of social policy which requires some account to be taken of Member States' diversity in prior provision and corresponding socio-economic variation.[171] It is nevertheless difficult to deny that the lack of a strong normative framework at the EU level exposes the operation of such measures to the danger of a prioritized objective of quantity over quality in job creation.[172]

This concern is echoed by Fredman's distinction between functional and numerical flexibility,[173] the former relating to the employer's ability to require employees to adjust their skills to match the demands of changes in technology or workload[174] and the latter resulting in the adjustment of labour inputs to meet fluctuations in employers' needs. Whereas functional flexibility relates to an investment in the human capital of an individual through the mutually beneficial enhancement of skills, numerical flexibility 'yields the precarious workforce: characterised by low pay, low status, and little by way of job security, training or promotion prospects' with the gains for employers in matching supply and demand resulting in direct costs to workers.[175] It is this process that has dominated European policy discourse with 'deep ambivalence on the part of policy-makers as to the extent to which the benefits employers gain from flexibility should carry with them social responsibilities'.[176] This point is illustrated by the provisions of

[169] Ibid, 93.

[170] Eg Ball, n 61 above.

[171] See N. Busby and D. Christie, 'The Regulation of Temporary Agency Work in the European Union', *The Cambrian Law Review* 36 (2005) 15.

[172] See Ashiagbor, n 66 above.

[173] Fredman, n 73 above, 177.

[174] In line with the personal development of human capital which, if supported by suitable and adequate training and other mechanisms is compatible with the capabilities approach—see Chapters 2 and 3.

[175] Fredman, n 73 above, 193.

[176] Ibid, 196. This ambivalence is reflected in the Court's jurisprudence in cases such as Case C-256/01 *Allonby v Accrington and Rossendale College and Others* [2004] ECR I-873 in which its reasoning for not allowing the claim to succeed on the basis of a tripartite arrangement under which female workers were employed demonstrates how 'flexiblisation functions to limit the reach of equal pay law'. The narrow view of responsibility implicit in EU law is illustrated by the Court's refusal to recognize the contractual nexus between the end user of the women's services and the agency as

the legislation themselves which, rather than providing self-standing rights aimed at improving the quality of jobs, adopt a particular application of the formal equality approach which serves more as a promotional tool in the use of such practices than as an antidote to the precariousness associated with non-standard work.

Although the atypical directives' shift in focus from an over-emphasis of the need to show sex-based differences overcomes some of the difficulties associated with indirect discrimination,[177] the denial of substantive rights in favour of the equal treatment approach has limited the potential application of their provisions. Both directives aim at providing 'non-standard' workers with a right to equal treatment with their 'standard' worker counterparts and, although they do not apply any sex-conscious criteria, they are more likely to be of benefit to female workers due to the nature of women's paid work and its relationship with unpaid care. However, the comparisons required by the legislation are narrowly construed so that the right is to equal treatment with standard workers engaged in broadly similar work, employed by the same employer at the same time under the same type of contract.[178] As well as excluding high numbers of otherwise relevant workers due to the segregated nature of labour markets,[179] the derivative nature of the rights severely limits their potential impact. The dependency on comparison with an appropriate 'standard' worker means that the directives do not provide any substantive rights to workers identified as being disadvantaged and vulnerable on their own account which, in turn, means that they provide no real challenge to the causes or nature of such disadvantage. In practical terms, the part-time worker who finds herself employed in a sector which is generally low paid has no redress as long as her pay is set at a similarly low rate as that of her full-time counterpart.

In short, this legislation illustrates the culmination of a process which seeks to provide protection to vulnerable workers by regulating or regularizing atypical work and accomplishing the EES's promotion of non-standard work as a means of increasing the labour supply[180] alongside the incompatible deregulatory stance deemed necessary to fend off enhanced competition from outside the EU. In the current context, this mismatch of aspirations further entrenches the distinction

sufficient grounds on which to base a dual set of responsibilities for the workers concerned. See also Case C-320/00 *Lawrence v Regent Office Care Ltd* [2002] ECR I-7325 and N. Busby, 'Equal Pay and Contracting Out: *Lawrence v Regent Office Care Ltd*', *Edinburgh Law Review*, 7/2 (2003), 233.

[177] See Chapter 6.

[178] The indications thus far are that the courts have interpreted the comparative requirements restrictively. Furthermore, Member States are given so much discretion that inequalities in contractual status can be transposed directly into the implementing provisions—see, for example, the UK's implementation of Directive 1999/70 which applies the equal treatment principle to *employees*, rather than the broader category of workers, in order to preserve the differentiation of those who work through tripartite agreements and are often deemed to be self-employed under national law and, thus, excluded from the scope of the Fixed-Term Employees (Prevention of Less Favourable Treatment) Regulations 2002, SI 2002/2034.

[179] See Chapter 3.

[180] Ashiagbor, n 66 above, 77.

between the dual goals of gender equality and the conciliation of personal and professional life on the one hand with the further integration of women into the labour market on the other. What is needed to instil some common purpose is a coherent and cohesive ideological stance. In the next section, the question of whether the EU Charter of Fundamental Rights, which post-Lisbon has acquired a constitutional status, is capable of fulfilling this function.

The Expression of Fundamental Rights in EU Law: The Constitutionalization of Norms

Alongside the developments that have taken place at supranational level over the past four decades, the influence of international law has continued to gather apace in the context of the categorization and regulation of 'work'. Central to this is the International Labour Organization's (ILO) concept of 'decent work' recognized through the individual aspirations of people in their working lives which is enshrined in its four strategic objectives encompassing fundamental principles and rights at work and international labour standards; employment and income opportunities; social protection and social security; and social dialogue and tripartism. The objectives are applicable to all workers in both formal and informal economies whether waged or working on their own account including those who provide unpaid work in the home. This broad-based approach to the concept of 'work' and its application across all aspects of life is in sharp contrast to the compartmentalization expressed in the language of EU policy which assumes a demarcation between 'work' and 'life'.

Furthermore, although the specific conceptualization of 'decent work' might be a relatively new addition to the ILO's strategic vision, the connection between paid and unpaid work has long been an acknowledged feature of its legal and policy framework with Convention No 156 providing that:

> Each Member shall make it an aim of national policy to enable persons with family responsibilities who are engaged or wish to engage in employment to exercise their right to do so without being subject to discrimination and, to the extent possible, without conflict between their employment and family responsibilities.[181]

The influence of such provisions of international law, based on a human rights paradigm, over EU law has been expressly recognized in recent years by the adoption of the CFR. The introduction of a catalogue of fundamental social rights was originally intended as a response to the threat of social dumping[182] and specifically as a means of breaking the Member States' deadlock over the further expansion of minimum social standards due to the reactionary stance adopted by

[181] ILO Convention No 156 1981, Art 3(1).

[182] See C. Barnard, 'Social Dumping and the Race to the Bottom: Some Lessons for the European Union from Delaware?', *European Law Review*, 25 (2000), 57, 57–63.

certain Member States in the 1980s.[183] This was initially achieved through the inception and implementation of the Community Charter of the Fundamental Social Rights of Workers—a soft law tool aimed at promoting the Commission's vision of a somewhat narrow 'European Social Model'.[184] However, despite its effectiveness as an 'impulse for change',[185] the Community Charter's influence was limited due to its narrow conception of social citizenship and its peripheral position within the legal order[186] and, in 1996, a 'Comité des Sages' called for a bill of rights to include both civic and social rights.[187] This was followed by the recommendation of a committee of legal experts appointed by the Commission that full recognition of fundamental rights should be achieved through consolidation of the rights contained, *inter alia*, in the European Convention on Human Rights (ECHR) and the ILO conventions in one single text to be inserted into the Treaties.[188] In making its recommendations, the committee acknowledged the crucial role played by the CoJ in integrating the provisions of the ECHR into EU law and stated that 'regardless of the means chosen to articulate and affirm fundamental rights' the Court would continue to 'exert paramount influence on their future interpretation and application'.[189]

In 1999, the Cologne European Council entrusted the drafting of a single text to be known as the Charter of Fundamental Rights of the European Union to a specially constructed body, 'the Convention', whose membership incorporated representatives of national governments, the Commission, the European Parliament, and Member State parliaments. The draft Charter was agreed in October 2000 and subsequently approved by the European Council, European Parliament, and Commission who jointly proclaimed it at the Nice Council in December of that year.[190] In its communication on the Charter, the European Commission stressed its relevance thus:

[183] See p 98 *et seq* above. The UK was the main culprit in this respect insisting, for example, that Art 100a (now 114 TFEU) provided that approximation measures concerning the establishment and functioning of the internal market did not apply to provisions 'relating to the rights and interests of employed persons' (see para 2). Art 118a's (ex 137 EC, now 153 TFEU) requirement for unanimity in all social policy areas except for those relating to 'the working environment, as regards the health and safety of workers' meant that the UK's resistance to the expansion of the working environment to include restrictions on working time ultimately resulted in Case C-84/94 *United Kingdom v Council (Working Time Directive)* [1996] ECR I-5755.

[184] See J. Kenner, 'Economic and Social Rights in the EU Legal Order: The Mirage of Indivisibility' in Hervey and Kenner (eds), n 76 above, 8–13.

[185] Ibid, 13.

[186] Ibid.

[187] *For a Europe of Civic and Social Rights*, report by the Comité des Sages chaired by Maria de Lourdes Pintasilgo (Brussels: Office for Official Publications of the European Communities, 1996).

[188] *Affirming Fundamental Rights in the European Union: Time to Act* (Brussels: European Commission, 1999).

[189] Ibid, 12–13.

[190] For the background documents see <http://www.europarl.europa.eu/charter/default_en.htm> and, for a scholarly analysis, see S. Peers and A. Ward, *The European Union Charter of Fundamental Rights* (Oxford: Hart Publishing, 2004).

The Charter is a major milestone for Europe as a political force, which is evolving into an integrated area of freedom, security and justice, simply as a consequence of citizenship. It is an indispensable instrument of political and moral legitimacy, both for the citizens of Europe in relation to politicians, administrations and national powers and for economic and social operators.[191]

The text[192] sets out the full range of civil, political, economic, and social rights of European citizens and all persons resident in the EU and, as well as encompassing the ECHR[193] and ILO principles, is also based on the constitutional traditions of the Member States, the Council of Europe's Social Charter, the Community Charter of Fundamental Social Rights of Workers, and the case law of the CoJ and of the European Court of Human Rights. In approving its establishment, the Council acknowledged its primary objective to make citizens' rights 'more visible'[194] through consolidation and restatement of pre-existing texts rather than to establish any new rights.[195] Consequently, although it applies to the European institutions, subject to the principle of subsidiarity, it does not extend the powers conferred on them by the Treaties and is not intended to require any amendment to the Member States' constitutional law.

The Charter's legal status was initially considered by the Cologne Council and it was subsequently drafted with a view to its insertion into the Treaty. Although sanctioned by a vote of the European Parliament with amendments tabled at the Nice Council in December 2000,[196] this proposal was later dropped and a decision taken to pay full consideration to the nature of its potential implementation as part of the general debate on the EU's future constitution initiated on 1 January 2001.[197] The Charter's legal status, thus, remained unclear—it existed in limbo as a standalone document without legal force although its contents were the

[191] Paragraph 2.1 of the Commission's *Communication on the Charter of Fundamental Rights of the European Union*, COM (2000) 599 final.

[192] For the final amended version of the 2000 text which became effective on the entry into force of the Lisbon Treaty on 1 December 2009, see OJ 2010 C 83/02. The Charter is accorded 'the same legal value as the Treaties' by Art 6(1) TEU.

[193] The Charter is intended to be fully compatible with the ECHR—see Art 52/3 which makes clear that the Charter respects the ECHR, its protocols, and the case law developed by the European Court of Human Rights, and that the rights and liberties shared by the Convention and the Charter have the same meaning in both texts even if the wording of the Charter is different, although this provision 'shall not prevent Union law providing more extensive protection'. For specific reference to the relationship between the ECHR and EU law, see also Art 6(2) and (3) TEU.

[194] Cologne Presidency Conclusions, Annex IV European Council Decision on the Drawing up of a Charter of Fundamental Rights of the European Union, para 1.

[195] See Article 51/2 which states 'This Charter does not establish any new power or task for the Community or the Union, or modify powers and tasks defined by the Treaties'. The fears of some Member States that it would provide a basis for new policies in specific areas are, thus, unfounded. On the contrary, the aim is to define the limits to the powers of EU or Member State authorities, and to enable their exercise of existing powers to be monitored more openly.

[196] See Annex I, para 11 to the Presidency conclusions at <http://www.consilium.europa.eu/ueDocs/cms_Data/docs/pressdata/en/ec/00400-r1.%20ann.en0.htm> accessed 7 December 2010.

[197] By the Nice Declaration, see in particular Declaration 23 which calls for further consideration of the status of the Charter of Fundamental Rights. For the emergence of subsequent detail regarding the debate itself, see COM (2001) 178 final of 25 April 2001, *Communication on Certain Arrangements for the Debate on the Future of the European Union.*

subjects of internationally and nationally approved standards many of which were already incorporated by EU legislation and the jurisprudence of the CoJ. Despite its uncertain status, its symbolic value as an aspirational statement or bill of rights gave it prominence and authority and it was soon cited in the national courts and in the CoJ.[198] The impetus necessary for its incorporation continued to grow and in December 2009 the Charter was finally given binding legal effect[199] by the entry into force of the Lisbon Treaty.[200]

The Charter's primary aim is to reaffirm and clarify the EU's commitment to democracy as expressed through the language of human rights with respect for the fundamental freedoms which lie at its core. It does this by articulating relevant principles in a series of statements which are divided up into six sections: dignity; freedoms; equality; solidarity; citizens' rights; and justice. In the current context, the most directly relevant provisions are to be found in Chapter IV Solidarity which contains most, but not all, of the economic and social rights covered by the Charter, in particular, Article 33 on Family and Professional Life.[201]

A notable feature of the Charter is its consolidation of modern economic and social rights with the more traditional and well established civil and political rights.[202] This does not automatically convey equality in application across the whole range of rights which is dependent on a range of factors, not least maintenance of the *status quo* which has developed over the EU's life time through the juridification of rights and which the Charter does little to disturb. However, the

[198] Initially by Advocates General—see, for example, AG Tizaros's opinion in Case C-173/99 *BECTU* [2001] ECR I-4881.

[199] The Charter was amended and proclaimed a second time in December 2007. Protocol (No) 30 to the Treaties on the application of the Charter to Poland and the United Kingdom restricts its interpretation by the Court of Justice and the national courts of these two countries, in particular regarding the rights relating to solidarity in Chapter IV. At the time of writing it is unclear how this restriction will affect the EU *acquis*.

[200] Detailed analysis of the Lisbon Treaty's long and difficult path to ratification is beyond the scope of this book and, at the time of writing, it is too early to present any substantiated conclusions about the effect of its provisions on the particular area of law and policy under review. However, the long period between the Charter's declaration and its ultimate incorporation into the EU *acquis*, provided ample time for scrutiny of its contents and consideration of their potential impact and the analysis presented in this Chapter is drawn from the resulting body of literature. It is submitted that the provision of the Charter and the nature of its incorporation into EU law provided the most directly relevant aspect of the Treaty's overall provision in the social sphere, a view which Hepple has endorsed, see, for example, his second Hamlyn Lecture 'Fundamental Rights in the European Union' published in B. Hepple, *Rights at Work: Global, European and British Perspectives* (London: Sweet and Maxwell, 2005) and his *Guardian* newspaper article, 'For the greater good' published 23 November 2004 in which he argues that, used in the context of the OMC, the Charter is capable of changing the focus of social policy to incorporate positive action giving it a greater potential for 'achieving superior outcomes for a larger number of people than adversarial litigation-based individual rights'.

[201] Which provides, '(1) The family shall enjoy legal, economic and social protection; (2) To reconcile family and professional life, everyone shall have the right to protection from dismissal for a reason connected with maternity and the right to paid maternity leave and to parental leave following the birth or adoption of a child.' Other relevant provisions include Chapter II Freedom, Art 7 on respect for private and family life, Art 9 on the right to marry and right to found a family, and Art 15 on freedom to choose an occupation and right to engage in work; and, in Chapter III Equality, Art 21 on non-discrimination, and Art 23 on equality between men and women.

[202] See Chapter 4.

placement of the full range of rights within a single document to which the EU has proclaimed its commitment does at least signify a process of deconstruction of the outdated and limiting hierarchy of rights. The Charter's constitutional recognition of social rights which are neither subordinated to their civil, political, and economic counterparts or hived off into a separate and inferior text, follows their treatment by the Court which has repeatedly emphasized the equal status of the EU's social goals and economic objectives.[203] In this respect, the Charter's significance in the social domain goes beyond the symbolic as, by its incorporation in the EU's constitutional law, 'the European market order can be said to incorporate a set of core social rights'.[204]

This alone does not guarantee that the recognition of those rights will necessarily be of sufficient robustness and consistency as to assist directly in providing a solution to the unpaid care/paid work conflict. In fact, substantial work will need to be done to bring the social provisions of the Charter closer to the citizens of Europe and the lack of any legislative dimension means that success will depend on their interpretation by the Court. Given that the Charter's inception was instigated by an acknowledgement of the EU's need to catalyse its legislative and programmatical activity at both supranational and national levels[205] and the fact that its apparently narrow function was already potentially fulfilled in the employment context at least by the pre-existing Community Charter, it is unsurprising that critics have been quick to question its relevance and purpose in light of its somewhat restricted objectives. Well-founded doubts about its significance and practical effect have tended to focus on the Charter's sketchy coverage[206] and its potential to privilege some rights over others.[207]

It is beyond the scope of this book to provide a full critique of the Charter but its significance in the context of the unpaid care/paid work conflict enables some optimism which should, nonetheless, be tempered with an equal dose of informed caution. The Charter's undoubted symbolic value may also have a practical use as its prominence illustrates that the EU's stated commitment to certain core values goes beyond the mere restatement of international standards and assures the Member States' governments that their own constitutional settlements incorporating such standards are not undermined by, but compatible with, their EU membership. This responds to the fears expressed by some Member States' senior judiciaries[208] that fundamental rights have not been adequately protected by the EU and, it is hoped, will result in greater confidence at the national level in instilling the relevant values through the dual processes of policy implementation

[203] Deakin and Browne, n 76 above, 27.

[204] Ibid.

[205] Kenner, n 184 above, 7.

[206] See, for example, M. Bell, 'The Right to Equality and Non-Discrimination' in Hervey and Kenner (eds), n 76 above, 91 and, in the same volume, T. Hervey, 'The "Right to Health" in European Union Law', 193.

[207] For example, J. Hunt, 'Fair and Just Working Conditions' in Hervey and Kenner (eds), n 76 above, 45; Fredman, n 129 above, 55–6.

[208] Notably Germany's Constitutional Court.

and juridification of EU law. Although such assurances are routinely provided in the preambles of secondary legislation, the transposition and application of EU law now carries a guarantee that affected individuals are able to challenge it on the basis of clear and legally binding fundamental rights. This process perhaps assumes greater relevance with the move away from norm-setting legally binding legislation towards a more nebulous system of bottom-up policy co-ordination as a means of regulating social relations.

Linked to this is the issue of legal certainty. For all those involved in the application of EU law,[209] its coherence depends on compliance with international human rights provisions as well as a guarantee that Member States' obligations under the EHRC will not be undermined. Whilst the protection of existing rights cannot be assured by the provisions of the Charter alone, the affirmed recognition of appropriate standards within the overall framework does, at least, provide some guarantee of uniformity as EU law increasingly engages in areas where individuals are directly affected emphasizing the need for parallel reinforcement of rights to ensure that State and supra powers do not eclipse social rights.

Perhaps the most compelling practical application of the Charter lies in its contribution to the identification of a unifying ideology and normalization of social standards, particularly within the overarching EES as implemented by the OMC. Without such a clear and unequivocal statement of common values, the task of interpreting the existing rights provided by EU law against the backdrop of the OMC's potentially deregulatory guidelines could be perilously vulnerable to ambiguity. This is as relevant to the apparently straightforward cases with which domestic courts are routinely engaged as it is to the hard cases with which the CoJ is on occasion confronted. It is unlikely that judges in either situation will refer directly to the guidelines themselves but because of the dynamic by which the EU *acquis* develops over time, particularly with regard to the Court's tradition of teleological reasoning,[210] it is expected that their content and related policy will have influence over judicial decision-making. Alongside the Charter's possible use in the judicial interpretation of employment policy, it has another role in the juridification of the soft law approach to employment regulation. This is perceptible in its guarantee of certain rights such as equality between men and women which amount to positive obligations whilst allowing for the progressive realization of associated rights. By placing such rights within the context of a statement of underlying principles, the Charter enables their realization through hitherto unchartered means, for example, by opening up the possibility at the inter-governmental level for the adoption of measures aimed at encouraging and incentivizing Member States to utilize positive action as a means of effecting real change.[211] By providing a clear statement of the guiding principles of EU law, the Charter has the potential to stimulate a valuable interplay between its contents and the

[209] Citizens, courts, national governments, and the EU institutions as well as nationals of third states.

[210] See Chapter 6.

[211] See Hepple, 'For the greater good', n 200 above.

implementation of the EU's employment strategy capable of giving renewed meaning to the rights-based provisions of the Treaties and related secondary legislation. When placed within its wider constitutional setting, the Charter is at least capable of producing a centrifugal effect by which pre-existing obligations are clarified and strengthened through their interrelationships with associated provisions so that rights beget rights.

This process places great emphasis on the CoJ's interpretive role and the assumption that it would be a central player in this respect, in conformance with its participation in the development of EU law through its 'constitutionalisation of the Treaties', was envisaged from the outset and implicitly incorporated into the arrangements surrounding the Charter's introduction into EU law. The provisions governing the Court's operation in terms of competence and procedure[212] allow for such a process and, based on previous observations of the Court's interplay with its partner institutions and of its dialogue with the national courts,[213] there is little doubt that it will be provided with requisite opportunities to make a difference in this respect. Such interplay is of particular relevance in the current context due to the wide diversity in individual needs requiring expression through the exercise of a right to care as a means of reconciling paid work with unpaid care commitments[214] so that the effective operation of such a right depends on the application of broad principles to individual circumstances and the development of normative standards for which the preliminary rulings procedure[215] provides an ideal vehicle. However, the enhanced importance of the Court's participation in establishing, interpreting, and upholding the norms and principles provided by the Charter is at odds with the policy-led movement away from hard law provision towards soft law compliance in which litigation assumes a marginal role in favour of the participation of key stakeholders in both setting and enforcing norms.[216] This apparent paradox, which is symptomatic of the lack of cohesion that characterizes EU provision in this area, places particular emphasis on the existing legislative provisions with which the Court will continue to engage through the preliminary rulings procedure.

Conclusions

This Chapter has considered the difficult road travelled by social rights in the development of Europe's legal framework. This has arisen largely due to the key founding objective of the Community as an economic entity which has posed a constant threat of subordination of Europe's social aims to its economic imperative. Expansion and further integration of the so-called 'social dimension' has served as a

[212] Section 5 TFEU and the Statute and the Rules of Procedure of the Court of Justice of the European Union.

[213] See Chapter 6 for a longitudinal study of the Court's relationship with the national courts and related expectations and opportunities.

[214] See Chapter 3.

[215] Art 267 TFEU.

[216] Fredman, n 129 above, 49.

catalyst in the ignition and stoking of Member States' fears regarding a perceived loss of sovereignty under an enhanced European order. Subsequently, despite some substantial progress in both the constitutional and juridical contexts, the Union lacks a clear and cohesive overarching strategy for social integration which continues to develop in a piecemeal and incremental way. In the context of the unpaid care/paid work conflict this has had a detrimental effect as any further progress depends on recognition of the need to 'join up' disparate aspects of the EU *acquis*[217] which is, in turn, reliant on the identification of a unifying ideology. This can clearly be seen in the, thus far, uncoordinated efforts to increase both the quantity and quality of jobs, which, in the context of those with caring responsibilities, can only be achieved by the alignment of the dual goals of gender equality and paid work and family reconciliation.

Despite the lack of a unifying ideology, there is some cause for optimism with regard to the recent developments relating to the management of employment policy. The overarching theme of the Lisbon Agenda's social context appears to point to an investment in human capital as a means of improving employability and enabling individuals to become more self sufficient which is, on the face of it, compatible with Sen's capability approach advocated by the current author as providing a suitable framework within which unpaid care/paid work conflicts might best be resolved. The movement from top-down harmonization of social standards, although lamented due to the threat posed to the future development of hard law initiatives and associated social rights, can also be viewed as an opportunity to move away from the stalemate all too often associated with attempts at further integration of Europe's social goals. The EES's adherence to policy co-ordination through the identification and imposition of self-regulated norms has much to offer, particularly to an enlarged Europe. However, as well as providing a source of potential strength, its voluntary nature could also pose its greatest threat as Member States find themselves faced with conflicting 'choices' in an increasingly competitive global environment.

The provision of the EU Charter of Fundamental Rights and its incorporation into the EU's constitution by the Lisbon Treaty is critical in this respect. As well as establishing a common set of values or 'norms' which have potentially broad application across the range of regulated activities, the Charter has a significance beyond its symbolic value in that it has the potential to overcome the differences in the status of rights and, thus, to further social integration by placing it on an equal footing with its economic counterpart and by removing the largely false distinctions between related rights and those more closely associated with political and civil freedoms.[218] Its potential in the current context is clear—as well as recognizing the fundamental nature of the social rights necessary to resolve the unpaid work/paid employment conflict, the Charter's provisions provide a normative framework which is capable of linking the existing employment rights with the development of the soft law approach provided by the EES in order to give recognition to the

217 For example, employment and social security policy.
218 See Chapter 4.

existence of a right to care under EU law. Realization of this exciting potential depends heavily on the participation of the CoJ and it is hoped that the Charter's recognition of the Court's considerable role in the prior incorporation of many of its provisions will instil confidence in the Court's own ability to continue on the path of social integration, but its co-operation in such a venture is by no means assured.

For one thing, the expectations surrounding the Court's continuing involvement in the furtherance of Europe's social goals is at odds with the move away from litigation under the EES which places greater emphasis on self-regulation and on the increased role of the social partners.[219] However, the Court has maintained a constant and apparently influential presence in all aspects of relevant legal provision and, consequently, in the development of related policy. It was, after all, the Court's intervention in the Treaty's provision of 'equal pay for equal work'[220] which led to the development of the dual principles of supremacy and direct effect[221] which have had an immeasurably positive impact on the integration of social rights in the overall schema of EU law. The Court's constitutionalization of social rights has been identified as a driving force in the attribution of their enhanced status so that they are no longer subordinated to but sit alongside their civil, political, and economic counterparts.[222] In acknowledging the Court's continuing influence, the committee responsible for drafting the CFR referred directly to the Court's innovation in integrating the provisions of the ECHR into EU law and used the resulting jurisprudence as a basis for much of the EU Charter's provision. More specifically, the recast Equal Treatment Directive codifies much of the Court's case law in this area and places a greater emphasis on the Court's interpretive role as a means of embedding core principles and instilling consistency in the now aligned areas of gender equality and reconciliation of work and family life. However, as noted in the context of maternity rights, expectations regarding the Court's ability and willingness to prioritize social rights over the Union's economic imperative must be tempered with regard to both its limited competence in adherence to the legislative provisions it is charged with interpreting and their relationship with the Treaties themselves as well as in relation to its own ideological stance. As noted above, the latter is at the forefront of attempts to analyse the underlying reasoning informing the Court's recent judgments in a line of cases concerned with the right of trade unions to organize freely against threats to their members' job security.[223]

All of this points towards consideration of the Court's potential as a driver of change and, hence, the work of the Court in the current context will provide the focus of Chapter 6 in which its role as an apparently neutral custodian of the Treaties capable of safeguarding their provisions in order to ensure that the law is

219 See also the provision of Article 21(2) of the Recast Directive which explicitly charges the Member States with the task of encouraging the social partners 'to promote equality between women and men... with the aim of facilitating the reconciliation of work and family life'.

220 See *Defrenne II*, n 20 above.

221 Ibid.

222 Deakin and Browne, n 76 above, 27.

223 See n 4 above.

observed will be considered alongside an exploration of the particular conceptualization that the Court has applied in its interpretation and application of the provisions of EU law surrounding the reconciliation of paid and unpaid work. The purpose of this particular analysis is to show that the Treaties' meaning is far from pre-determined by the stark words of their texts but relies on a positivist approach to law-making with which all of Europe's citizens are potentially engaged by virtue of the social conventions that represent our acceptance or rejection of the particular way in which it is played out. The CoJ, rather than the independent adjudicator synonymous with the perceived image of domestic courts (often more imagined than real), is actually the gatekeeper of Europe's morality and has, through its unique relationships with the domestic courts and with its fellow EU institutions, the administrative capacity to influence the application of the Treaties in order to ensure that their meaning correlates with the lives of Europe's citizens.

6

The Case Law of the Court of Justice of the European Union

Introduction

Chapter 5 considered the legal and policy framework relevant to the treatment of unpaid work in European employment law. As that analysis showed, despite a move away from hard law regulation towards the soft law and policy approach proffered by the European Employment Strategy (EES) through the open method of co-ordination (OMC), EU policy- and law-makers have continued to place an increasing emphasis on the role of the Court of Justice in interpreting the social provisions of the Treaties and associated legislation. This is in line with the Court's position at the forefront of the development of Europe's social dimension from its earliest days. However, the Court's continued involvement, although clearly anticipated, is at odds with the new legal environment within which it now finds itself, in which self-regulation is favoured over litigation as a means of establishing and enforcing social standards through, for example, the involvement of the social partners at national level. This produces a paradox, whereby the Court's involvement is explicitly sought to give meaning to the principles relevant to further social integration but, at the same time, is inhibited by the policy approach adopted.

Whatever the effect of this inconsistency on the Court's future involvement, the method of bottom-up policy co-ordination espoused by the OMC leaves little space for the initiation of new social legislation and this is likely to mean that the existing Treaty provisions and secondary legislation retain a particular significance in the Court's jurisprudence. Of special note in this respect are the provisions of the Charter of Fundamental Rights (CFR) which have recently been elevated in status to provide, in theory at least, a fundamental right to reconcile family and professional life.[1] How this constitutional promise is ultimately recognized will, no doubt, be largely determined by the Court, which has a tradition of contextual interpretation by which it is able to draw on the widest range of instruments in order to give meaning to the Treaties' provisions. In the current context that the normative development of a catalogue of social rights has been placed in the hands of the Court carries certain concerns because, despite its

[1] See Art 33(2) CFR.

reputation as a socially progressive institution, the Court has had a somewhat inconsistent approach to resolving specific unpaid care/paid work conflicts to date with this aspect of its jurisprudence escaping detailed scrutiny.[2]

This Chapter will consider the Court's jurisprudence in the field of the reconciliation of paid work and unpaid care starting with an assessment of how its specific methods of interpretation and legal reasoning may have particular value in this context. Its proactive stance in applying teleological reasoning to give meaning to the Treaties' provisions, criticized by some as judicial activism, is in fact the expression of a crucial function which ensures the effective operation of the general schema of EU law. Whether the Court has always utilized its potential effectively in reconciling unpaid care and paid work is the main focus of this Chapter and this question will be considered in the context of the Court's jurisprudence. The effectiveness of the constitutional and legislative provisions interpreted by the Court, which were considered in Chapter 5, are not the focus of this analysis which is, rather, intended to explore the Court's specific treatment of those claims essentially linked to the conflict between unpaid care and paid employment with two main aims: to identify the specific issues with which the Court has been confronted and to identify the particular ideology underpinning its conceptualization of the relationship between unpaid care and paid work. The cases themselves are concerned with a range of activities across the life cycle including career progression, personal development, and pension provision which are all reliant on the ability to combine work and care. The purpose of identifying the underlying ideology of the Court's jurisprudence is to explore how this has influenced its interpretation of key provisions. In cases where the Court has been faced with a range of possible conceptual tools, the application of which may produce conflicting results, it is possible to ascertain whether certain principles have trumped others, for example, to prioritize market-making over the pro-regulatory stance necessary for the attainment of substantive equality. The overall objective is to discover whether the Court has taken advantage of its unique position and interpreted the law creatively in recognition of a right to care which, as argued in Chapter 5, is potentially compatible with the current provisions of EU law.

[2] This is not to overlook explorations of related areas such as McGlynn's work on EU law's ideological treatment of motherhood, see 'Ideologies of Motherhood in European Community Sex Equality Law', *European Law Journal*, 6 (2000), 39; 'Reclaiming a Feminist Vision: The Reconciliation of Paid Work and Family Life in European Union Law and Policy', *Columbia Journal of European Law*, 7 (2001), 241; 'Work, Family and Parenthood: The European Union Agenda' in J. Conaghan and K. Rittich (eds), *Labour Law, Work and Family* (Oxford: Oxford University Press, 2005), 217–36, or Fredman's consideration of the effects of flexible labour markets on women's employment (eg S. Fredman, 'Women at Work: The Broken Promise of Flexicurity', *Industrial Law Journal*, 33/4 (2004), 299) which provide insightful assessments of the Court's contributions to the areas under review. What is highlighted is the lack of focused considerations of the reasoning underpinning the Court's decision-making in the specific context of unpaid care/paid work reconciliation.

The Court of Justice's Interpretive Methods: A Unique Institution?

The Court's interpretive method is generally described as purposive or teleological meaning that, when interpreting a rule, account is taken of the purpose, aim, and objective that the rule pursues. The Court has confirmed this approach in *CILFIT*,[3] by declaring 'every provision of Community law must be placed in its context and interpreted in the light of the provisions of EC law as a whole, regard being had to the objectives thereof and to its state of evolution at the date on which the provision in question is to be applied'.[4] This approach is consistent with the dynamic and evolving nature of the EU within which the once exclusively economic imperative has been expanded significantly to encompass a much broader system of values incorporating social issues and the protection of human rights. However, the narrow scope of the Treaties' aims, which restrict the EU's competence, and the relative immaturity of the European legal order itself have combined to ensure that the Court is always conscious of its place in the greater scheme so that it has taken great care to justify its decision-making on the basis of the overall aims and intentions of the Treaty provisions. That is not to say that it has always been confined and uncreative in its decision-making. On the contrary, the Court has attracted criticism on the grounds that, driven by the desire to meet political objectives rather than interpreting the law for its own sake, it has overstepped the judicial mark and become law-maker.[5] Such charges raise serious questions concerning judicial independence which strike at the heart of the Union's democratic legitimacy. In order to determine whether such criticism is valid, the Court's reasoning must be considered. This is a difficult undertaking as not much has been written on the subject,[6] probably because little guidance exists on how the individual judges should reach a collective decision and the Court is obliged not to make its deliberations public, so '[a]ll we know about the Court's reasoning is written in its judgments'.[7] As far as the processes applied in order to arrive at these judgments are concerned, they have been characterized as 'sometimes firmly grounded and clearly

[3] Case 283/81 *CILFIT v Italian Ministry of Health* [1982] ECR 3415.

[4] Ibid, 3430.

[5] See H. Rasmussen, *On Law and Policy in the European Court of Justice: A Comparative Study of Judicial Policymaking* (Copenhagen: Martinus Nijhoff, 1986); H. Rasmussen, 'Between Self Restraint and Activism: A Judicial Policy for the European Court', *European Law Review*, 13 (1988), 28; P. O'Neill, *The European Court of Justice: a Case Study in Judicial Activism* (London: European Policy Forum, 1995).

[6] A small body of literature exists, eg A. Bredimas, *Methods of Interpretation and Community Law* (Amsterdam: North Holland, 1978); J. Bengoetxea, *The Legal Reasoning of the European Court of Justice* (Oxford: Oxford University Press, 1993); T. Koopmans, 'The Theory of Interpretation and the Court of Justice' in D. O'Keeffe and A. Bavasso (eds), *Liber Amicorum in Honour of Lord Slynn of Hadley, Vol 1, Judicial Review in European Union Law* (London: Kluwer International Law, 2000); J. Bengoetxea, N. McCormick, and L. M. Soriano, 'Integration and Integrity in the Legal Reasoning of the European Court of Justice' in G. De Búrca and J. Weiler (eds), *The European Court of Justice* (Oxford: Oxford University Press, 2001), 43.

[7] H. Schepel, 'Reconstructing Constitutionalization: Law and Politics in the European Court of Justice', *Oxford Journal of Legal Studies*, 20/3 (2000), 457, 466.

spelled out, sometimes maddening Delphic offerings, always the product of judicial negotiation and compromise'.[8]

Although the judges themselves have acknowledged that, as with all judicial decision-making, poor legal reasoning attracts criticism which can be damaging to the Court's authority and legitimacy,[9] the human element cannot be eradicated or ignored as 'Judges are humans of flesh and blood, their motives for arriving at certain decisions are probably political and moral as much as legal, they probably settle differences with each other for strategic reasons or sheer lack of time rather than in the belief that they have arrived at the correct legal solution'.[10] Law is a subjective discipline:[11] it is not scientifically objective and the thought processes of individual judges are but one manifestation of this. Furthermore, the various ways in which the law evolves and operates are deeply ideological. In the current context, the judicial treatment of particular issues derives from a combination of the application of legislative provisions, themselves the result of political compromises, and the particular theoretical perspectives of the Court's judges. To think that judicial decision-making takes place in a 'black box' where all external factors are (and should be) suspended, is both naïve and illusory.

In seeking to understand why the Court has arrived at a particular decision, it is necessary to unpack its various elements by systematic means capable of enabling broad comparisons to be drawn between separate but related judgments. Such elements arise out of various sources, some express, such as the Treaty provisions themselves, others more opaque but, nonetheless, implicit in the EU legal order, such as the perceived objectives of the legislature and the institutions' overall vision of the EU's aims and aspirations. The interpretation afforded to these sources is not static but has evolved over time alongside the development of the EU itself and can only be fully understood through a process of contextualization requiring an holistic approach which places the decisions in the time and place in which they were reached with regard to the political climate and external pressures faced by the Court and its fellow institutions. Furthermore, the rich cultural fabric of the Court itself has undoubtedly had an impact on the decision-making process, so that different compositions have given rise to differences in the understanding of what 'legal reasoning' is.[12]

[8] Ibid, 466.

[9] U. Everling, 'Zur Begründung der Urteile des Gerichtshofes der Europäischen Gemeinschaften', *Europarecht* 29 (1994), 127.

[10] Ibid, n 7 466.

[11] See Chapter 2.

[12] For example, Judge Everling's observation that the Court's shift in its approach from the establishment of general principles to a more case-specific stance in the 1970s was partly due to changes in its composition by the arrival of judges from the common law tradition, 'schooled in case law'. U. Everling, 'The Court of Justice as a Decisionmaking Authority' in Michigan Law Review Association, *The Art of Governance: Festschrift zu Ehren von Eric Stein*, 156 (1987), 163. See also Advocate General Jacob's assertion that criticism of the Court's politicization is misconceived as it overlooks the notion of constitutional jurisprudence on which the Court is founded and arises from a lack of familiarity with this conception of the judicial role within some Member States—F. Jacobs, 'Is the Court of Justice of the European Communities a Constitutional Court?' in D. Curtin and

Despite being prevented from breaking the secrecy of deliberations,[13] the Court's judges have been fairly forthcoming about what goes on in Chambers.[14] Furthermore, however they arrive at their decisions, they are obliged to provide a legal justification.[15] Although an account of the reasoning applied cannot deconstruct the role of the judges, it can identify the range of possible choices and impose specific criteria of validity. Despite such restrictions on the decision-making process, the charge that courts, from time to time, engage in judicial activism rather than legal interpretation remains. The operational features of the Court, its position as a supranational institution, and the aspirational nature of many of the provisions which it is responsible for interpreting have made this charge particularly resonant in critiques of its activities.[16] Responses to such criticism have focused on the repositioning of the judicial function so that, rather than the out-dated reductive concept, which places the judges in an ascertaining role without personal responsibility or creative means, they are viewed as interpreters and creators of law.[17] This shift in focus has been attributed to the radical transformation of the role of law and government in modern welfare states[18] by which a 'revolt against formalism'[19] has emerged. From this perspective, the judicial function is characterized as a way of providing meaningful contemporary solutions to legal problems which require systematic contextual interpretations of rules and must also take account of the impact these rules will have on human conduct in society.[20] This movement towards enhanced judicial creativity encompasses an acceptance of the element of choice in the judicial function, whereby abstract logic must sit alongside concerns involving economic, political, ethical, sociological, and psychological factors as the

D. O'Keeffe (eds), *Constitutional Adjudication in European Community and National Law* (London: Butterworths, 1992), 25, 32.

[13] Art 35 of the Statute of the Court of Justice provides that '[t]he deliberations of the Court shall be and remain secret'.

[14] U. Everling, 'The Court of Justice as a Decision-making Authority', *Michigan Law Review*, 82 (1984), 1294; D. Edwards, 'How the Court of Justice Works', *European Law Review*, 20 (1995), 539.

[15] Bengoetxea, n 6 above, distinguishes between 'context of discovery' and 'context of justification'. The former relates to the process of uncovering what caused the Court to arrive at one decision in favour of other possible outcomes. Although the secrecy of deliberations means that this will always be a matter of conjecture, the published output (the judgment and the Advocate General's opinion) provide something more than an account of the Court's decision-making process, rather, they provide an account of what makes the decision the right legal decision by stating legal reasons for what is opined or answered. This is known as the context of justification.

[16] See Rasmussen and O'Neil, n 5 above.

[17] O. Pollicino, 'Legal Reasoning of the Court of Justice in the Context of Equality: Between Judicial Activism and Self-restraint', *German Law Journal*, 5/3 (2004), 286.

[18] By which the significant growth in State intervention in fields previously the domain of self-regulation has led to a corresponding increase in judicial activity.

[19] This phrase was originally coined by the French lawyer F. Geny, who argued in favour of revealing the voluntaristic, discretionary element of judicial choice rather than merely focusing on the pure, mechanical logic of judicial reasoning in response to the excessive legalism of the post-codification era.

[20] See T. Koopmans, 'The Theory of Interpretation and the Court of Justice' in D. O'Keeffe and A. Bavasso (eds), *Liber Amicorum in Honour of Lord Slynn of Hadley, Vol 1, Judicial Review in European Union Law* (London: Kluwer International Law, 2000), 48.

available means by which decisions are reached.[21] If this approach is considered in the context of the Court's jurisprudence, two factors emerge which, together, provide a compelling justification for its engagement in creative decision-making: the institutional framework, and the language and nature of the Treaties themselves.

The charting of the various political phases that have shaped the Union's history[22] reveals an interrelationship between the relevant law-making mechanisms and the Court's perceived activism so that, on occasion, the legislature's inactivity has compelled the Court to engage in problem-solving more usually the role of law and policy-makers.[23] For example, the political inertia which characterized the first half of the 1980s led to the Court's increased activism with creative decision-making utilized to fill the void.[24] By referring to the aims and general principles of the EU, the Court has sometimes found itself 'compelled to interpret from the standpoint of the existential necessities of the Communities and ensure the maintenance of their capacity to function'.[25] Furthermore, the difficulty in linking the electorate's wishes with political decision-making within the EU has conferred legitimacy upon judicial creativity which would not necessarily apply in legal systems within developed democracies.[26]

The legal instruments which form the objects of the Court's deliberations have themselves encouraged its creative interpretation. Their compromised nature, the result of bargains struck on the basis of common goals between Member States with divergent political and legislative traditions, has resulted in a framework which reads as little more than a series of aspirational statements and lacks the requisite detail on which to base clear, sustainable legal solutions. The Court is left with little choice but to '[tease] out the meaning and implications of the treaties (or of instruments enacted pursuant to the treaties), [to show] how they support one view or line of action rather than another'. This process 'must be the very stuff of justification in this context'.[27] The aims-driven nature of directives by which the national legal systems are entitled to implement suitable provisions in line with the principle of subsidiarity, adds further to the amorphous quality of the texts which the Court is compelled to interpret so that it may, at times, have to provide 'a creative answer to questions when there is no obvious answer'.[28] Added to this dynamic, the apparent difficulties in linguistic interpretation inherent in the

[21] See M. Cappelletti, 'The Law Making Power of the Judges and its Limits', *Monash University Law Review*, 8 (1981), 15, 22.

[22] See Chapter 5.

[23] H. Kutscher, *Methods of Interpretation as seen by a Judge of the Court of Justice* (Luxembourg, 1976), 2, sect 6(a).2.

[24] See Chapter 5.

[25] Pollicino, n 17 above, 288.

[26] T. Koopmans, 'The Roots of Judicial Activism' in F. Matscher and H. Petzold (eds), *Protecting Human Rights: The European Dimension, Studies in Honour of Gerard J. Wiarda* (Kluwer, 1988), 327.

[27] Bengoetxea *et al*, n 6 above, 44.

[28] D. T. Keeling, 'In Praise of Judicial Activism, but What Does it Mean? And Has the European Court of Justice Ever Practiced It?' in C. Gialdino (ed), *Scritti in Oncore di G.F. Mancini* (Milan: Bellini, 1998) 505, 512.

drafting of legal texts, which must have application across the range of European languages, mean that the resulting texts are sparse and imprecise in comparison to national legislation.

All of these factors conspire to make some of the usual methods employed in case analysis particularly unsatisfactory. The concepts of judicial activism and judicial self-restraint as normative or interpretive ideology are not particularly helpful devices when attempting to explain or justify the decision-making processes of the CoJ which are better explored through its legal reasoning.[29] By focusing on how the Court takes account of reasons, identified as 'legal norms, values, principles, policies' to justify its decisions, attention is drawn to 'whether and by what considerations its decisions are justified or, at the very least, rationally justifiable'.[30] Rather than the 'context of discovery', emphasis is placed on the 'context of justification'[31] which enables an assessment of the extent to which the Court has consciously developed an underlying strategy in relation to the issues under review.

Motherhood and Parenting: The Dominant Ideology of the Court of Justice

Despite the wide literature on the Court's purpose and activities, there has been a lack of specific focus on the justifications on which the Court's decision-making is based in cases concerning the reconciliation of unpaid care and paid work. However, a review of the relevant literature does uncover some pertinent observations which can usefully inform a deeper understanding of its reasoning in the current context. In her work on paid work and family life within EU law, McGlynn has found evidence of a dominant conservative ideology underpinning the particular conceptions of motherhood[32] and, more generally, parenthood[33] adopted by the Court in its jurisprudence which has reinforced traditional assumptions surrounding the role of women within the family and, thus, inhibited their progress.

This ideology has manifested itself in the context of the Court's justification for the restriction of adoption leave[34] and a period of optional leave eight weeks after the birth of a child[35] to women only. In the former case, the Court's concern for the Italian state's attempt 'to assimilate as far as possible the conditions of entry of the child into the adoptive family to those of the arrival of a new-born baby in the family during the delicate initial period'[36] which was used to justify its decision is based on the assumption that only mothers are capable of providing care for an infant. In giving its judgment in the latter case, the Court specified its belief that it

[29] J. Bengoetxea *et al*, n 6 above, 44.
[30] Ibid.
[31] Ibid.
[32] McGlynn (2000), n 2 above.
[33] McGlynn (2005), n 2 above, 229–35.
[34] Case 163/82 *Commission v Italian Republic* [1983] ECR 3273.
[35] Case 184/83 *Hofmann v Barmer Ersatzkasse* [1984] ECR 3047.
[36] Case 163/82, n 34 above, at para 16.

was 'legitimate to protect the special relationship between a woman and her child'.[37] In its adherence to the traditional view that a woman's place (at least in the early months of motherhood) is in the home, the Court declined to endorse an early move towards substantive equality founded on the laudable basis of the mutual benefits of gender-neutral parenting for both sexes.[38] That the earlier case arose from a challenge by the Commission that Italian legislation was contrary to the Equal Treatment Directive (76/207) illustrates the willingness of that institution at least to test the boundaries of the non-discrimination principle and its compatibility with the realization of equality between the sexes.

In keeping with its restrictive view that parental benefits could legitimately be confined to mothers, the Court found in *Abdoulaye*[39] that a payment made in addition to the woman's full salary during maternity leave did not constitute direct discrimination against men despite the fact that, in cases of adoption, the payment was available to either parent. The Court sought to justify its decision on the basis that the payment constituted a form of compensation due to the 'occupational disadvantages inherent in taking maternity leave'[40] experienced by women. That its own prescription that women should bear exclusive responsibility for the care of an infant leaving fathers' careers unaffected by parenthood might perpetuate such disadvantage appears to have passed the Court by.

In *Lewen*[41] the Court considered the wider implications of the Parental Leave Directive[42] for the first time in considering a claim that an employee on parental leave should be eligible to receive a Christmas bonus. In her claim, the employee concerned sought to rely on Clause 2(6) of the framework agreement on which the Directive is based which provided that rights acquired at the start of a period of parental leave 'shall be maintained as they stand until the end of parental leave.' However the Court held fast to its restrictive approach in finding that Directive 96/34 did not provide any specific right to receive such a payment and that the applicant's eligibility for the payment was based instead on her gender, as women are likely to 'be on parenting leave far more often that male workers'.[43] Thus, the exclusion of women on such leave from eligibility for related bonuses amounted to indirect sex discrimination. This reinforces the Court's earlier stance that childcare is primarily the responsibility of mothers and seriously undermines the purpose and effectiveness of the parental leave provisions which were, after all, intended to encourage men 'to assume an equal share of family responsibilities'.[44] Through its judgment in *Lewen,* the Court has differentiated between the rights applicable to mothers on parental leave and those applicable to fathers on the same leave who will

[37] Case 184/83, n 35 above, at para 26.
[38] McGlynn (2005), n 2 above, 218–24.
[39] Case C-218/98 *Abdoulaye and others v Renault SA* [1999] ECR 1-5723.
[40] Ibid, para 18.
[41] Case C-333/97 *Lewen v Denda* [1999] ECR I-7243.
[42] Directive 96/34, see Chapter 5.
[43] *Lewen,* n 41 above.
[44] See para 8, Annex to The Framework Agreement on Prenatal Leave, Directive 96/34.

enjoy a reduced level of protection.[45] This is of no long-term benefit to either sex as women seeking protection of the rights relating to caring responsibilities find themselves consigned to reliance on sex-specific rather than on gender-neutral criteria which reinforces the stereotypical assumptions about their role within the family, whereas men, unable to rely on the same sex-specific argument, are refused any right to claim similar work-related bonuses during periods of parental leave.[46]

However, as two recent cases show, the Court's approach to the use of sex-specific criteria as a means of gaining benefits under the Directive has been somewhat inconsistent. In *Gómez-Limón Sánchez-Camacho*,[47] the Court was asked whether national legislation which provides for a reduction in social security benefits proportionate to a reduction in contributions as a result of part-time parental leave is precluded by the framework agreement annexed to Directive 96/34. The applicant had reduced her working hours in line with a national system enabling part-time parental leave to be taken in order to care for a child under six, when the applicant became unable to work due to illness. Her invalidity benefit was calculated on the basis of her reduced contribution following her reduction in hours which, she contended, negated the effectiveness of parental leave which was intended to promote equality and to eliminate sex discrimination. The Court held that, as the current provision was applicable to both men and women, it did not amount to direct discrimination. That the acquisition of entitlement to benefits was a matter for regulation by the Member States under the auspices of Directive 79/7 which did not oblige national authorities to grant advantages in respect of social security to those who had brought up children meant that the provision in question was not indirectly discriminatory.

In a contrasting judgment, the issue of compensatory payment for redundancy during a period of parental leave was considered by the Court in *Meerts*.[48] The applicant had been dismissed while participating in a reduced-hours parental leave scheme (not unlike that in operation in *Gómez-Limón*) and her compensation was paid at the rate of her reduced salary. This, the Court held, was contrary to the objectives of the Framework Agreement on Parental Leave which covers all the rights and benefits derived from the employment relationship and which is intended to make it easier to reconcile working and family life. Thus the compensatory payment in the event of a dismissal should be based on the full-time salary provided for by the contract of employment. This a welcome (and gender-free) interpretation of the wider aims of the parental leave provisions which, although distinguishable from the harsh judgment in *Gómez-Limón,* is difficult to reconcile in principle with the earlier case which appears to provide that, as long as gender neutrality is maintained, the purpose of parental leave will carry varying

[45] See E. Caracciolo di Torella, 'Childcare, Employment and Equality in the EC: First (False) Steps of the Court', *European Law Review*, 25 (2000), 310.
[46] See further, McGlynn (2005), n 2 above, 233.
[47] Case C-537/07 *Gómez-Limón Sánchez-Camacho v Instituto Nacional de la Seguridad Social (INSS) and Others* [2009] ECR I-6525.
[48] Case C-116/08 *Meerts v Proost NV* [2009] ECR I-10063.

influence on the Court's decision-making depending on the relevance of such matters as national procedural autonomy.

Alongside the protection arising in respect of periods of related leave, the ongoing challenges of balancing care commitments during times of 'active employment'[49] have also been the subject of the Court's consideration. In *Lommers*[50] the Court was confronted with a dispute over the legitimate allocation of State-funded nursery places. Under the Dutch scheme in question, the places were reserved for the children of women employees, except in cases of emergency when they could be offered to male employees. In justifying the discriminatory effect of these provisions, the Court relied on Article 2(4) of the Equal Treatment Directive (76/207) in finding that they amounted to a legitimate use of the concept of positive discrimination as they were 'specifically designed to authorise measures which, whilst being discriminatory, were intended to eliminate or reduce material inequality of opportunity'. The provision of childcare primarily for mothers' use would assist in addressing the underrepresentation of women within the relevant sectors of the Dutch civil service and 'allow women to pursue their careers on an equal footing with men'.[51] The measure was found to be proportionate as it was sufficiently flexible so as to be able to accommodate fathers who were bringing up children on their own. Under the guise of progressive decision-making based on the concept of positive discrimination, the Court, once again, placed primary responsibility for childcare on the mother's shoulders whatever her domestic circumstances and regardless of the father's willingness to assume some of that responsibility.[52] Men, on the other hand, are only to be supported in their pursuit of childcare where they have no alternative in the form of a female partner with whom responsibility would presumably otherwise rest. This approach provides a short-term solution to the symptoms of discrimination but does not deal with their causes such as the reasons underpinning women's underrepresentation within certain employment sectors.[53]

The Court's dominant ideology of motherhood is rooted in the essentialist notion of woman's existence as being predetermined by her biological and psychological predication for all things care-related[54] which makes her homemaker and man breadwinner.[55] For this reason the Court has struggled less in its development of a 'relatively clear set of principles'[56] in relation to its jurisprudence surrounding pregnancy and maternity than in other areas of its case law in which the divisions

[49] See *Lewen*, n 41 above (eg at para 15) in which the German provisions under review drew a distinction between a worker who was on maternity or parental leave and one who was not and was, thus, in 'active employment'.

[50] Case C-476/99 *Lommers v Minister van Landbouw, Natuurbeheer en Visserij* [2002] ECR I-2891.

[51] Ibid, para 32.

[52] Which the applicant in *Lommers* apparently was.

[53] McGlynn (2005), n 2 above, 235.

[54] See Chapter 2 and Chapter 5.

[55] See Chapter 4.

[56] A. Masselot and E. Caracciolo di Torella, 'Pregnancy, Maternity and the Organisation of Family Life: An Attempt to Classify the Case law of the European Court of Justice', *European Law Review*, 26/3 (2001), 239, 245.

between women's and men's employment experiences are gender rather than sex-based.[57] However, as the Court's judgments in the above cases demonstrate, its concern for the protection of maternity assumes, at times, a paternalistic tone that is unhelpful in the Union's pursuit of its dual goals of gender equality and 'work and family reconciliation'. Read alongside its own judgments, the Court's proclamations that Community law was not intended to interfere with the 'organisation of the family' or to 'alter the division of responsibility between parents'[58] clearly support its adherence to the *status quo* through the perpetuation of 'separate spheres'[59] rather than the accommodation of individual arrangements pertaining to the sharing of responsibility. This is illustrated by the *Lommers* case in which one family's attempt to do just that was cast aside in favour of a prescriptive ruling which inferred that childcare remains the responsibility of the mother regardless of her own career aspirations.[60]

Despite the outward appearance of a clear division in its classification of the issues before it as being sex-based (for example, pregnancy) or gender-based (for example, related to the social arrangements such as childcare), the Court has consistently applied the same purposive approach to upholding the division of labour within families in all of its related case law regardless of the issue at stake. In the context of pregnancy and maternity, the resulting outcomes are generally more palatable to feminist critics simply because of the proximity of the resulting protection to the event of childbirth so that women are (rightly) protected when they are deemed to be at their most vulnerable physically and psychologically.[61] For example, the Court has been consistent in the development and application of its mantra that, as pregnancy is a state unique to women, to use it as justification for a refusal to employ[62] or to dismiss[63] will amount to direct discrimination for which there is no need for a male comparator.[64] Likewise, access to certain work-related

[57] See Chapter 2 and the analysis of atypical work cases below.

[58] *Hofmann*, n 35 above, para 24.

[59] See further T. Hervey and J. Shaw, 'Women, Work and Care: Women's Dual Role and Double Burden in EC Sex Equality Law', *Journal of European Social Policy*, 8 (1998), 43, 50.

[60] The fact that the applicant's partner in *Lommers* might have had difficulty in pursuing her career because of the necessity to take care of the couple's young children, was held to be of 'no relevance for the assessment of the validity of the measure at issue in relation to Art.2(1) and (4) of the Directive' see n 50 above, para 49. This was justified on the basis that the principle of equal treatment can only be applied between the employees working for the employer who is responsible for the measure.

[61] See, for example, Masselot and Caracciolo di Torella, n 56 above, who found (at 11) that in cases relating to pregnancy and maternity in the workplace, the Court 'did not hesitate to take the part of women' in contrast to cases concerning wider issues of family responsibility where the Court had been 'less proactive'.

[62] For example, Case C-207/98 *Mahlburg v Land Mecklenburg Vorpommern* [2000] ECR I-549.

[63] For example, Case C-421/92 *Habermann-Beltermann v Arbeitwohlfahrt Bezirksverband* [1994] ECR I-1657; Case C-32/93 *Webb v EMO Cargo* [1994] ECR I-3567; Case C-394/96 *Brown v Rentokil* ECR I-4185 (which overturned the Court's previous decision in Case C-400/95 *Handels-og Kontorfunktionaerernes Forbund i Danmark v Dansk Handel & Service (Larsson)* [1997] ECR I-2757).

[64] The Court's judgment in Case C-177/88 *Dekker v Stichting Vormingscentrum voor Jonge Volwassenen Plus(Dekker)* ECR I-3941 and the accompanying opinion of Advocate General Darmon is the earliest exposition of this aspect of its jurisprudence. On this point, see R. Wintemute, 'When is Pregnancy Discrimination Indirect Discrimination?', *Industrial Law Journal*, 27 (1998), 23, in which the author argues that the technical explication of the equality principle as formulated under the

benefits[65] will flow from the special protection that lasts from the beginning of pregnancy up to the end of the period of maternity leave.[66]

Although the Court's jurisprudence in this area is ostensibly based on the application of the equality principle as expressed in the Recast Directive (2006/54/EC) there is an underlying rationalization which has its roots in traditional perceptions of women's biological and social functions and which is echoed in the related legislative provisions of EU law.[67] Through this association, the protection of pregnancy and maternity is justified and, in the context of EU law, justifiable on the basis of the woman's physical state, particularly in relation to her health and safety and that of her unborn child or infant. Although this might be seen as the appropriate approach to the development of a normative framework relating to the treatment of pregnancy and early motherhood in employment, it is not conducive to the conferment of suitable principles in other care-related contexts, including the longer-term provision of childcare. The difficulty arises where the rationalization of protection on the grounds of physical well-being—particularly that of the unborn child—does not provide a clear enough link to the right being sought. In other words, the further away in time from the physical states of pregnancy and childbirth that the woman is, the more her behaviour at work is expected to conform to that of the standard (male) worker,[68] so that protection from dismissal on the grounds of illness outside of the maternity leave period is restricted even where it is directly linked to pregnancy or childbirth.[69] Correspondingly, the more tenuous the connection between the right claimed and the physical state of pregnancy, the less receptive the Court is in recognizing that right so that, for example, payment during maternity leave need not be linked to normal earnings.[70]

In adopting this particular formulation, the Court has extended the dominant ideology of motherhood discernible in its case law on gender equality to its jurisprudential treatment of pregnancy and childbirth and their resulting effects so that its message, at least subliminally, is that women are the primary providers of care with which any explicit attempts to combine paid employment will attract punitive measures.[71] Aligned with this is the intimation that a woman's mind and

relevant legislation will always require a comparator and that the focus should, therefore, be on the identification of an appropriate comparator. Further, Wintemute contends that the Court's categorization of pregnancy discrimination as always amounting to direct discrimination does not aid the coherent development of case law.

[65] Such as consideration for promotion, see Case C-136/95 *Caisse Nationale d'Assurance Vieillesse des Travailleurs Salariés (CNAVTS) v Thibault* [1998] ECR I-2011.

[66] See *Brown v Rentokil*, n 63 above.

[67] See the discussion of Directive 92/85/EEC and its proposed amendment in Chapter 5.

[68] Hence the loss of the special protection surrounding pregnancy and maternity beyond a certain specified time limit, see *Brown v Rentokil*, n 63 above.

[69] Case C-179/88 *Handels-og Kontorfunktionaerernes Forbund I Danmark v Dansk Arbejdsgiverforening (Hertz)* [1990] ECR I-3879 and *Larsson*, n 63 above.

[70] Case C-342/93 *Gillespie and Others v Northern Health and Social Services Board and others* [1996] ECR I-475 discussed in Chapter 5.

[71] For example, in specific terms, the loss of earnings during maternity leave and, in general terms, the reduction in status and precariousness associated with atypical work—see Chapter 5.

body are not her own[72]—she is protected when 'with child' and is prevented from having the freedom to make her own choices about how to combine employment with care for her child once it is born.

An alternative view would result in the conferment of substantive rights on the basis that women (and men) should be entitled to seek to combine paid employment with their parental and, for that matter, their other caring responsibilities on their own terms.[73] In order to discover whether the Court has been at all receptive to this way of thinking requires a shift of focus away from its case law which is directly concerned with the issues of pregnancy and childbirth towards its jurisprudence in a group of cases where the relationship between unpaid care and paid employment is, perhaps, less transparently linked to essentialist notions of sex but arises in respect of individual attempts to balance these two apparently conflicting sets of responsibilities. Of course, given the organization of work and care within contemporary society, it is impossible to distinguish between women's roles as the bearers of children and as the providers of care[74] as the two are inextricably linked through corresponding social arrangements as much as they are in the Court's psyche. However, by moving from the Court's treatment of claims which are closely related to the event of childbirth and/or explicitly require its consideration of motherhood toward its consideration of issues arising from the general reconciliation of paid and unpaid work, it is at least possible to make some assessment of its ideological stance on the place of unpaid care in European employment law. This requires analysis of its treatment of a series of cases relating to atypical working arrangements.

The Social Context of Atypical Work

The Court's teleological approach to interpretation and the non-binding nature of its own judgments gives it a wide discretion when faced with decision-making, as long as the decision reached can be justified on the basis of the Treaties' provisions.[75] The Court's constitutionalization of the EC Treaty led to its landmark decision in *Defrenne II* in which Article 119 (ex 141, now Art 157 TFEU) was found to be directly effective, thus extending its scope in ways not previously envisaged. The national courts have responded by making extensive use of the preliminary rulings procedure provided by Article 267 TFEU (ex 234) ever since. The determination of litigants and legal advisors and the willingness of national courts to make referrals, have, on many occasions, provided the Court with opportunities to utilize its discretion in order to apply creative judicial decision-making to a range

[72] See Chapter 2.

[73] And in fulfilment of the full range of normal human activities—see the discussion of the capabilities approach in Chapter 2.

[74] See Chapter 3.

[75] This applies in the broadest sense and could be interpreted as encompassing the 'spirit' of the Treaties as well as their 'black letter' provision.

of related issues. Furthermore, the categorization of non-discrimination as a fundamental principle of Community law ascribed it a very high status when set against a range of possible outcomes enabling the Court, if inclined, to use its furtherance as justification for deciding a case in a particular way.

As discussed in Chapters 3 and 4, the deregulated nature of global labour markets has led to the emergence of new ways of working, requiring a reconceptualization of work. This has fundamentally changed the relationship between employer and worker, once founded on mutual dependency, to a range of diverse arrangements based primarily on the needs of the organization and increasingly met by means of dispensable, short-term contracts lacking any clear commitments on the part of the employer to the welfare and well-being of the worker. This shift, which has taken place alongside an increase in the labour market participation rates of women, has led to greater economic dependency with a decline in social protection resulting, in some circumstances, in legal independence from the employing organization. Furthermore the gendered nature of labour markets which is inextricably linked to the provision of unpaid care, places women more often than men in low status employment categorized as 'atypical'.

These developments are mirrored in a group of cases with which the Court has been confronted over the past 30 years, which deal with the rights of part-time workers. These cases have been the subject of referrals due, in some respects, to the novelty factor—the new methods of working are as different from traditional working arrangements as those filling them are different from the normative concept of 'worker'. Consequently, the provisions of national law are insufficient and, faced with new legal claims, little guidance, and a whole range of possible outcomes, national courts have grasped the opportunity to refer specific questions for adjudication by the European Court. Some of these cases relate to workplace practices based on assumptions regarding levels of employee commitment and economic necessity which have been used to justify different rates of pay for those working part-time. Some are based on national legislation and policies aimed at distinguishing atypical workers from the standard (male breadwinner) model by providing them with lower standards of social protection. Such actions can, on the face of it, be rationalized if the primary objective of EU law is assumed to be the furtherance of economic goals as provided by the Treaty, within whose context the provision of equal pay was rationalized on the basis of economic integration between Member States. Indeed, supranational labour market policy has supported the deregulation of labour markets as a means of job creation in the face of rising unemployment.[76]

Confronted with stark choices concerning the interpretation of the substantive provisions of a legal system founded on the basis of the economic imperative on the one hand, and the chance to apply Community law creatively in order to further social integration on the other, what choices has the Court made? What theoretical perspective has it adopted in its conceptualization of the normative values required

[76] See Chapters 4 and 5.

to interpret such provisions? When faced with a range of possible conceptual tools, some of which may, in application, produce conflicting results, have certain principles trumped others? If so, which ones and on what basis? Finally, in seeking to interpret the relevant provisions consistently in line with the requirements of the principles of legal certainty and legitimate expectation, has the Court developed a philosophical position on the unpaid care/paid work conflict which is capable of identification as a specific jurisprudence?

Laying the Conceptual Foundations: *Jenkins, Bilka-Kaufhaus*, and *Rinner-Kühn*

The first three cases on atypical work to come before the Court led to the establishment of certain key features of what is now accepted as EU law's treatment of part-time workers' sex discrimination claims. In common with the other cases under review, *Jenkins*,[77] *Bilka-Kaufhaus*,[78] and *Rinner-Kühn*[79] were concerned with inequities in pay rates between full and part-time workers with the domestic courts seeking clarification of the scope and meaning of Article 119 EC (now 157 TFEU).[80] Consideration of these cases in chronological order enables some assessment of the incremental development of the interpretation of those provisions and invites analysis of the choices made by the Court. Given its relative infancy at the time that these cases came before it and the untested nature of the relevant provisions, it is asserted that we are looking at a stage in the development of EC law when everything was up for grabs: the Court's definition of its own judicial role; the underlying meaning of the aspiration of equality articulated by the Treaty; the identification, position, and interpretation of the principles which would emerge as the guiding lights of EU law and the place of gender relations within European integration.

Jenkins v Kingsgate

In *Jenkins*, the applicant was employed on a part-time basis for 30 hours per week. Her employers, Kingsgate (Clothing Productions) Ltd, employed 83 full-time workers, whose normal working week was 40 hours per week, and six part-time workers, five of whom were women. The one male part-time worker was viewed as an exceptional case in that he had been allowed to stay on past normal retirement age and worked 16 hours per week.[81] Before the joint enactment of the Sex

[77] Case 96/80 *Jenkins v Kingsgate (Clothing Productions) Ltd* [1981] ECR 911.

[78] Case 170/84 *Bilka-Kaufhaus GmbH v Karin Weber Von Hartz* [1986] ECR 1607.

[79] Case 171/88 *Rinner-Kühn v FWW Spezial-Gebäudereinigung GmbH & Co. KG* [1989] ECR 2743.

[80] Which had been found to have both vertical and horizontal direct effect in Case 43/75 *Defrenne v SABENA* [1976] ECR 455, '*Defrenne II*'.

[81] The male worker in the *Jenkins* case may be seen as the fly in the ointment with regard to the argument that the Court's acceptance of the claim as indirect discrimination is flawed (see below at

Discrimination Act (SDA) and the Equal Pay Act (EqPA) in 1975, male and female employees had been paid at different rates but there was no difference in the hourly rates of pay of full-time and part-time workers. However, in response to the requirements of the legislation, new rates of pay were introduced which equalized full-time rates for men and women but distinguished those working for less than 40 hours per week who were categorized as 'part-time' and paid 10 per cent less per hour. Mrs Jenkins claimed that the difference between her pay and that of a full-time male employee contravened the equality clause inserted into her contact of employment by the EqPA. In response, her employers asserted that the differential rates of pay were not related to the sex of the workers concerned but were intended as a disincentive to part-time working so that the optimum use could be made of machinery.[82] This defence was accepted by the industrial tribunal and Mrs Jenkins appealed to the EAT which referred the case for consideration by the Court.

Before considering the subsequent judgment and reasoning of the Court of Justice, it is important to place the case in its historical context. The concept of indirect discrimination was still very much in its infancy, having been introduced into UK statute law just five years earlier by the SDA whose enactment, rather than relating directly to the UK's membership of the Community, had been strongly influenced by the approach adopted in the United States' prohibition of race discrimination. The relationship between the US Supreme Court's decision in *Griggs v Duke Power Co*[83] and the development of the UK's legal framework is demonstrated by the inclusion and framing of the concept of indirect discrimination in s 1(1)(b) of the Act. Indirect discrimination, although recognized by the ECJ in its earlier case law,[84] was not expressly provided for in the Treaty or in secondary legislation until much later.[85] And although the concept of indirect discrimination was applied by the European Court in *Jenkins*, the statutory provision itself was not under consideration. This is because, the claimant had originally sought to rely on the EqPA by arguing that her engagement on like work with a male comparator employed on a full-time basis entitled her to equal pay and the industrial tribunal had accepted the employer's defence under s 1(3) of the EqPA, that the difference in pay was attributable to a material difference unrelated to sex.

p 151) since his existence mitigates against Jenkins's treatment and that of her female co-workers as direct discrimination. However, it is asserted that his arrangements which were classified as 'exceptional' by the employer should not disturb the essence of the argument that where women, because of their sex, find themselves in different situations from men, any detriment suffered amounts to direct discrimination—see Chapter 5 at p 111. I am indebted to Evelyn Ellis for pointing out the need to articulate this.

[82] Striking an interesting contrast with recent attempts to *increase* the amount of part-time work (see Chapter 5) illustrating how employers and the State make strategic use of workers' contractual arrangements depending on factors extraneous to the relationship and thus manipulate 'market factors'.

[83] 401 US 424 (1971).

[84] See, for example, Case 152/73 *Sotgiu v Deutsche Bundespost* [1974] ECR 153.

[85] In Council Directive 97/80/EC of 15 December 1997 on the burden of proof in cases of discrimination based on sex, OJ 1998 L 14/6, now provided for by Directive 2006/54.

In its reference to the Court, the Employment Appeal Tribunal (EAT) asked, *inter alia,* whether the principle of equal pay required that pay for work at time rates should be the same irrespective of the hours worked each week, or whether the employer's aim of attaining a commercial benefit by encouraging workers to do the maximum possible hours justified the payment of different rates dependent on hours of work.[86] Furthermore, the Court was asked whether, and in what respects, the application of Community law would differ 'if it were shown that a considerably smaller proportion of female workers than of male workers is able to perform the minimum number of hours each week required to qualify for the full hourly rate of pay'.[87]

Given its lack of experience in dealing with the relevant provisions, the EAT displayed an impressive insight into the issues at stake in framing the questions for referral. By inviting consideration of the employer's policy as an acceptable justification for *prima facie* discrimination, the Court's reference opened the door, perhaps regrettably (see below), to the application of the concept of indirect discrimination. The identity and role of Jenkins's Counsel is noteworthy at this juncture. Anthony (now Lord) Lester QC acted on her behalf and she was assisted throughout the proceedings by her trade union and the Equal Opportunities Commission. Lester's involvement is particularly relevant to the conduct of the case: as one of the chief architects of the UK legislation, he would have had a far greater degree of familiarity with its intended purpose and approach than the majority of practitioners at that time.[88] Following his client's failure before the industrial tribunal, 'counsel for Mrs Jenkins conceded that . . . he could not succeed [at the EAT] on the basis of the British legislation alone', hence the invocation of Article 119 and the Equal Pay Directive.[89]

The Court's judgment in *Jenkins* has been the subject of criticism (see below) on the basis that it revealed little of the reasoning applied and, consequently, its wider application is difficult to discern. In contrast, the Advocate General's opinion, with which the Court appears to have concurred, sets out the various theoretical and conceptual grounds relevant to the case and so is worthy of specific attention.

The Advocate General's Opinion

In its submission, the Commission had argued that 'the very wording of Article 119 required that pay for work at time rates should be the same irrespective of the numbers of hours worked each week'[90] Advocate General Warner asserted that in order to read Article 119 in this light, the phrases 'the same job', 'the same work',[91]

[86] Question 1.
[87] Question 3.
[88] See the Advocate General's opinion, at 4 in which he contrasts Mrs Jenkins' representation with that of the unrepresented employer commenting that her case is 'fully represented'.
[89] Ibid, 596.
[90] AG's Opinion at 598.
[91] Para 3.

and 'equal work'[92] would all have to be accorded the same meaning enabling their interchangeable use. With regard to the phrases 'equal work' and 'the same work', this was unproblematic. However, the distinction in terminology between 'equal' (the same) 'work' and the 'same job' appeared to be deliberate as it occurred in all the different language texts of the Treaty, thus, although a part-time and full-time worker may perform equal work, they do not have the same job.[93] This distinction between the 'work' and the 'job', if accepted by the Court, would effectively close off the possibility that an employer's policy of differentiating pay rates on the basis of hours of work could amount to direct discrimination. Following this reasoning, the jobs performed are 'different' and the gender of the incumbents becomes irrelevant giving way to the possibility of justification.

Turning to the employer's defence that the differential pay rates were based on the desire to facilitate the optimum use of machinery rather than the sex of the workers, AG Warner disputed the approach proffered by the claimant which was based on the '*Clay Cross* approach'. In that case, Lord Denning MR[94] had opined that the intention of the employer must be set aside if his actions resulted in unlawful discrimination. To accept market-based 'excuses' such as a woman's willingness to work for less than a man or a man's request for higher wages than a woman's would result in the UK legislation being a 'dead letter' as '[t]hey are the very circumstances in which the statute was intended to operate'.[95] AG Warner found 'no support in the Clay Cross case for the wide proposition that counsel for Mrs Jenkins sought to derive from it'[96] and rejected the supposition that 'differentiation was a hangover from the days when Kingsgate paid all its female employees at lower rates than its male employees'.[97] This was despite the fact that the change in policy from differentiation on grounds of sex to hours of work had occurred a month before the deadline for compliance with the EqPA and the SDA. Even the industrial tribunal, despite finding against Mrs Jenkins as a matter of law, had remarked that if differential rates of pay were could be legally justified, 'this in itself smacks of inequality among the sexes because by the very nature of things the part-time workers are bound to be mostly women'.[98] It is regrettable that the Advocate General, and ultimately the Court itself, were not more accepting of Denning's approach in *Clay Cross* that the defences advanced by employers should be interpreted purposefully in light of the intention of the statute, as to do otherwise would seriously undermine its effect.

[92] Para 1.

[93] In its submission, the Commission rejected this approach arguing that it was the 'post' and not the number of hours worked which determine whether or not two jobs are the same. This line appears to be supported by the Court in its judgment in Case 129/79 *Macarthys Ltd v Smith* [1980] ECR 1275 in which it was found that, in deciding whether a female worker is performing the same work as a male worker, regard should be had to the *nature of her services*.

[94] *Clay Cross (Quarry Services) Ltd v Fletcher* [1979] ICR 1, CA.

[95] Ibid, 5A, D.

[96] AG's Opinion at 599.

[97] Ibid.

[98] Ibid, 596.

Having opened the door for a potential justification by the employer, AG Warner turned to the concept of disparate impact. The claimant's position before the EAT had been that, were her primary claim of direct discrimination to fail, the disproportionate adverse impact of the employer's policy to encourage a 40-hour week should be considered in light of its effect on women who would be less able to comply due to family responsibilities. This line of argument in support of which Jenkins's counsel cited the US Supreme Court's judgment in *Griggs*[99] is now familiar as indirect discrimination. Interestingly, the Commission had rejected this approach out of hand describing it as a 'half-way house' and questioning its enforcement as being 'difficult to monitor in practice'.[100] Nonetheless, this was the approach favoured by the Advocate General and, ultimately, by the Court itself and has remained the accepted formulation for dealing with equal pay and treatment claims by part-time (and other 'atypical') workers under the sex discrimination provisions of EC law ever since. Drawing support from the Court's jurisprudence on the application of the principle of non-discrimination in the context of nationality,[101] AG Warner approved this approach as the only one 'that reconciles the need to prevent discrimination between full-time and part-time workers with the need to prevent injustice to an employer who differentiates between [such] workers for sound reasons unconnected with their sex'.[102]

The Judgment in *Jenkins*

In concurring with the findings of the Advocate General, the Court held that as the purpose of Art 119 was to ensure the application of the principle of equal pay for men and women for the same work, prohibited differences in pay are, therefore, based exclusively on the sex of the employee. Thus, differential pay rates for full and part-timers do not offend the Article provided the difference is due to factors which are objectively justified on grounds unrelated to sex. The provisions of Article 119 would be directly effective in circumstances where the national court could apply the criteria of equal work and equal pay to establish that different pay rates for full and part-time workers amounted to sex discrimination.

Criticism at the time of the judgment centred on its opaqueness rather than its reasoning, so that 'it was thought from the decision . . . that the ECJ had a narrow understanding of the concept of indirect discrimination, namely that an action was only discriminatory when it was intended to be so'.[103] The President of the EAT had such difficulty trying to apply the judgment that he used his own interpretation

[99] See n 83 above.
[100] AG's opinion at 599.
[101] Case 152/73 *Sotgiou v Deutsche Bundespost* [1974] 1 ECR 153; Case 61/77 *Commission v Ireland* [1978] ECR 417; Case 237/78 *Caisse Regionale d'Assurance Maladie (C.R.A.M.), Lille v Palermo* [1979] ECR 2645.
[102] Ibid, 601.
[103] C. Barnard and B. Hepple, 'Indirect Discrimination: Interpreting Seymour Smith', *Cambridge Law Journal*, 58 (1999) 2, 399, 401. See also C. Kilpatrick, 'Community or Communities of Courts in European integration? Sex Equality Dialogues between the UK Courts and the ECJ', *European Law Journal*, 4/2 (1998), 121, 140 in which the judgment is described as being 'extremely confused'. For

of national law in finding that unintentional indirect discrimination against part-time female workers was contrary to the EqPA even if it was not prohibited by Article 119.[104] It is unfortunate, given how much was at stake and in light of its subsequently wide application, that the judgment in *Jenkins* was not based on more solid foundations.

Although hailed as the case in which the Court enabled part-time workers to utilize Article 119 as a basis for claims before national courts, the confused reasoning underpinning the judgment had set the law on a path which has become increasingly contentious over the years. One cannot help but wonder how things might have turned out if the Court had accepted the claimant's primary argument that her treatment amounted to *direct* discrimination. From a vantage point of nearly 30 years, this may at first consideration seem entirely inappropriate. However, if the incremental development of the law in this respect is set aside and a deconstructed analysis of the facts applied, it emerges as being as much of a possibility as the Court's actual finding that such cases should be dealt with as *indirect* discrimination claims.

When stripped back to its bare essentials, the categorization of the claim in *Jenkins* as direct discrimination does not, in fact, necessitate a huge leap in terms of reasoning but merely requires the setting aside of the hours of work performed as a relevant criterion for the establishment of 'different' jobs. If the hours of work are deemed to be irrelevant in determining the nature of the job, a straightforward comparison between the pay received by Mrs Jenkins and her male comparator for the same work amounts to a direct breach of the principle of equality as provided by Article 119. This was the essence of the claimant's primary argument and was accepted as the correct approach by the Commission. The wording of the Article appears to support this approach in its provision that 'pay for work at time rates shall be the same for the same job'.[105] Given the different sexes of the workers, the comparison struck between the hourly pay received by the part-time worker and that of her full-time comparator would have enabled a finding of direct discrimination with no opportunity for justification.

It is important to clarify that the criticisms set out here in relation to the suitability of indirect discrimination as a means of dealing with the claim in *Jenkins* should not be read as a rejection of the use of indirect discrimination in all related circumstances. On the contrary, it is clear that indirect discrimination is the most appropriate means of dealing with cases covering a wide range of issues,[106] and the use of disproportionate impact as a means of assessing employer and State policies

confirmation of the belief that *Jenkins* applied only to circumstances where there had been an intention to discriminate, see the UK's submission in *Bilka-Kaufhaus*, n 78 above.

[104] *Jenkins v Kingsgate* [1981] IRLR 388.

[105] Article 119, para 3.

[106] Specifically those arising from 'equal value' claims which necessitate comparisons between different jobs or professions—see, for example, Case C-127/92 *Enderby v Frenchay Health Authority and another* [1993] ECR I-5535—and those in which the discrimination arises from a combination of factors such as the application of a collective agreement which limits the effects of national legislation or *vice versa*—see below at p 164 *et seq*.

has been a very welcome addition to anti-discrimination law. What is contentious is the Court's explicit assumption in its case law since *Jenkins,* that the principle of equality is only applicable to 'atypical' workers if it is derived from the application of a 'neutral' policy (imposed by an employer or the State—see *Rinner-Kühn* below) which cannot be justified on non-gender grounds. This prevents a thorough assessment of the factual basis against non-justifiable provisions by the national courts and enables claims to succeed only if a number of technical procedural hurdles can be cleared, often through the application of wholly subjective criteria.[107]

The Relationship between Women's Employment and Unpaid Care

The most significant shortcoming of the Court's approach in *Jenkins* is its refusal to consider the actual cause and effect of the employer's policy of paying less to part-timers. Although it is not within the Court's jurisdiction to establish the factual basis of the case, nor to consider the application of the national provisions under review, some assessment of the motive informing the employer's behaviour would surely have permitted a more pragmatic view to have been taken. In framing the questions for referral, the EAT did invite this. The employer's claim that the policy was for reasons of 'commercial benefit' meant merely that the lower pay rates saved money—a 'justification' which would have applied equally to a policy concerned with the explicit payment of women at lower rates than men. The conferment of the principle of sex equality through its enshrinement in the Treaty carried a financial cost for employers, but it was accepted that this was a price worth paying. To subordinate this principle so early on to employers' prerogative over wages costs has had a profound effect on the rights of those engaged in 'women's work'[108] and, consequently, on the reconciliation of paid employment and unpaid care.

If the Court had been minded to take a wider view of the issues raised by the case, the reasons why the part-timers worked the hours that they did would have been directly relevant to the outcome. This would have necessitated some consideration of their need to balance paid employment with unpaid care and the employer's decision to employ them at a lower pay rate would have emerged as the punitive measure it effectively was. In fact, the relationship between part-time work and care commitments *was* implicitly accepted by the Court as a relevant factor in its finding of indirect discrimination. If Mrs Jenkins' reasons for working part-time had been directly attributed to her gender, her case could surely have succeeded as a direct discrimination claim.[109] Of course, the inherent difficulty in ascribing unpaid care as exclusively the concern of women carries with it

[107] See D. McCann, *Regulating Flexible Work* (Oxford: Oxford University Press, 2008), 63.

[108] See Chapter 3.

[109] This has been how the jurisprudential approach to cases concerning dismissal on the grounds of pregnancy and maternity has evolved—see *Webb v EMO Cargo*, n 63 above These types of claims only succeeded latterly, once the woman's sex was viewed as the reason for any discrimination on the grounds of pregnancy and maternity.

stereotypical assumptions that all women are mothers and/or have primary responsibility for childcare. Subsequently, where such assumptions inform the application of legal doctrine, there is a danger that they will become embedded in the normative concepts on which policy and law-making are based and, thus, be perpetuated.[110] This difficulty illustrates the important dividing line between the biological categorization of sex and the social construction of gender.[111] However, by not harnessing sex discrimination law to the root causes of such discrimination at such a pivotal stage in its development, the Court missed a valuable opportunity to effectively challenge the construction of gender roles. If female part-time workers had been recognized as the victims of direct sex discrimination and had won the right to equal pay with male full-timers, perhaps the place of unpaid care in paid employment would have been the subject of informed legal debate, rather than merely providing justification for the marginalization of so-called 'atypical work'.

Bilka-Kaufhaus

In the second case to come before it on the issue of equal pay and part-timers, the Court revisited the specific issue of justification in cases of indirect discrimination. *Bilka* was referred by the German Federal Labour Court three years after the Court's judgment in *Jenkins* and, despite the infancy of the Court's jurisprudence, the application of indirect discrimination in such cases had become accepted to such an extent that direct discrimination is not even considered in the later case. The German court, having heard the case as an indirect discrimination claim, asked the ECJ for clarification of the application of Article 119 to an employer's policy which excluded part-timers from membership of a pension scheme and guidance on what might qualify as an acceptable justification in this context. The questions on which the reference was based were all explicitly framed around the Court's decision in *Jenkins* and, like the EAT before it, the German court displayed both insight and open-mindedness in their construction.

In *Bilka* part-time employees were excluded from a non-contributory pension scheme, available to full-time workers, unless they had been employed for at least 15 years at the time of their retirement. The employer contended that their exclusion was to discourage part-time employment and to make full-time work more attractive so that evening and Saturday opening times could be covered which, following *Jenkins,* amounted to an economic reason capable of justifying the differential pay rates. In response, the claimant argued that the encouragement of full-time work arose as a matter of choice and was not justified as the employer would be entitled not to recruit part-time workers but could not, without infringing

[110] See the discussion of the Court's dominant ideology of motherhood and resulting jurisprudence, this Chapter at p 139.

[111] See Chapter 1.

Article 119, worsen the situation of such workers 'who are already at a disadvantage'.[112]

In its reference the German court asked whether the exclusion of part-time workers from an occupational pension scheme amounted to an infringement of Article 119 if it had a disproportionate effect on more women than men;[113] whether the exclusion of part-timers could be objectively justified on the grounds of a policy to deter part-time working arrangements, even if such a policy is not necessary for reasons of 'commercial expediency'[114] and, whether the undertaking is under a duty to structure its pension scheme so as to take account of the 'special difficulties experienced by employees with family commitments in fulfilling the requirements for an occupational pension'.[115]

The confusion caused by the judgment in *Jenkins* is apparent in the UK's submission in which it opined that Article 119 did not apply to 'indirect discrimination' and that Article 119 was only applicable where an element of intention on the part of the employer was present, so that 'the court cannot step into the shoes of the employer in assessing his choice of business policy'.[116] The distinction between direct and indirect discrimination was also central to the Commission's submission which took the opposite view that *Jenkins* inferred that a lack of intent on the employer's part was not enough to justify a provision which in fact placed women at a disadvantage.[117] Furthermore, the Commission submitted that the social objective of Article 119, following *Defrenne II*, can 'be effective only if employers' pay policy does in fact take into account the living and working conditions of women employed part-time'.[118] This would have enabled a wide consideration incorporating the promotion of improvements in such conditions as articulated in what were Articles 117 and 118.[119] In his opinion, Advocate General Darmon, citing the respondent's view, had referred to the relationship between care and employment in his observation that '[p]art-time work consolidates the traditional roles between men and women, without making women economically independent [and] . . . is thus . . . a manifestation of the conflict inherent in the situation faced by women: home and family on the one hand, employment on the other'.[120]

In its judgment, the Court considered the applicability of Article 119 to the pension scheme in question, holding that its contractual nature[121] meant that it did amount to 'consideration' and, thus, fell within the scope of Article 119. The Court held that Article 119 was infringed by the exclusion of part-time employees from an occupational pension scheme where that exclusion affects a far greater

[112] *Bilka*, n 78 above, 710.
[113] Question 1.
[114] Question 2(a).
[115] Question 2(b), (paraphrased from the case report).
[116] AG's Opinion at para 10.
[117] Ibid, para 11.
[118] Ibid.
[119] (Ex 136 and 137) now Arts 151–3 TFEU.
[120] AG's Opinion at 117.
[121] As distinguished from a statutory scheme which would fall outside of the scope of Article 119—see Case 80/70 *Defrenne v Belgium* [1971] ECR 445.

number of women than men, unless it could be objectively justified.[122] The Court then set down what has become the definitive test for objective justification by holding, in line with the Commission's submission, that justification will be possible only where the measures chosen correspond to a real need on the part of the undertaking, are appropriate with a view to achieving that objective and are necessary to that end. Finally, Article 119 did not impose an obligation on employers to organize their occupational pension schemes so as to take into account the particular difficulties faced by those with family responsibilities.

The Test of Objective Justification

The court's decision in *Bilka* has been widely welcomed as establishing a right of access to occupational pension schemes for part-time workers and the guidance it provided has been used extensively in the intervening years.[123] However, there are certain weaknesses in the reasoning applied which have had a far-reaching impact on the development of the equality principle. First and foremost, the Court's reliance on the shaky foundations of *Jenkins* has meant that the success of related claims depends on the claimant's ability to show group impact in order to prove indirect discrimination. The requirement that all part-time workers' equal pay claims must be supported with statistical data presents particular difficulties in sectors where women predominate in both full and part-time work[124] and, even where such 'proof' is available, the applicant must ensure that the discrimination cannot be justified.

The test for objective justification established by the Court in *Bilka* represents an amalgam of the principle of proportionality which is present in the national legal systems of several Member States.[125] In German law, the relevant test rests on an assessment of three factors: suitability of the measure under review for the attainment of the desired objective; the necessity of the disputed measure (ie there is no alternative measure available which is less restrictive of the individual's freedom); and the proportionality of the measure to the restrictions that are thereby involved.[126] The *Bilka* test differs substantially from this formulation through its self-justifying stance that the measure be both 'appropriate' and 'necessary' in its achievement of the objective ('the real need of the business'). Use of the German test is qualified only by weighing up the effect of the measure and the restriction of the individual's freedom, whereas no such requirement is present in the test as stated in *Bilka*. In fact, the *Bilka* test can be interpreted clearly as favouring employers' interests: once a 'real need' is identified, the measures chosen to support

[122] Judgment at para 28.

[123] Although, depending on the circumstances of the case, with varying degrees of success—see the section below on Retirement and Work-related Benefits, at p 169.

[124] Such as teaching and nursing.

[125] France and Germany being the most prominent examples.

[126] See P. Craig and G. De Búrca, *EU Law Text, Cases and Materials* (Oxford: Oxford University Press, 2003), 372.

it are self-justifying by being both appropriate and necessary to ensure it is achieved. Although the Court made it clear that the use of the test should always be considered by national courts in light of the specific facts of each case, its conceptual foundations are questionable as a means of furthering the principle of equality with its main weakness being the lack of any requirement to balance the employer's needs against those of the individual disadvantaged by the imposition of the measure. In *Bilka* these components amounted to the gaining of a commercial advantage by a business pitched against the denial of an individual's pension rights. If the loss suffered by the claimant due to the discrimination caused is weighed up against the consequences of deprivation of the business need (as required by the German test), it is at least possible to make an assessment of the relative values of the factors at stake. In the context of the relationship between employer and employee, it also becomes apparent that some rights may be more fundamental in securing the well-being and security of workers than others, with entitlement to a pension coming high up this list.

Turning to the Court's response to the question of whether, in formulating policies, employers should take any account of the 'special difficulties experienced by employees with family commitments in fulfilling the requirements for an occupational pension', it is revealing that the Court found this to be beyond the scope of Article 119. In *Bilka* it had been argued that employers should be obliged to ensure that periods spent meeting family responsibilities should count as periods of full-time employment for the purposes of calculating pension entitlement.[127] The Court's refusal to entertain the possibility that the impact of unpaid care on paid employment could not be mitigated by the provision of Article 119 clearly illustrates the low value that it ascribed to the former. Given the apparently wide application of Article 119 as set out in *Defrenne II*, it seems wholly plausible that the Court *could* have established this important link between the principle of equality and living and working conditions by applying a contextual approach incorporating the Treaty's social aims as articulated by Article 119's near neighbours, Articles 117 and 118.[128] More fundamentally, the Court's finding that to exclude part-time workers from occupational pension schemes is contrary to the principle of equality as articulated by Article 119 is undermined by its refusal to consider the reasons for women's inability to work full-time as being relevant to its interpretation. This is conceptually perverse as the adverse impact required for such claims to be accepted as indirect discrimination arises as a direct consequence of women's unpaid care commitments. It appears, from its reasoning in *Bilka*, that the Court was prepared to go only so far in interpreting Article 119 in the context of the group impact of certain measures and no further. The future success of claimants would depend on their ability to advance statistical data illustrating the existence of group impact with discrimination, even where it could be shown, vulnerable to the possibility of justification.

[127] Judgment in *Bilka*, n 78 above, para 40.
[128] Ex Arts 136 and 137, now 151–3 TFEU.

Proving Disproportionate Impact

The use of statistical data as evidence in discrimination cases has its origins in the US case *Griggs v Duke Power Co.*[129] Although *Griggs* was referred to by both of the Advocate Generals in *Jenkins* and *Bilka* and by the Court in *Jenkins* as authority, the reasoning applied by the Supreme Court has little in common with the ECJ's approach in either case. In *Griggs*, the practice of applying the criteria of a high school education or passing a general intelligence test as conditions of employment were found by the Supreme Court to be prohibited[130] if they were not significantly related to job performance and operated to 'freeze' the *status quo* of prior discriminatory employment practices. The reasoning of the Court was that the practical effect of the criteria was to disqualify black applicants at a substantially higher rate than white applicants because, under the conditions pre-dating the passing of the Civil Rights Act, black people had received inferior educations in segregated schools. Furthermore, the jobs to which the criteria were attached had formerly been filled only by white employees as part of a longstanding practice of giving preference to white applicants. Although *Griggs* was brought as a class action and the petitioners' claim was demonstrable by the use of statistical data, the Supreme Court's decision did not rest on the presentation of that data[131] but rather on the nature and effect of the criteria. In deciding whether such a policy could be justified *despite* its impact, the Court held that the 'touchstone is business necessity',[132] meaning the necessity of the application of the criteria. In the circumstances, the criteria were not found to be necessary as they were not significantly related to job performance. Although the Court recognized that a balance must be struck between the attainment of equality and the pursuit of satisfying genuine business needs, it gave preference to the elimination of historical disadvantage suffered by black people in line with the overriding objectives of the legislation.

This approach can be fundamentally distinguished from the reasoning applied by the ECJ. By expressly stating in *Bilka* that it was not necessary for account to be taken of the particular difficulties faced by those with family responsibilities in the formulation of employers' policies, the Court closed off the possibility that such issues could be raised as relevant factors in subsequent claims. The guidelines set down by the European Court on the test for objective justification differ fundamentally from those established by the Supreme Court for disparate impact justification by way of which 'the posture and condition of the job-seeker [should] be

[129] See n 83 above.

[130] By Title VII of the Civil Rights Act 1964.

[131] The data was in fact necessary to prove the validity of the claim, as the failure of one black individual to graduate from high school or pass the intelligence test could have been merely indicative of the fact that the individual was of below average intelligence. However, by presenting a statistical analysis showing that all of the applicants who had not completed high school or taken the test had continued to perform satisfactorily, the petitioners were able to show that the criteria were irrelevant in assessing job performance. In *Bilka*, in contrast, the act of excluding part-time workers from the pension scheme and its effects on the individual were obvious without statistical proof.

[132] Judgment in *Griggs*, n 83 above, 431.

taken into account'.[133] Furthermore, the European Court's interpretation of the phrase 'commercial expediency' appears to be substantially different from that of the Supreme Court's reading of 'business necessity', with the former being established as a 'real need on the part of the undertaking' and the latter arising from a job-centred necessity measurable by the performance (actual or potential) of the incumbent.

Due to the European Court's treatment of the claims in *Jenkins* and *Bilka*, the application of the equality principle to those who combine paid employment with unpaid care became fettered by the technical hurdles presented by the concept of indirect discrimination. Furthermore, the subjective nature of objective justification coupled with the wide discretion given to national courts looked set to be the cause of different standards of application across Member States. Despite the recognition of sex equality as a legislative aim within the national legal systems, the development and application of policy in many areas is still heavily influenced by the public/private dichotomy.[134] This is apparent in many of the State-led policy strands relevant to public and private sector employment in relation to which Article 119 (ex 141, now Art 157 TFEU) has direct effect.[135] Following the 'success' of the claims in *Jenkins* and *Bilka*, it was only a matter of time before a case came before the Court in which a worker sought to review the legality of a State measure which had an adverse impact on her pay due to her status as a part-time employee.

Rinner-Kühn

The claimant, who was employed by an office cleaning business for 10 hours per week, was informed during a period of illness that she was not entitled to sick pay in accordance with national legislation which excluded those who worked 10 hours or less per week. She asserted that the provision was contrary to Article 119 as the number of women in part-time employment was considerably higher than the number of men. In response, the German Government stated that part-time workers were excluded on the grounds that they were not as integrated in or dependent on the undertaking as full-time workers. Consequently, the Labour Court asked the ECJ to consider the compatibility of the relevant legislative provision with Article 119 and Council Directive 75/117 (the Equal Pay Directive) as the proportion of women adversely affected by the provision was considerably greater than the proportion of men.[136]

133 Ibid, 430.

134 See Chapter 2.

135 See *Defrenne II*, n 80 above.

136 Statistics requested by the Court from the Commission showed that the category of employees whose normal working week was less than 10 hours was made up of significantly more women than men in seven Member States with Germany at the top of the table with 89% of such workers being women.

Rejecting Advocate General Darmon's suggestion that the use of objective justification might not be appropriate in the case of State policy, the Court applied essentially the same test as that formulated in *Bilka* which had equal application regardless of whether the measure was a State provision or an employer policy. However, in variance from the terminology adopted in *Bilka,* the 'real need of the business' became 'a necessary aim of social policy'[137] and rather than the means chosen to achieve that aim being 'appropriate and necessary', the Court in *Rinner-Kühn* stated that they must be 'suitable and requisite'.[138] Although it was for the national court to determine whether a legislative provision was justified on objective grounds, the Court did proffer an opinion regarding the suitability of the justification advanced by the German Government regarding the part-time workers' integration in and dependency on the employing undertaking. Such assumptions, the Court found, amounted to 'generalisations about certain categories of workers'.[139] However, if the Member State could show that the means chosen met a 'necessary aim of its social policy', the 'mere fact' that part-timers' exclusion affected a much greater number of female workers than male workers could not be regarded as constituting an infringement of Article 119.[140]

Social Policy as a Ground for Justification

The Court's approach in *Rinner-Kühn* was broadly consistent with that in *Jenkins* and *Bilka* in line with the principles of legal certainty and legitimate expectation. However, the entrenched classification of such claims as individual indirect discrimination defensible through the advancement of an objective justification meant that the law on atypical workers' rights was now written. Article 119 would not be extended to provide an absolute right to the same pay for men and women regardless of their hours of work or other contractual arrangements which deviated from those of the normative model of the 'standard worker'.[141] Furthermore, the Court's treatment of justifications for State provisions in *Rinner-Kühn* gave Member States an apparently wide discretion as long as they could show that such measures amounted to a necessary aim of social policy. This enabled the development of self-fulfilling strategies based on the differentiation of groups of workers to encourage or discourage certain labour market behaviour on economic or social grounds, with Community law providing no clear protection for those who were disadvantaged. In this respect, the *status quo* remained intact with the further

[137] *Rinner-Kühn,* n 79 above, judgment at para 14.
[138] Ibid.
[139] Ibid, para 13.
[140] Ibid, para 14.
[141] Specifically those exhibiting the 'typical' characteristics of the (male) norm, ie full-time and permanent.

deregulation of labour markets deemed potentially compatible with the principle of equality as provided by Article 119. In the years since *Rinner-Kühn,* Member States have sought to utilize this potential with varying degrees of success and some of those attempts will be considered in the proceeding analysis.

The Place of Unpaid Care in the Court's Jurisprudence on Sex Discrimination and Atypical Workers

The Court's reasoning in *Jenkins*, *Bilka*, and *Rinner-Kühn* undermined the application of the equality principle to those whose unpaid care commitments impact on their engagement with paid employment by preventing their compliance with the normative model of the 'standard worker'. The ability of (most) men to conform to this model is largely dependent on women's conformity to an equally traditional model of female behaviour through the provision of essential unpaid care within the family. All three judgments make clear that Article 157 TFEU (ex 119, ex 141) does not impose an obligation on employers to take account of the relationship between labour market behaviour and care arrangements in the formulation of policy, but the reasoning informing this aspect is confused and sends a mixed message to employers as the imposition of certain measures may give rise to indirect sex discrimination which will only be justifiable if the *Bilka* test can be met. As a consequence, although the reasons for women's 'different' labour market behaviour need not explicitly inform employer behaviour, the reverse appears to be true as strategies promoting seemingly 'neutral' policies should implicitly take account of their likely or possible impact on women as a group or on specific groups of women. In addition, the Court did not determine that any authority (employers, the State, or the courts) should be expressly required to consider the effects of historical disadvantage born of a recent past of lawful discrimination on women's employment or on the social construction of gender. The Court's jurisprudence supports the continuation of traditional gendered roles within families and workplaces by consistently finding in its early cases that the right to equality is largely dependent on the ability of the individual to exhibit traditionally male characteristics in her labour market behaviour, failing which it cannot be guaranteed.

In the following section, the Court's case law following *Jenkins*, *Bilka*, and *Rinner-Kühn* will be assessed chronologically to discover whether its own evolution has enabled a more progressive stance. The cases tend to have been clustered around certain issues such as the (predominantly German) use of collective agreements, the application of national legislative measures, and retirement-related rights. However, it is the Court's treatment of their recurring themes that is of most interest in the current context; these are identified as: the reasons why part-timers work 'non-standard' hours; the linear relationship between time served and the acquisition of skills and knowledge; and conceptions regarding the utilization of part-time workers' 'non-working' time.

Assumptions Regarding Part-time Workers

In *Kowalska*,[142] the Court found that a contractual entitlement to severance pay on retirement which was based on a collective agreement[143] did fall within the scope of Article 119 and amounted to indirect discrimination. The relevant scheme excluded those who worked less than 38 hours per week on the grounds that 'part-time workers do not provide for their needs and those of their families exclusively out of their income from their employment'.[144] Thus, the employers contended, there was no duty to provide temporary assistance for such employees on termination of employment. In contrast to its judgment in *Rinner-Kühn*,[145] the Court remained silent on the appropriateness of this defence which depended on a stereotypical view of part-timers' attachment to the labour market and the classification of such workers' income as 'pin money' subsidiary to that of a 'breadwinner'.

In *Nimz*,[146] the Court was confronted with the differential use of length of service for the purposes of incremental progression. As in *Kowalska*, the scheme in question had been collectively agreed and provided that length of service for those who worked for more than 50 per cent and less than 75 per cent of 'normal' working hours[147] should be calculated at half the actual period of employment. The employers sought to justify this practice on the grounds that full-time workers acquired the abilities and skills relating to their job more quickly than those classified as part-time. The Court followed *Kowalska* in its finding of indirect discrimination, noting that the employer's defence amounted to 'generalisations about certain categories of workers'.[148] Whilst acknowledging that 'experience goes hand in hand with length of service',[149] the Court held that establishment of the objectivity of such a criterion required consideration of 'the relationship between the nature of the work performed and the experience gained from the performance of that work upon completion of a certain number of working hours'.[150] This at least acknowledges the potential value of a more rigorous assessment in place of length of service and measured working time which, although still widely used in public sector employment, will generally disadvantage those with care commitments who are more likely to experience labour market mobility and to work part-time.[151] In this respect, the Court's judgment is progressive and signals a move

[142] Case 33/89 *Kowalska v Freie und Handsestadt Hamburg* [1990] ECR I-2591.
[143] Namely the Bundesangestelltentarifvertrag (Federal Civil Service Employees' Collective Agreement) hereinafter referred to as the 'BAT'.
[144] Judgment at para 14.
[145] See n 79 above.
[146] Case 184/89 *Nimz v Freie und Hansestadt Hamburg* [1991] ECR I-297.
[147] Defined as 35 hours per week.
[148] Judgment at para 14.
[149] Ibid.
[150] Ibid.
[151] See Chapter 3.

away from its position in *Jenkins* that once a job is performed on a part-time basis, it differs in some fundamental way from its full-time counterpart.[152] By its acceptance that pay structures should take account of the levels of competence acquired through completion of tasks rather than the number of hours worked, the Court recognized part-time workers as autonomous post-holders, capable of achievement on their own terms rather than as a tolerable aberration from the normative model of the standard worker.

The progress discernible from the Court's reasoning in *Nimz*, however, was short-lived.[153] In *Helmig*,[154] the Court backtracked on this advancement by finding that an overtime supplement, payable under a collective agreement to full-time staff who worked more than their ordinary working week,[155] was not payable to part-time workers who worked in excess of *their* normal working week. The employers claimed that the overtime premium payment was intended to compensate for an 'increased physical burden and to prevent the imposition of excessive demands upon employees' which were not applicable to a part-time worker who 'merely exceeds the contractually agreed working hours'.[156] Furthermore, the resulting 'restriction on leisure time affects employees employed for normal working hours . . . more than part-time employees'.[157] Although provided with an opportunity to challenge the presumptive basis of the employer's defence that time spent away from part-time employment was 'leisure time', the Court chose to sidestep the issue by finding the agreements in question to be compatible with Article 119 as they enabled part-time employees to receive the same pay as full-timers if they worked more than the normal working hours.[158]

The Court's reasoning displays the somewhat limited conceptual foundations of its jurisprudence on part-time workers in its failure to take specific account of the relationship between paid employment and unpaid care which was at least acknowledged in its findings of indirect discrimination in previous cases.[159] In *Helmig*[160] the Court reasserted the subordination of part-timers' rights to the 'normal' working practices of their full-time counterparts by its implicit acceptance that the double burden of paid employment and unpaid care is insignificant when

152 See *Jenkins*, n 77 above.

153 Although the Court's recognition of the need to view part-time workers independently from their full-time counterparts in certain respects did re-emerge in its later judgments in Case C-1/95 *Gerster v Freistaat Bayern* [1997] ECR I-5253, Case C-243/95 *Kathleen Hill and Ann Stapleton v Revenue Commissioners and Department of Finance* [1998] ECR I-3739, and Case C-285/02 *Elsner-Lakeberg v Land Nordrhein-Westfalen* [2004] ECR I-5861, all discussed further below.

154 Cases C-399/92, C-409 and 425/92, C-34, 50 and 78/93 *Stadt Lengerich v Helmig* [1994] ECR I-5727.

155 In this context 38.5 hours per week.

156 Question 3 in *Helmig* (n 154 above)—see judgment at para 4.

157 Question 2(b) in Case C-34/93—see judgment at para 4.

158 Judgment at para 29.

159 See, for example, *Jenkins*, n 77 above, *Bilka*, n 78 above, *Rinner-Kühn*, n 79 above, *Kowalska*, n 142 above, and *Nimz*, n 146 above.

160 See n 154 above.

pitted against the effort expended by the standard worker and the consequential linkage of part-time 'work' and extended 'leisure time'.[161]

The Member States' 'Broad Margin of Discretion'

In *Krüger*[162] the Court was asked to consider the applicability of Article 141 to a Christmas bonus scheme governed by a collective agreement which excluded part-time workers.[163] In contrast to *Kowalska,*[164] *Nimz,*[165] and *Helmig,*[166] in which the alleged discrimination resulted solely from the terms of collective agreements, the scheme in *Krüger* was based on such an agreement *and* the provision of national legislation, thus enabling the use of a 'social policy' justification.[167] In considering whether the State's assertion that 'persons in minor employment are not required to pay social insurance contributions'[168] amounted to a potential justification, the Court referred to its social security case law[169] which had established that Member States had 'a broad margin of discretion'[170] in selecting the measures capable of achieving the aims of their social and employment policy. However, the Court distinguished the current case from those in the social security context as the differential treatment of part-timers arose from the terms of the collective agreement rather than from a legislative measure and thus amounted to indirect discrimination. The reasoning applied reveals much about the development of the social policy justification since its establishment in *Rinner-Kühn.* In the intervening 10 years, the Court had considered the discriminatory impact of national measures on three occasions and, although willing to apply a generally consistent approach to employers' policies, it appeared reluctant to apply the same interpretation of the equality principle in deference to the 'broad margin of discretion' afforded to Member States.

The cases were all concerned with the payment of compensation for attendance at staff committee training courses. In *Bötel,*[171] national legislation made no provision for part-time workers' attendance at such training in excess of their usual working hours. This appears to have arisen by accident rather than design

[161] This position appears to have been partially mitigated in Case C-300/06 *Voss v Land Berlin* [2007] ECR I-10573 in which the Court held that the payment of overtime at a lower rate to part-time workers than that paid to their full-time counterparts would, on the basis of relevant statistics, amount to indirect discrimination unless justified by objective factors.

[162] Case C-281/97 *Krüger v Kreiskrankenhaus Ebersberg* [1999] ECR I-5127.

[163] The BAT, see n 143 above.

[164] See n 142 above.

[165] See n 146 above.

[166] See n 154 above.

[167] See *Rinner-Kühn,* n 79 above.

[168] AG Léger's Opinion at para A43.

[169] In cases C-317/93 *Nolte v Landesversicherungsanstalt Hannover* [1995] ECR I-4625 and C-444/93 *Megner and Scheffel v Innungskrankenkasse Rheinhessen-Pfalz* [1995] ECR I-4741—see judgment in *Krüger* (n 162 above) at para 28.

[170] See n 162 above, judgment at para 28.

[171] Case C-360/90 *Arbeiterwohlfahrt der Stadt Berlin NV v Bötel* [1992] ECR I-3589.

as 'the BetrVG envisaged only the case of full-time workers'.[172] The Court observed that their exclusion for payment would be likely to dissuade part-time workers from participating in staff committees, thus making their representation difficult. Accordingly, it had no hesitation in finding the national legislation in question to be contrary to Article 119 and Directive 75/117 unless the Member State could establish that it was justified by objective factors.

In *Lewark*,[173] the German Labour Court claimed that the judgment in *Bötel* was based on a misunderstanding of the relevant legislation which provided that staff council functions were performed on an unpaid basis 'outside of any relationship of subordination'.[174] Accordingly, their performance did not constitute 'work' within the meaning of Article 119 and the compensation provided did not constitute pay but was intended to ensure that those attending training did not lose wages. Furthermore, it contended that the legislation did not differentiate between staff working part-time and full-time as they were all protected in the same way against loss of earnings. The measure in question was justified as, if payment was more generous than the actual wages lost, this might compromise the independence of staff council members.[175]

The ECJ held on in part to its reasoning in *Bötel* by stating that, although the compensation was not contractual in nature, it was 'nevertheless paid by the employer by virtue of legislative provisions and under a contract of payment'[176] and, accordingly, did fall within the scope of Article 119. Furthermore, following *Helmig*,[177] the Court found that unequal treatment arose wherever the overall pay of full-time employees is higher than that of part-time employees for the same number of hours worked. Consequently, the legislative provisions under review did amount to indirect discrimination. The Court was less emphatic on the issue of objective justification leaving the door ajar to the possibility that the 'the concern to ensure the independence of the members of [staff] councils . . . reflects a legitimate aim of social policy'[178] deemed to be of greater importance than the representation of part-time workers on such councils.

A similar approach was taken in *Freers*[179] in which the Court went one step closer in condoning the German government's line of defence by agreeing that the aim of assuring the independence of staff council members appeared to be 'unrelated to any discrimination on grounds of sex'.[180] Although a strict interpretation might support this finding, it is the Court's change in direction from its judgment in *Bötel*[181] that is the most striking feature of these cases. In finding that the apparent oversight which had excluded part-timers from the legislative arrangements for

[172] Facts at para 451.
[173] Case C-457/93 *Kuratorium für Dialyse und Nierentransplantation v Lewark* [1996] ECR I-243.
[174] Judgment at para 14.
[175] Judgment at para 16.
[176] Judgment at para 22.
[177] See n 154 above.
[178] Judgment at para 38.
[179] Case C-278/93 *Freers and Speckamnn v Deutsche Bundespost* [1996] ECR I-1165.
[180] Ibid, para 27.
[181] See n 171 above.

compensatory payment potentially amounted to a legitimate aim of social policy, the Court appears to have backed down under the pressure exerted by the German legislature.

The defence advanced in these cases is reminiscent of *Helmig*[182] at least in the presumption that time outside of employment is at the disposal of part-time workers. As well as overlooking the reasons why such workers generally engage in part-time work, the denial of compensation for participating in work-related activities outside of normal hours fails to acknowledge the costs incurred for replacement care. That compensation for what amounts to working overtime would incentivize participation in works councils and, thus, undermine the independence of participants, is an irrational assertion if applied to part-time workers who, if they wished to increase their income and had the time available, would simply increase their usual contractual hours.

As envisaged from the Court's early jurisprudence on part-time workers' rights, the imposition of discriminatory State measures has presented the Court with particular difficulties. The need to accommodate the Member States' broad margin of discretion has resulted in inconsistency at odds with the principles of legal certainty and legitimate expectation. Added to this is the potential scope for circumvention of the equality principle available to Member States in their dual role as legislature and employer. The following group of cases highlight the Court's treatment of the justifications advanced by various State departments and consideration will be given to whether the State's role as law-making authority has compromised its obligations as employer.

The State as Employer

In *Gerster*[183] and *Kording*[184] the ECJ considered the compatibility of Article 119 and Directives 75/117 and 76/207 with statutory rules which distinguished between part-time and full-time civil service workers for the purposes of calculating length of service as a prerequisite for promotion (*Gerster*) and for the granting of exemption from a qualifying exam for tax consultants (*Kording*). Although caught by different provisions,[185] both cases shared a common approach in differential calculations under the statutory rules for length of service in respect of full and part-time workers.

In *Gerster*, periods of employment of those who worked for at least half of the full-time hours were counted as being equal to two-thirds of normal working time.[186] Progression to a higher grade and accompanying pay rise depended on

[182] See n 154 above.
[183] See n 153 above.
[184] Case C-100/95 *Kording v Senator Für Finanzen* [1997] ECR I-5289.
[185] The Laufbahnverordung (Bavarian Regulations on Career Structure) in *Gerster* and the Steuerberatungsgesetz (Act on Tax Consultancy) in *Kording*.
[186] For those who worked less than 50% of full-time hours, there was no calculation made for length of service (see AG Pergola's Opinion at fn 3), presumably meaning that such workers were

the completion of six years' employment at normal working hours[187] on completion of which individuals were automatically placed on a waiting list and considered for promotion when they reached the top of the list. The applicant had been employed by the civil service since 1968 and had taken three years' unpaid leave on care-related grounds, returning to work part-time in 1987. In 1993 her request that her six years' part-time employment be treated as full-time for the purposes of calculating length of service for promotional purposes was rejected.

The Court held that Articles 1 and 3 of Directive 76/207 were relevant to the measures under review which had a disproportionate impact on the promotional prospects of part-time workers and amounted to unlawful indirect discrimination.[188] In considering the Bavarian State's justification[189] that part-time workers would take longer than full-time workers to acquire the professional skills and abilities necessary for higher level employment, the Court repeated its criticism in *Nimz*[190] of the subjective nature of 'an alleged special link' between length of service and the acquisition of knowledge and experience which amounted to no more than a generalization concerning certain categories of worker.[191] Thus, it was up to the national court to decide whether part-time employees were 'generally slower than full-time employees in acquiring job-related abilities and skills'[192] and to consider whether the measures chosen complied with the test for objective justification in accordance with *Rinner-Kühn*.[193] It is unclear whether the Court intended the question of justification to rest on the State's establishment of a clear connection between the prescribed hours and the acquisition of the necessary skills and experience or whether the statutory rules could be justified by alternative means so long as they amounted to a legitimate social policy aim and were proportionate to the achievement of that aim.

In *Hill and Stapleton*[194] the relevant measure differentiated between those employed on a job-share basis[195] and full-time employees in calculating length of service for the purposes of incremental progression up a pay scale. The general rule that 'increments are granted annually provided an officer's services are satisfactory'[196] was subject to an exception in the case of job-sharers whose pay was calculated as 50 per cent of that of full-time staff. The Irish Labour Court referred the case to determine whether the scheme was contrary to EU law if its effect was

completely excluded from consideration for promotion under the appropriate rules. However, as Ms Gerster was included in the category of those who worked between 50 and 75% of full-time hours this aspect was never investigated.

[187] This case differed from *Nimz* (n 146 above), as promotion to the higher grade was not based solely on the completion of a specific period of service.

[188] Ibid, para 34.

[189] Judgment at para 36.

[190] See n 146 above.

[191] Judgment at para 39.

[192] Ibid.

[193] See n 79 above.

[194] See n 153 above.

[195] Who worked one week on, one week off.

[196] Circular 9/87 as quoted at para 9 of judgment.

that employees who convert from job-sharing to full-time work 'regress on incremental scale and hence on their salary scale'[197] or whether such a measure could be objectively justified.

The national court had already considered the relationship between time served and the acquisition of experience and was satisfied that 'a job-sharer could acquire the same experience as a full-time worker' within the same timeframe.[198] Thus, the CoJ was denied the opportunity to rely on this aspect as a possible justification for the differences in pay as it had done in *Gerster*[199] and was compelled to reject as irrelevant the employer's defence that the established practice of only rewarding actual service maintained staff motivation, commitment, and morale.[200] Further attempts to justify the differential pay rates on economic grounds were also rejected as 'an employer cannot justify discrimination arising from a job-sharing scheme solely on the ground that avoidance of such discrimination would involve increased costs'.[201] In acknowledging that almost all of those who worked under job-share arrangements in the Irish Republic were women who did so in order to combine paid employment and unpaid care, the Court held that 'Community policy in this area is to encourage and, if possible, adapt working conditions to family responsibilities'.

In *Elsner-Lakeberg*[202] a teacher who normally worked for 60 hours per month was prevented from receiving payment for working an additional 2.5 hours by a rule that excluded civil servants from receiving overtime payments unless the additional hours worked exceeded three hours a month. The Land Nordrhein-Westfalen as employer, backed by the German Government, defended the scheme on the grounds that it treated part-time teachers and full-time teachers in exactly the same way as both groups were eligible for overtime payments only in circumstances where the overtime worked exceeded three hours in one month. The Court took a different view in finding that the requirement to work an additional three hours before the entitlement to extra payment was triggered represented a 'greater burden for part-time teachers than . . . for full-time teachers'.[203] Since the number of additional teaching hours used to calculate entitlement to pay was not reduced for part-timers in proportion to their working hours, their treatment differed from that received by full-time teachers.

The Court's reasoning in *Gerster*,[204] *Hill and Stapleton*,[205] and *Elsner-Lakeberg*[206] represents, to some extent, a continuation of its recognition in *Nimz*[207] that the autonomy of those who work part-time is compromised if their treatment

[197] Part (b) of the question referred as quoted in para 15 of judgment.
[198] Judgment at para 27.
[199] See n 153 above, in which the national court had not considered this issue.
[200] Judgment at para 38.
[201] Judgment at para 40.
[202] See n 153 above.
[203] Judgment at para 17.
[204] See n 153 above.
[205] See n 153 above.
[206] See n 153 above.
[207] See n 146 above.

at work is defined by their difference from those who work full-time. This acknowledges the labour market contribution of such workers in contrast to the Court's previous judgments in *Helmig*,[208] *Lewark*,[209] and *Freers*.[210] The reasoning and judgment in *Hill and Stapleton*[211] illustrate the Court's explicit acceptance of the relationship between unpaid care and the need to work part-time as articulated by its acknowledgement that EU policy is aimed at adapting working conditions to fit family circumstances. In *Elsner-Lakeberg*[212] the Court's reasoning recognizes that providing the same treatment to individuals who are differently situated can, in certain circumstances, result in discriminatory outcomes.

The possibility of objective justification was left open in each of these cases as a matter to be decided by the national court with State discretion providing an ample opportunity for justification on the grounds of social policy. However, the reasoning informing these judgments, at least, demonstrates a move towards the application of the equality principle as a means of providing self-standing rights to part-time workers with their treatment assessed independently of that received by full-time workers with, at least, some consideration given to the relationship between paid employment and unpaid care. In each of these cases, the Court considered the impact of the policies in question on the claimants in order to inform its decision-making. Furthermore, that the policies under review were essentially imposed by the State appears to have made no difference to the Court's robust approach.[213] However, the area of policy that has been the most contentious in this respect is that concerned with retirement benefits on which the Court's interpretation has been sought on several occasions and it is this aspect of its jurisprudence to which attention will now be paid.

Retirement and Work-related Benefits

The Court's jurisprudence on part-time workers' pension entitlement has evolved through its consideration of the equality principle to two separate but related strands: State pension schemes and occupational or contracted-out schemes. As the focus of this book is on the regulation of the employment relationship, the former group of cases, which have as their legal base the social security provisions of EU law, are outside of its scope and will not be specifically considered.[214] However,

[208] See n 154 above.
[209] See n 173 above.
[210] See n 179 above.
[211] See n 153 above.
[212] See n 153 above.
[213] For an alternative to the assumed linear relationship between time served and the acquisition of skills and knowledge, see Case C-17/05 *Cadman v Health and Safety Executive* [2006] ECR I-9583, involving a full-time worker's claim for equal pay with longer serving male colleagues, in which the Court held (at 36) that employers are 'free to reward length of service without having to establish the importance it has in the performance of specific tasks'.
[214] For an up-to-date assessment of EU social security law, see F. Pennings, *European Social Security Law* (Oxford: Hart, 2010).

the Court's jurisprudence in cases concerning part-time workers' rights of access to occupational pension schemes provides a fascinating insight into its reasoning where the principles of equality, effectiveness, and legal certainty converge to reveal much about its conceptualization of gender relations and, consequently, its perception of the place of unpaid care within European employment law.

Following *Bilka*, the Court's first opportunity to consider part-time workers' access to occupational pension schemes was presented by *Vroege*[215] and *Fisscher*[216] in which it was asked to interpret the effect of the temporal limitation imposed by the Barber Protocol[217] on the applicability of Article 119 to benefits under such schemes. The current claims concerned the payment of backdated benefits to part-time workers denied membership due to a collective agreement which excluded those who worked less than 80 per cent of full-time hours and Dutch legislation which had excluded married women from such schemes. Following *Barber*,[218] the legislation and the agreement had been amended and the claimants sought to have their membership backdated to the date of the Court's judgment in *Defrenne II*.[219]

In *Vroege*,[220] the Court held that Article 119 'covers not only entitlement to benefits paid by an occupational pension scheme but also the right to be a member of such a scheme'.[221] The temporal limitation in *Barber* had resulted from the Court's finding that Member States had been reasonably entitled to consider that Article 119 did not apply to pensions paid under contracted-out schemes due to the transitional derogations in the determination of pensionable age which were permitted by Directives 79/7 and 86/378. However, there was 'no reason to suppose that the professional groups concerned could have been mistaken about the applicability of Article 119' to occupational pension schemes[222] which had been settled without any temporal limitation since the Court's judgment in *Bilka*,[223] thus enabling retroactive membership from 8 April 1976.[224] The same reasoning was applied in *Magorrian*[225] in order to grant rights of access to additional benefits payable under such a scheme. In *Fisscher* the Court was asked whether EU law precluded the imposition by national legislation of time limits which could restrict the effectiveness of the remedies available. The Court upheld

[215] Case C-57/93 *Vroege v NCIV Instituut voor Volkhuisvesting BV and Stichting Pensioenfunds NCIV* [1994] ECR I-4541.

[216] Case C-128/93 *Fisscher v Voorhuis Hengelo BV and Stichting Bedrijfspensioenfunds voor de Detailhandel* [1994] ECR I-4583.

[217] Which restricted the consideration of such benefits as remuneration for the purposes of Article 119 if they related to periods of employment prior to 17 May 1990, except where they arose in respect of claims instigated before that date, see Case C-262/88 *Barber v Guardian Royal Exchange Assurance Group* [1990] ECR I-1889.

[218] Ibid.

[219] See n 80 above.

[220] See n 215 above.

[221] Ibid, judgment at para 15.

[222] Ibid, para 25.

[223] See n 78 above.

[224] The date of the judgment in *Defrenne II.*

[225] Case C-246/96 *Magorrian and Cunningham v Eastern Health and Social Services Board and Department of Health and Social Services* [1997] ECR I-7153.

the use of such rules as long as they were no less favourable in their effect on Community provisions than those relating to similar actions of a domestic nature.[226]

Preston[227] was concerned with UK legislation[228] which implied an equality clause into every contract of employment with a provision that related claims would be time-barred unless brought within a period of six months following the cessation of employment.[229] Furthermore, retroactive claims in respect of failure to comply were restricted to a period of two years prior to the date on which proceedings were instigated.[230] The stakes were high as the pension entitlement of thousands of UK public and private sector workers rested on the outcome of the case[231] which incorporated claims for retroactive membership dating back, in some cases, to before 8 April 1976.[232] In its reference, the House of Lords sought to determine the compatibility of the national time limits with 'the principle of EC law that national procedural rules for breach of Community law must not make it excessively difficult or impossible in practice for the claimant to exercise her rights under Article 119'.[233]

In relation to the 'six-month rule', the Court found that, where such time limits were reasonable, it was settled in case law that they represented an application of the principle of legal certainty by preventing administrative decisions from being vulnerable to legal challenge indefinitely.[234] On this basis, following the reasoning of Advocate General Léger,[235] the Court upheld the six-month limitation.[236] Turning to the two-year rule, the Court acknowledged that, although its application did not completely deprive the claimants of their rights, it did severely reduce the practical effect of the right to claim retroactive membership[237] and was, thus, precluded by Community law. In this respect, the Court's judgment appears to be consistent with its earlier jurisprudence in *Vroege*[238] and *Fisscher*.[239] However, the Court's separate consideration of the six-month time limit and the two-year limitation in time seriously detracted from the practical application of its judgment.

[226] The judgment in *Vroege and Fisscher*, n 215 above, at para 39.

[227] Case C-78/98 *Preston and Others v Wolverhampton Healthcare NHS Trust* [2000] ECR I-3201.

[228] EqPA 1970, s 1(1).

[229] EqPA 1970, s 2(4).

[230] EqPA 1970, s 2(5) as amended by the Occupational Pension Schemes (Equal Access to Membership) Regulations 1976, reg 12(1).

[231] The 22 claimants had been denied membership of various contracted-out pension schemes at some time in the past on the grounds of their part-time status and were representative of some 60,000 part-time workers in the UK who had instigated proceedings following the Court's judgments in *Vroege* and *Fisscher*, discussed below.

[232] The date of the judgment in *Defrenne II*, n 80 above.

[233] Question 1 in *Preston*.

[234] See Case 33/76 *Rewe* [1976] ECR 1989; Case C-261/95 *Palmisani v Instituto Nazionale della Previdenza Sociale* [1997] ECR I-4025.

[235] In his opinion delivered on 14 September 1999. See also AG Léger's opinion and the judgment of the ECJ in the related case C-326/96 *Levez v Jennings (Harlow Pools) Ltd* (1998) ECR I-7835.

[236] Ibid, 34.

[237] *Preston* judgment, n 227 above, 35.

[238] See n 215 above.

[239] See n 216 above.

The fact that all of the appropriate pension schemes had been amended between 1985 and 1996 to admit part-time workers, ironically, presented insurmountable difficulties for many of the women. Those whose employment had ceased on retirement or other grounds, following their admittance to the appropriate scheme, had been prevented from initiating proceedings by the application of the two-year rule. In this respect the judgment changed nothing as failure to initiate proceedings in the six months following cessation of the employment rendered any potential claims time-barred despite the otherwise potentially retroactive nature of the claims.

That failure to instigate proceedings arose out of the imposition of a statutory rule makes the outcome particularly unjust. The Court's separate consideration of the two rules was based on the terms in which the referred questions were framed, but the award of an effective remedy was dependent on an integrated approach.[240] The lack of informed reasoning in the *Preston* judgment is evidenced by the failure to consider the implications of the maintenance of national procedural rules which are in conflict with the Court's case law. By denying part-time workers the right to benefit from the Court's jurisprudence on occupational pension schemes, the UK had arguably been in breach of EC law since *Defrenne II*,[241] certainly since *Bilka*[242] but this appears to have had little bearing on the resulting judgment. Consequently, rather than achieving the stated aim of preserving legal certainty, the judgment in *Preston*[243] resulted in an uneven application of available remedies for those directly involved in the litigation and confusion surrounding the legitimate expectations of those with potentially worthy claims.

The Court's deference to Member States' authority over procedural policy-making is all the more surprising given the fundamental issues at stake in the application of the equality principle which, in this case, affected the pension entitlements of a generation of part-time workers. The apparent disregard for the welfare rights of women in old age results from the Court's reluctance to interpret Community law in order to remedy past discrimination. The failure to explicitly acknowledge the economic contribution made by those who combine paid employment with unpaid care enabled the Court, when faced with choices regarding the relative importance of various legal principles, to subordinate the equality principle to the procedural autonomy enjoyed by Member States.

The plight of worker-carers caught in the post-*Defrenne* era, many of whom face retirement with reduced pensions or no entitlement at all, was further illustrated by *Grau-Hupka*.[244] The claimant who was in receipt of a State pension and worked

[240] For an analysis of the practical effects of the judgement on the various categories of workers represented by the test case, see N. Busby, 'Only a Matter of Time', *Modern Law Review*, 64/3 (2001), 489–99.

[241] See n 80 above.

[242] See n 78 above.

[243] See n 227 above.

[244] Case C-297/93 *Grau-Hupka v Stadtgemeinde Bremen* [1994] ECR I-5535.

part-time, was paid at a lower rate than comparable full-timers in line with national legislation aimed at those who combined part-time work with a full-time occupation.[245] She argued that her own loss of earnings which resulted from time away from paid employment due to child rearing necessitated her continued employment and distinguished her pension from wages earned through full-time employment. The Court held that the relevant Community provisions on social security[246] did not oblige Member States to grant advantages in respect of pension schemes to those who had brought up children or to provide benefits where employment had been interrupted to bring up children.[247] Consequently, the resulting reduction in pension entitlement did not preclude payment at a lower rate for part-time work than full-time work under Article 119.[248]

The Normalization of Fundamental Rights: The Tide Turns?

In *Schröder*[249] the Court was again asked to consider the applicability of the Barber Protocol to national rules permitting part-time workers access to occupational pension schemes. Although the scheme in question, which had excluded part-timers, had subsequently been amended to give such workers access, the temporal limitation had been applied from the date of the *Barber* judgment in 1992. The claimant sought to obtain the benefits that she would have accrued if she had been granted retroactive membership of the scheme from the date that her employment commenced in 1975.

The employer contended that Article 119 had precedence over the German Constitution in which the principle of equality between men and women was enshrined[250] and, thus, the limitation imposed by the Barber Protocol should also limit the application of national law. This was the first time that the Court had been asked to interpret EU law in order to *reduce* the rights available to atypical workers under national law. Furthermore, it was provided with its first opportunity, since its articulation of its 'dual purpose' in *Defrenne II,* to explicitly consider a potential conflict between Article 141's social and economic aims. If applied, the constitutional provision would enable access to the scheme as a basic right with no

[245] The national court acknowledged that most of the workers in this category were men as women's 'twin responsibilities of career and family' made it unlikely that they would be able to engage in full and part-time work concurrently—see judgment at para 15.

[246] Contained in Directive 79/7 on equal treatment in matters of social security.

[247] Judgment at para 27.

[248] Although see also Case C-77/02 *Steinicke v Bundesanstalt für Arbeit* [2003] ECR I-9027 in which the Court found that a statutory rule which restricted the right of public sector workers to work part-time upon retirement to those who had worked in a full-time capacity for three of the five years preceding retirement was prohibited by Arts 2(1) and 5(1) of Directive 76/207.

[249] Case C-50/96 *Deutsche Telekom v Schröder* [2000] ECR I-743.

[250] Article 3 of the Grundgesetz für die Bundesrepublik Deutschland (the Basic Law) provides: '(1) All persons shall be equal before the law. Men and women shall have equal rights. (2) The State shall encourage effective attainment of equal rights for men and women and shall take actions to remove existing disadvantages'.

retroactive restrictions[251] which, as not all national legal systems provided such rights, would distort competition between Member States by putting German employers and pension administrators in a less favourable position than comparable organizations in other States.

In holding that Article 119's (ex 141, now 157 TFEU) economic aim is secondary to its social aim,[252] the Court ruled that the right not to be discriminated against on the ground of sex is 'one of the fundamental human rights whose observance the Court has a duty to ensure'.[253] Accordingly, the retroactive membership of occupational pension schemes was unfettered by either of the temporal restrictions applicable under Community law.[254] The Court's position, although expressly linked to its own jurisprudence,[255] surely owes much to the Member States' approval and subsequent adoption of the Charter of Fundamental Human Rights (CFR).[256] Given the high number of cases previously referred by German courts to determine the compatibility of Article 119 with the provisions of national law,[257] it is surprising that the explicit articulation of the equality principle under German constitutional law had not been directly raised before in this context. However, even if it had, it is not a certainty that the Court would have given priority to its social, rather than economic, aim. By the time *Schröder*[258] was considered by the Court, the environment within which it operates was changing with EU law's formal recognition of human rights standards placed high up the political agenda.[259] Faced with an inescapable challenge to articulate the relationship between such standards and the principles of EU law,[260] the Court was left with little option but to acknowledge the prevalence of the former.

Whether this will translate into substantive developments in the Court's jurisprudence remains to be seen and, despite the fact that the CFR has subsequently been given legal effect by the Lisbon Treaty according it the same legal status as the Treaties, it is too early at the time of writing to draw any conclusions about the Charter's impact on the Court's case law. However, one recent case merits a mention in the current context. In *Chatzi*[261] the Court was asked to interpret

[251] See Question 6 referred by the Landesarbeitsgericht (Regional Labour Court). The Grundgesetz predates the Court's judgment in *Defrenne II* and, if applied, would provide rights for women in Germany with less retroactive restrictions than those applicable in any other Member State.

[252] Judgment at para 57.

[253] Judgment at para 56.

[254] In respect of the dates of the Court's judgments in *Defrenne II* (n 80 above) or *Barber* (n 217 above).

[255] Specifically Case 149/77 *Defrenne v SABENA* [1978] ECR 1365; Joined Cases 75 and 117/82 *Razzouk and Beydoun v EC Commission* [1984] ECR 1509 and Case C-13/94 *P v S and Cornwall County Council* [1996] ECR I-2143.

[256] See Chapter 5.

[257] Albeit through its articulation in collective agreements.

[258] See n 249 above.

[259] Illustrated by the development of the 'new' Art 13 (now Art 19 TFEU) as an enabling measure intended to significantly broaden the grounds of discrimination prohibited under EU law and the subsequent adoption of the CFR—see Chapter 5 at p. 100.

[260] Now one and the same since the CFR, which articulates international human rights standards as fundamental principles of EU law, was given legal effect by the Lisbon Treaty on 1 December 2009.

[261] Case C-149/10 *Chatzi v Ipourgos Ikonomikon*, judgment of the Court 16 September 2010, nyr.

the Framework Agreement on Parental Leave essentially to determine whether the parents of twins should be entitled to separate and distinct periods of leave in respect of each child. In making its application for a reference, the Greek court asked specifically for interpretation of the relevant provisions of the CFR.[262] In its judgment, the Court referred to the principle of equal treatment 'whose fundamental nature is affirmed in Article 20 of the Charter of Fundamental Rights' and which 'is all the more important in implementing the right to parental leave because this social right is itself recognised as fundamental by Article 33(2) of the Charter of Fundamental Rights'.[263]

In applying the principle of equal treatment which 'requires that comparable situations must not be treated differently and that different situations must not be treated in the same way unless such treatment is objectively justified',[264] the Court held that the national legislature are obliged to establish parental leave regimes which take account of the particular needs of the parents of twins and that it is up to the national courts to determine whether this obligation has been discharged. The typification of the most salient features of the reference procedure makes this otherwise unremarkable case a worthy note on which to finish this analysis. As well as invoking the crucial dialogue between the national courts and the CoJ, which in this instance was the source of the specific reference to the CFR's provisions, *Chatzi* illustrates the continuing interrelationship between the articulation of the principles of EU law at constitutional level, their clarification through the process of litigation, and their subsequent realization at national level. The importance of this process and its potential in the current context cannot be overstated but its ultimate yield depends entirely on the Court's use of the opportunities it is presented with.

Conclusions

In considering the Court's jurisprudence in the field of unpaid care and paid work reconciliation, this Chapter has sought to uncover evidence of its recognition of a right to care within European employment law. The constitutional provisions with whose interpretation it is charged combined with the Court's distinct operational features mark it out as the only institution capable of giving effect to the Treaties' promises of the elimination of discrimination between men and women alongside improvements in living and working conditions. It is through this function that the Court's apparent activism is justified. However, an assessment of its jurisprudence in related areas reveals certain features that cast doubt over the Court's ability to make full use of its unique position.

[262] Namely, Arts 20 on equality before the law and 33(2) on the reconciliation of family and professional life.

[263] Judgment at para 63.

[264] The 'Aristotelian formula', see Chapter 2.

The dominant ideology of motherhood founded on traditional assumptions regarding women's and men's roles within the family is pervasive in the Court's case law on maternity, parental, and family-related rights. Although providing a basis for apparently progressive decision-making concerning the status of pregnancy and maternity rights, the influence of this essentialist notion of women's being on the Court's jurisprudence has been restrictive in areas where the biological differences between the sexes are less apparent. In circumstances where such differences are attributable to gendered rather than biological criteria, the Court appears to have had more difficulty in recognizing the disadvantages experienced by women in the labour market and has, thus, been less inclined to take account of the relationship between unpaid care and paid work in formulating its judgments. Correspondingly, the further removed from childbirth and its effects that the case-specific issues are, the less cohesive and coherent the Court's jurisprudence, culminating in unclear and, at times, oblique reasoning in its case law on part-time workers' pension entitlement. Although hidden from view in the context of the Court's judgments, the silent impact of unpaid care is that the low value ascribed to it has a devaluing effect on the Court's treatment of paid work when performed alongside it.

This is not to say that the Court has always been unreceptive to arguments based on the unpaid care/paid work conflict in giving effect to the principles of equality and non-discrimination. In its jurisprudence on part-time workers' employment, the Court has, on occasion, been willing to recognize the reasons why part-time workers engage in such work and accordingly to provide self-standing rights which recognize the economic and social value of those individuals who combine paid work with the provision of care. However, this is matched by a general reluctance to utilize the provisions of EU law to remedy the effects of past discrimination and, even where the duty to do so has been inescapable, the resulting rights have been qualified by their possible justification with reductive effect. The overwhelming impression is that the standard worker's normative model is pervasive in the Court's reasoning and that unpaid care and paid employment are deemed incompatible if the former impacts on the latter in any discernible way. As well as resulting in disincentives to the normalization of non-standard work, this translates into a resistance to women's integration into the labour market and is at odds with policy attempts to increase part-time work.

In order to overcome these difficulties, the Court will need to develop a clear normative framework within which to situate its decision-making with the aim of achieving EU law's dual goals of sex equality and work/family reconciliation. This is possible but requires its explicit endorsement and expression of a right to care which, although observant of the need for non-discrimination between the sexes, is not reliant on sex- or gender-based difference for its expression. The Charter of Fundamental Social Rights, although far from a panacea in this regard, has a potentially valuable application and early indications are that it is capable of wielding the necessary level of influence over the Court's decision-making so that its provisions might form the basis for just such a normative framework. In conclusion, although the jurisprudence of the CoJ has suffered from the same conceptual flaws apparent in the constitutional and legislative provisions of EU law generally and has not always lived up to the promise of its early judgments, there are certainly grounds for optimism that the Court will use its undoubted influence within the new constitutional framework to give effect to a specific right to care in European employment law.

7

Conclusions: Solving the Unpaid Care/Paid Work Conflict

Introduction

This book has considered how the current conflict between paid work and unpaid care could be solved by the development of a right to care in European employment law which would provide employment protection for those who combine both. It is asserted that the current law and policy provisions of the European Union do in fact sanction such an approach and that there is potential for its operation within the current regulatory framework. However, it is also recognized that in order to give effect to such a right it is necessary to co-ordinate the relevant but disparate law and policy strands.

In Chapter 2, which considered the appropriate theoretical perspective from which a right to care might best be advanced, Sen's capabilities approach (CA) was identified as a potentially useful framework due to its compatibility with the current EU regulatory context in that it is essentially a liberal theory which recognizes and values the principles of autonomy, freedom, and equality. Furthermore, it has the requisite conceptual flexibility for recognizing each individual's right to freedom as its central tenet is the accommodation of human diversity. Thus, the approach places the needs of individuals at its centre by enabling and encouraging involvement in the selection of the very tools required for policy appraisal and design. Furthermore, by rejecting the use of a single factor or a narrow set of indicators for the purposes of measuring success, Sen's CA avoids the potential traps of both the utilitarian focus on mental state and the Rawlsian emphasis on income and wealth enabling inclusion of a broader set of capabilities than those associated with neo-liberal conceptions of the good life and facilitating an evaluation of the full range of human activities intrinsic to both parties to the care relationship—carer and cared for.

Chapter 3 explored the nature of care and argued that its explicit incorporation in the employment law paradigm would facilitate improvements in so-called 'women's work' as well as the normalization of atypical employment arrangements such as part-time work. The effect of its current exclusion is that it is deemed to be of no economic value and consequently renders the paid work undertaken alongside it of less worth than other types and configurations of 'market' work. It is therefore desirable to seek alternative ways of conceptualizing and organizing 'work' which are capable of taking account of the full range of human activities relevant to the regulation of paid work, including its intersection with unpaid care. This challenges the dominant neo-liberal conceptualization of the traditional liberal values of equality, autonomy, and freedom in order that they might be achievable for *all* members of society. As well as responding to the moral questions posed by the current conflict between unpaid care and paid work, this quest for alternative approaches is necessary in order to realign labour law with the substantial changes that are taking place in the context of the employment relationship and the world of paid work generally.

Chapter 4 asserted that market forces, rather than resulting from a mysterious and spontaneous process, are the products of a range of interrelated factors including human decision-making. The democratic function of labour law has traditionally provided a stabilizing influence over the balancing of power in the management of industrial relations to which its distinct yet interrelated goals can contribute, through the private law regulation of the employment relationship and through the application of public law principles, to fulfil its wider social justice objectives as well as serving a more fundamental democratic end. What is required to intercept the operation of the market to enable more equal and fairer outcomes is legal intervention aimed at facilitating individual opportunity and decommodifying labour with the ultimate goal of enabling individuals to develop the capacity to be free to make effective choices and thus participate in genuine and dynamic interaction in the market. However, the very real threat in this respect comes from the ideological appropriation through which needs and respective rights are traded off on the basis of prioritization of economic over social goals—a threat which is exacerbated by the current lack of a normative framework within which to evaluate developments in labour law in either its vocational or theoretical forms. In this respect, the CA can make a useful contribution as, by placing the values by which individuals are able to reach their potential at its centre and focusing on outcomes rather than the means by which such achievement might be possible, it protects itself against such manipulation through the infiltration of political dogma. Furthermore its reflexive nature makes it particularly well suited as, in order to be effective, a right to care must take full account of the full range of needs which result from attempts to combine unpaid care with paid employment which will vary depending on individual circumstances.

As argued in Chapter 5, the European Union's founding objectives as a primarily economic entity have meant that it has not always been receptive to the development of social rights. This has resulted in a continued threat of subordination of the Treaty's social aims to its economic imperative which has been bolstered by the perceived fear among Member States of a loss of autonomous decision-making in the social area. Consequently, despite some substantial progress in both the constitutional and juridical contexts, the Union lacks a clear and cohesive overarching strategy for social integration which has continued to develop in a piecemeal and incremental way. This has stifled progress in attempts to reconcile the unpaid care/paid work conflict as further progress in this context depends on the co-ordination of the various aspects of the EU *acquis*[1] which, in turn, requires the identification of a unifying ideology. This can clearly be seen in the, thus far, uncoordinated efforts to increase both the quantity and quality of jobs,[2] which, in the context of those with caring responsibilities, can only be achieved by the alignment of the dual goals of gender equality and work and family reconciliation. The regulatory model exemplified by the European Employment Strategy (EES)[3] as implemented through the open method of co-ordination (OMC) has potential in this respect, particularly in an enlarged Europe, as it is targeted at the achievement of broad policy aims through the identification and imposition of self-regulated norms. However, as well as providing a source of opportunity to develop a more responsive method of regulation at the European level, its voluntary nature also poses its greatest threat as Member States are faced with conflicting 'choices' in an increasingly competitive global environment.

The incorporation of the EU Charter of Fundamental Rights into the constitutional provisions of EU law by the Lisbon Treaty is critical in this respect as it articulates a common set of values or 'norms' which have broad application across the range of regulated activities. As well as its normative potential, the Charter could have significance in the context of the EU's future legislative programme due to its levelling effect on the hierarchy of rights in which civil and political rights have traditionally been prioritized over their social and economic counterparts. Thus, in the context of the unpaid work/paid employment conflict, the Charter has a dual role: to enhance the status of social rights generally through its provision of a catalogue of such rights which are recognized as fundamental and through its normative effect which has the potential to embed and develop the requisite set of values necessary to resolve the conflict. Furthermore, the Charter's status means that it is capable of linking existing employment rights with the development of the soft law approach provided by the EES[4] in order to give recognition to the existence of a right to care under EU law. Furthermore, the relatively recent recognition within the EU policy context that investment in human capital is a viable means of improving employability[5] and enabling individuals to become more self-sufficient corresponds with the ideological foundations of Sen's capability approach and enhances its potential use as a suitable framework within which legal and policy interventions aimed at resolving the unpaid care/paid employment might be evaluated.

The Court of Justice has been heralded as an important driver in the EU's realization of its social goals. Rather than taking the role of independent adjudicator more synonymous with domestic courts, the Court has become the

[1] For example, employment policy and social security provision.

[2] See the Lisbon Agenda, Chapter 5.

[3] The EES is to be phased out from 2010 and, at the time of writing, discussions were ongoing regarding its replacement which it is envisaged will incorporate a broadly similar approach.

[4] Under the OMC. As Hepple has noted, the Charter gives some teeth to the soft law approach currently dominating social law and policy in the EU, see B. Hepple, 'For the greater good', *The Guardian*, 23 November 2004.

[5] See the Lisbon Agenda's social context.

moral gatekeeper of the EU and has, through its unique relationships with the domestic courts and with its fellow EU institutions, the administrative capacity to influence the application of the Treaties in order to ensure that their interpretation has resonance with the lives of Europe's citizens.

Its jurisprudence on EU social law was influential in the drafting of the Charter and, in the context of gender equality, in the provisions of the Recast Directive which codifies much of the Court's decision-making. It is hoped that this recognition of the Court's contribution will instil confidence in its own ability to continue on the path of social integration but its ability or willingness to co-operate in such a venture is by no means assured. At a constitutional level, the expectation surrounding the Court's continuing involvement is at odds with the move away from litigation heralded by the EES which has placed greater emphasis on self-regulation and on the increased role of the social partners. Furthermore, expectations regarding the Court's ability and willingness to prioritize social rights over the Union's economic imperative must be tempered with regard to both its limited competence in adherence to the legislative provisions it is charged with interpreting as well as in relation to its own ideological stance, in which context its recent jurisprudence has not been particularly inspiring.[6]

In Chapter 6, the Court's jurisprudence in the field of work and family reconciliation was specifically considered with a view to uncovering whether the Court has been particularly receptive to representations concerning the relationship between unpaid care and paid employment in cases in which the arrangements in respect of the latter, which are a direct consequence of the applicant's care commitments, have given rise to allegations of unequal treatment or discrimination. The Court's work is of particular interest due to its position as the only institution capable of giving effect to the Treaty's promises of the elimination of discrimination between men and women alongside improvements in living and working conditions. Furthermore, the emphasis that has been placed on its contribution by those responsible for developing the relevant body of law and policy places it in a pivotal position within the resulting regulatory framework. However, far from uncovering a mine of progressive decision-making in this respect, the resulting analysis found the Court's reasoning to be lukewarm and, at times, resistant to the idea that the domain of unpaid care should be integrated with that of paid employment through the recognition of an implicit right to care within European employment law. Rather than providing a particular challenge to the dominant ideology surrounding gender relations and its impact on the reconciliation of professional and private life, the Court's jurisprudence has tended to accept the basic tenets on which that ideology is grounded without question so that the central misconceptions are replicated through application of its case law. This has led to some progress in the form of enhanced rights in relation to pregnancy and maternity for which an

[6] See the judgments in Case C-438/05 *Viking Line ABP v The International Transport Workers' Federation, the Finnish Seaman's Union* [2007] ECR I-10779; Case C-341/05 *Laval un Partneri Ltd v Svenska Byggnadsarbetareförbundet* [2007] ECR I-11767; Case C-346/06 *Dirk Rüffert v Land Niedersachsen* [2008] ECR I-1989; Case C-39/06 *European Commission v Luxembourg* [2009] ECR I-4323.

essentialist approach is generally required, but has not been useful in advancing claims in areas where the biological differences between the sexes are less apparent. In circumstances where such differences are attributable to gendered rather than biological criteria, the Court appears to have had more difficulty in recognizing the disadvantages experienced by women in the labour market and has, thus, been less inclined to take explicit account of the relationship between unpaid care and paid work in formulating its judgments. The low value ascribed to unpaid care has, thus, implicitly had a devaluing effect on the paid work performed alongside it. It is hoped that the new constitutional provision of the Charter of Fundamental Rights (CFR) will have some impact in this respect through its normative capacity. However, the simultaneous achievement of EU law's dual goals of sex equality and work/family reconciliation is likely to require an endorsement and clear expression of a right to care which go beyond what the current provisions of the Charter are able to deliver.[7] It is, thus, asserted that the right should be provided by secondary legislation. The final section will set out some suggestions for the form and nature of such provision.

What Would a Right to Care Look Like?

In order to facilitate and encourage gender-free care and contribute towards the normalization of atypical work arrangements, such a right is required to be observant of, but not reliant on, pre-existing anti-sex discrimination legislation. The formulation of such a right necessitates law's consideration of the full range of human activities with the ultimate social goal identified as autonomy for all citizens regardless of personal characteristics such as gender, race, age, sexuality, or degree of physical or mental ability. The introduction of a specific right to care would require the status of carer to be added to this list. This vision for the future regulation of work, although apparently at odds with the current conception of liberalism as perceived through the neo-liberal policy lens, is in fact perfectly compatible with its underlying and sustainable ethos.

In seeking to identify what such a right would look like, attention is drawn to current examples of regulatory intervention which seek to accommodate a wide range of diverse needs through the prism of a reflexive right. Such examples do exist—in the European context in the form of the UK's disability discrimination legislation which provides a flexible approach to accommodation of difference[8] and, drawing from international experience, the Australian state legislation of New South Wales and Victoria which offer specific rights for carers within employment. Although far from perfect models on which to base such a right, these examples do provide an opportunity to explore what such a right might look like and how it might operate as well as enabling some assessment of the potential pitfalls and they

[7] See Chapter 5.
[8] Disability Discrimination Act 1995, s 4A(1).

will be briefly considered to identify what can be gleaned from them that might be used in developing the form of regulatory approach proposed in this book.

The Accommodation of Difference: The UK's Disability Discrimination Act

The UK's Disability Discrimination Act 1995 (DDA) which applies, *inter alia*, in the employment field, imposes an obligation on employers to make adjustments in circumstances where a provision, criterion, or practice applied by or on behalf of the employer or any physical feature of the premises occupied by the employer places a disabled person at a substantial disadvantage in comparison with persons who are not disabled. Although it was always a provision of the Act, the duty has developed since its introduction in line with case law and changes to the nature of equality legislation generally[9] and is a key element of the legislation which distinguishes it from other UK anti-discrimination legislation as it recognizes difference and enables such difference to inform decision-making. This is in contrast to the equal treatment approach adopted in most of the UK's anti-discrimination law, and indeed in the EU provisions as discussed in Chapter 5, although both approaches share common conceptual roots in the Aristotelian formula that 'likes should be treated alike and different cases should be treated differently'.[10] The European Employment Framework Directive[11] makes a similar provision in that Article 5 provides that employers should take appropriate measures, where needed in a particular case, to enable a person with a disability to have access to, participate in, or advance in employment.[12]

The provisions of the DDA, by which employers are required to take special measures, represent a manifestation of the social model of disability which is based on the premise that external barriers which prevent participation in employment should be removed wherever practicable and possible.[13] This requires the employer's intervention as the disadvantage suffered by the disabled worker entitles her to different treatment from those who are not disadvantaged as long as she can show that it was necessary to achieve parity with non-disabled workers in the particular circumstances in which she found herself. Its situation alongside the more traditional non-discrimination approach enables account to be taken of the specific causes of such disadvantage in the provision of remedial action which will vary

[9] Most recently by the Equality Act 2010.

[10] See Chapter 2.

[11] Council Directive No. 2000/78 establishing a general framework for equal treatment in employment and occupation, OJ 2000 L 303/16.

[12] This should be read alongside Art 7 of the Directive which allows for positive action 'to prevent or compensate for disadvantages' or, in the case of disabled workers, 'for safeguarding or promoting their integration into the working environment'. However, whether such action is taken does not arise as an obligation on Member States but depends on national implementing legislation.

[13] N. Bamforth, M. Malik, and C. O'Cinneide, *Discrimination Law: Theory and Context* (London: Sweet & Maxwell, 2008), 1072.

dependent on the nature of the individual's disability and her particular circumstances.

Whether this intervention amounts to *positive* discrimination or arises as a *remedy for* discrimination has been a matter of some conjecture. This distinction is important in the current context because the application of a similar approach to carers would, if effected by secondary legislation, require the attainment of political consensus from across the Member States which may be difficult to achieve if couched as a means of positive or even affirmative action leaving it vulnerable to political attack. Furthermore, even if the realization of such a right is deemed to be solely a matter of interpretation for the Court of Justice, reliance on the well-established principle of non-discrimination would be more likely to achieve the necessary result. Waddington and Hendriks argue that failure to make a reasonable adjustment is a form of discrimination as it amounts to a failure to provide equal opportunities in line with the traditional expectation of the anti-discrimination legislation.[14] Furthermore, in direct reference to the Framework Directive itself, Waddington has asserted that the reasonable accommodation requirement recognizes that 'where people's impairments result in them being differently situated regarding employment opportunities, identical treatment may be a source of discrimination, and different treatment may be required to eliminate it'.[15] This is a persuasive argument for substantive rather than procedural equality which is only measurable by output and, therefore, requires the identification and removal of specific barriers which will vary depending on the nature of the disability and the particular circumstances in which the individual finds herself.

When applied to the worker-carer, this approach has far-reaching potential as it offers the type of conceptual flexibility necessary to encompass the wide range of care arrangements and working practices that are relevant to the unpaid care/paid work conflict and which can only be remedied by adjustment or accommodation. Thus, the use of reasonable accommodation on the grounds of a recognized carer status has the potential to respond to discrimination which arises where individuals find themselves differently situated from those without caring responsibilities without the need to revert to the sex discrimination provisions, the restrictive interpretation of which has tended to focus on biological difference rather than social construction.[16] Furthermore, in market terms, this approach is capable of improving economic efficiency in some circumstances as the removal of unnecessary barriers to participation in employment would facilitate the integration of those previously excluded from the labour market. On this basis, the use of such an approach has the potential to reconcile the EU's dual goals of gender equality and the conciliation of personal and professional life with the further integration of

[14] L. Waddington and A. Hendriks, 'The Expanding Concept of Employment Discrimination in Europe: From Direct and Indirect Discrimination to "reasonable accommodation" Discrimination', *The International Journal of Comparative Labour Law and Industrial Relations*, 18/4 (2002), 403.

[15] L. Waddington, *Implementing and Interpreting the Reasonable Accommodation Provision of the Framework Employment Directive: Learning from Experience and Achieving Best Practice*, EU Network of Experts on Disability Discrimination (Brussels: European Commission, 2004), 31.

[16] See Chapter 6.

women into the labour market.[17] However, the duty to make such adjustments under the DDA is not absolute but depends on the interpretation of what is 'reasonable' in the circumstances which, in turn, is reliant on the prioritization of competing claims on the distribution of resources.

In *Archibald v Fife Council*,[18] the House of Lords considered the extent of the duty and found it capable, at least, of requiring employers to amend policies and procedures that pose an insurmountable barrier to a disabled person which may engender making special provisions in certain circumstances. As Lady Hale noted, 'It is common ground that the Act entails a measure of positive discrimination, in the sense that employers are required to take steps to help disabled people which they are not required to take for others.'[19] Although mindful of the fact that employers are only required to take those steps 'which in all the circumstances it is reasonable for them to have to take', their Lordships nevertheless found the duty to be extensive and capable of including 'all adjustments which might be made to the particular job—adapting the premises, reallocating duties, altering the hours, modifying equipment or providing training, interpretation or supervision' in order to clear any identifiable obstacles out of the disabled person's way. The duty does not arise only when the disability makes it impossible for the individual to do the job at all and 'there is no adjustment to the arrangements for that job which can make any difference'.[20] This approach, which requires the matching of the job to the individual and stresses the fluidity and flexibility of the former rather than the latter, who is deemed incapable of adjusting or adapting due to personal circumstances, heralds a move away from insistence on conformity to a specified norm which is of inestimable importance if the ultimate goal of equality is to be achieved.[21]

Of course, the DDA is not without its faults, the main issue having been identified in the case law as the definition of disability used in the legislation, but nevertheless, it has been recognized as 'a very important legislative instrument, which has made a gradual but significant contribution to breaking down some of the barriers to full and equal participation by persons with disabilities in society'.[22] Fredman, although generally positive about the significant contribution that the Act has made to existing anti-discrimination legislation, notes that its operation remains too individualistic to give effect to the 'universalist' approach required to promote more proactive means of ensuring access to social goods for all.[23] The

[17] See Chapter 5. Although the attainment of greater labour market integration carries obvious attractions in economic terms, the main justification for this policy development lies, in the current author's view, in its claim to equality of opportunity for those who seek to combine paid employment with unpaid care.

[18] [2004] UKHL 32.

[19] Ibid, para 57.

[20] Ibid.

[21] See S. Fredman, 'Disability Equality: A Challenge to the Existing Anti-Discrimination Paradigm?' in C. Gooding and A Lawson (eds), *Disability Rights in Europe* (Oxford: Hart Publishing, 2004) at 212. Although it still relies on *comparison against* a specified norm—see below at p 188.

[22] Bamforth, Malik, and O'Cinneide, n 13 above, 1098.

[23] Fredman, n 21 above, 214.

concept of reasonable adjustment is a particular feature of the individualism that prevents the application of a more substantive notion of the attainment of equality, so how can this be reconciled with the genuine need to provide tailor-made solutions to the specific conflicts between social arrangements (such as employment policies and specific workplace requirements) and individual circumstances which arise through disability or caring responsibilities? In Fredman's view, such development is possible through a 'group dimension of duty of accommodation'[24] by which the duty is generalized to embrace all grounds of discrimination. This requires reconfiguration of the concept of equality 'so that the norm itself is refashioned to incorporate social diversity'[25] and which, in turn, necessitates the restructuring of social institutions to reflect this widened norm. Such development, as well as overcoming the difficulties arising out of the compartmentalization of anti-discrimination law by enabling claims on multiple grounds, would also be capable of knocking down the largely false distinctions that exist between the various legal paradigms such as employment law, social security law, and family law.[26] Its application in the current context, however, would depend on legal recognition of carers as a specific social group capable of attracting protection. This is the approach taken by the state law of New South Wales which will now be considered.

Specific Protection for Carers: Carers' Responsibilities Legislation in Australia

A distinct legal model, used in the legislation of the Australian state New South Wales,[27] recognizes carers as a protected category. The legislation in question places a duty on employers to take reasonable steps to accommodate requests for alternative work arrangements from those with care-giving responsibilities, including childcare and care for elderly or sick relatives irrespective of whether the relationship is formed by marriage or a *de facto* relationship.[28] The approach is anti-discriminatory as such workers are expressly identified as a distinct category to be protected against direct and indirect discrimination. The same approach was subsequently adopted by the legislature in Victoria.[29]

[24] Ibid, 218. In support of this proposal, Fredman cites South African employment equity legislation which places a duty on designated employers to take affirmative action including making reasonable accommodation for blacks, women, and disabled people.

[25] Ibid.

[26] See Chapter 4.

[27] Following a 2001 amendment to the New South Wales Anti-Discrimination Act 1977 which operates alongside the prohibition of sex discrimination.

[28] Section 49S indicating that children can include grand-children, immediate family members can include a spouse, a parent, or a step-parent, a grand-parent, or sibling, and that relationships can be hetero- or homosexual in nature.

[29] The Equal Opportunity Amendment (Family Responsibilities) Act 2008, Victoria, which places employers under an obligation not to unreasonably refuse to accommodate the responsibilities that a

Bourke has identified the objectives of the NSW legislation as being gender equity, support for the privatization of care, and acknowledgment of the diversity of caring relationships and the promotion of flexible work practices, all of which are 'implicit in the legislative form' which 'also reflects a frustration with the limited capacity of existing models of anti-discrimination regulations to produce substantive gender equality and a desire to encourage employers to proactively engage in implementing flexible work practices'.[30] The introduction of the new provisions was accompanied by extensive mandatory training for all legal practitioners, including tribunal members, involved with the operation and interpretation of the provisions[31] with specific training on the carers' amendment extended to the commissioners of the NSW Industrial Relations Commission.[32] The objective of such training was to ensure familiarity with the policy background, the range of potential flexible work arrangements, and the barriers to their introduction, thus enabling expert assessment of both employer and employee claims.[33]

The non-discrimination approach, which requires the bringing of individual claims, denies worker-carers a self-standing right to care and means that the protection that does exist suffers from the same weakness of individualism rather than universalism as the UK's disability discrimination legislation which has a restrictive effect on its potential reach.[34] However, its undoubted advantage lies in its non-reliance on sex discrimination as the basis for a claim and the relatively wide scope of its provisions which ensure equal treatment for women and men, parents and carers regardless of the nature of the relationship.[35] This is bolstered by the reasonable adjustment provisions which indicate an important shift from the requirement for individuals to justify their need for reasonable adjustments onto employers to justify their refusal to make such adjustments[36] which potentially cover all aspects of work organization including home-based work, relocation, notice periods, and overtime requirements. Only one of the 140 claims decided in the first two years after the

person has as a parent or carer. Failure to comply with this obligation constitutes unlawful discrimination.

[30] J. Bourke, 'Using the Law to Support Work/Life Issues: The Australian Experience', *Journal of Gender, Social Policy and the Law*, 12/1 (2004), 19, 29.

[31] A. Hegewisch, *Flexible Working Policies: A Comparative Review* (Equality and Human Rights Commission, 2009), 7.

[32] The administrative agency charged with conciliation in relevant cases.

[33] J. Bourke, 'Caregiver discrimination in Australia in law and litigation'. Presentation at Working time, discrimination and the law: the family responsive workplace in Europe and the United States Conference, American University Washington College of Law; Washington, DC, 21–22 March 2005, cited in Hegewisch, n 31 above.

[34] See Fredman, n 21 above.

[35] Although, in relation to the NSW legislation, Bourke has called for the definition of 'caring responsibilities' to be expanded to include employees who provide care for people who are not immediate family members, or people who do not live in the same household, such as those in homosexual relationships living apart—see n 30 above, 68.

[36] See Australian Human Rights Commission, *Submission of the Human Rights and Equal Opportunity Commission to the Senate Legal and Constitutional Affairs Committee on the enquiry into the effectiveness of the Sex Discrimination Act 1984 in eliminating and promoting gender equality* (Sydney: AHRC, 2008), para 284. Available at <http://www.hreoc.gov.au/legal/submissions/2008/20080901_gender_equality.html> accessed 7 December 2010.

introduction of the NSW legislation was appealed[37] although predictably the gender-free formulation of the right did not initially result in any discernable change in the nature of claims with 77 per cent of those 140 complaints lodged by women, primarily by mothers seeking part-time work on return from maternity leave.[38] However, according to Bourke, the composition of complaints has become less traditional over time, with more male parents and carers bringing claims.[39]

From Recognition of Difference to Self-Actualization

The UK's disability provisions and the Australian states' carers' legislation both provide models which are capable of contributing to the inclusion of those traditionally excluded from or denied full access to the physical and social arrangements surrounding paid work. Both share a similar approach in their identification of specifically targeted groups whose individual members are entitled to reasonable accommodations in respect of their particular needs in order to remove potential or actual barriers to their self-actualization. Although this approach contributes to the reprioritization of needs by incorporating what are ostensibly non-market considerations into market-based solutions through the media of employment law, it falls somewhat short of the provision of self-standing rights which recognize the social value and related contributions of the individuals they are intended to protect. Both the Australian and UK provisions rely on identification of the differences of their subjects as a starting point in the accommodation of such difference which, although a necessary step in the recognition of substantive equality for such individuals, is nevertheless ultimately reliant on comparison against a specified norm which is unencumbered by the disability or caring responsibilities which, by implication, afflict the protected individual. Full realization and attribution of the worth of all individuals and the accommodation of the wide diversity that characterizes the human race ultimately rests on Fredman's vision of a refashioned norm.[40] What this tells us in the current context is that a right to care which, as this book has argued is potentially compatible with the current provisions of EU law, is merely an important initial step in a much longer process aimed at solving the current conflict between unpaid care and paid work. This book has advocated the use of the capability approach (CA) as a valuable evaluative framework within which to assess the ongoing development of a right to care and it is on the use of that framework in the specific context of the EU regulatory system that it will conclude.

The Ongoing Development of a Right to Care: Concluding Remarks

In her work on the application of the CA, Nussbaum has sought to develop a partial theory of justice by seeking to identify certain political principles that should be

37 Bourke, n 30 above. 38 Ibid, 66. 39 Bourke, n 33 above.
40 See n 21 above.

universally guaranteed and which, therefore, 'citizens have a right to demand from their governments'.[41] To this end, she has identified a well-defined but general set of 'central human capabilities' that, she argues, should be incorporated in all constitutions.[42] Sen, in contrast, has always desisted from endorsing a specific list of capabilities, preferring to leave decisions about what should or should not be included to those responsible for conducting specific evaluative exercises within the CA's paradigm through the 'act of reasoning'. This emphasizes Sen's desire to retain the CA as a normative framework rather than a fully formed theory of justice, thus enabling its use in a variety of contexts alongside specific complimentary social theories, the use of which will lead to different selections of valuable functionings depending on the context.[43] Furthermore, Sen argues that the use of the CA in the development of policy should be predicated on the outcomes of democratic processes and social choice procedures so that the requisite valuable capabilities are specifically defined by those who will be affected by the resulting policy.

The question of whether Sen should, as Nussbaum contends,[44] endorse a specific list of capabilities is open to interpretation. It is worth bearing in mind that the different views taken by the two foremost proponents of the CA in this respect owe much to their own respective interests in and uses of the CA: Nussbaum from her political and moral philosophical perspective is instinctively interested in conceptions of the good life and has focused her attention on constitutional design which requires the identification and defence of well-defined political principles, whereas Sen, as an economist interested in social choice theory, has advanced the argument that agency should play a central role in policy design so that the subjects of collective evaluations and related decision-taking should be involved in the fundamental design of evaluative frameworks. However, one could argue that, rather than being a matter of personal preference, this issue does have a particular significance in the field of policy design—Nussbaum's advocacy for a set of constitutional guarantees does at least establish a basis on which policy might be grounded, whereas the attraction of Sen's resistance to such specification has obvious merit in the reflexive nature of resulting measures.

In the context of European employment law, both approaches have direct application. Nussbaum's articulation of certain fundamental values on which we should all be able to depend regardless of transient but dominant political ideology or economic circumstance is echoed in the constitutional promises of the Treaties and the corresponding fundamental principles of EU law. Alongside this, Sen's advocacy of reflexive regulation, itself the result of a democratic process, is

[41] See M. Nussbaum, *Women and Human Development: The Capabilities Approach* (Cambridge: Cambridge University Press, 2000), 12.

[42] See ibid, in which Nussbaum lists the relevant capabilities as being: 1. Life; 2. Bodily health; 3. Bodily integrity; 4. Senses, imagination and thought; 5. Emotions; 6. Practical reason; 7. Affiliation; 8. Other species; 9. Play; 10. Control over one's environment. This list is always open for revision so should be checked against her most recent formulation.

[43] A. Sen, 'Capability and Well-being' in *The Quality of Life*, M. Nussbaum and A. Sen (eds) (Oxford: Clarendon Press, 1993).

[44] M. Nussbaum, 'Capabilities as Fundamental Entitlements: Sen and Social Justice', *Feminist Economics*, 9/3 (2003), 33.

representative of the broad development of the secondary sources incorporating legislation, soft law, policy, social partner initiatives, and judgments of the Court, all of which are capable of bringing the constitutional commitments to life and whose realization will ultimately depend on the moral choices we should all be free to make.

Bibliography

Alstott, A., *No Exit: What Parents Owe their Children and What Society Owes Parents* (New York: Oxford University Press, 2004).

Aristotle, *Nicomachean Ethics*, D. Ross (trans) (Oxford: Oxford University Press, 1925).

Ashiagbor, D., *The European Employment Strategy: Labour Market Regulation and New Governance* (Oxford: Oxford University Press, 2005).

——'Promoting Precariousness? The Responses of EU Employment Policies to Precarious Work' in J. Fudge and R. Owens (eds), *Precarious Work, Women and the New Economy: The Challenge to Legal Norms* (Oxford: Hart Publishing, 2006).

Atkins, S., and Hoggett, B., *Women and the Law* (Oxford: Blackwell, 1984).

Australian Human Rights Commission, *Submission of the Human Rights and Equal Opportunity Commission to the Senate Legal and Constitutional Affairs Committee on the enquiry into the effectiveness of the Sex Discrimination Act 1984 in eliminating and promoting gender equality* (Sydney: Australian Human Rights Commission, 2008).

Ayres, I., and Braithwaite, J., *Responsive Regulation: Transcending the Deregulation Debate* (Oxford: Oxford University Press, 1992).

Badgett, M. V. L., and Folbre, N., 'Assigning Care: Gender Norms and Economic Outcomes', *International Labour Review*, 138/3 (1999), 311.

Baer, S., 'Citizenship in Europe and the Construction of Gender by Law' in K. Knopp (ed), *Gender and Human Rights* (Oxford: Oxford University Press, 2004).

Ball, S., 'The European Employment Strategy: The Will but not the Way?', *Industrial Law Journal*, 30/4 (2001), 353.

Bamforth, N., Malik, M., and O'Cinneide, C., *Discrimination Law: Theory and Context* (London: Sweet & Maxwell, 2008).

Barbera, M., 'The Unsolved Conflict: Reshaping Family Work and Market Work in the EU Legal Order' in T. Hervey and J. Kenner (eds), *Economic and Social Rights under the EU Charter of Fundamental Rights: A Legal Perspective* (Oxford: Hart Publishing, 2003).

Barnard, C., 'The Economic Objectives of Article 119' in T. Hervey and D. O'Keeffe (eds), *Sex Equality Law in the European Union* (Chichester: John Wiley, 1996), 321.

——'Social Dumping and the Race to the Bottom: Some Lessons for the European Union from Delaware?', *European Law Review*, 25 (2000), 57.

——and Deakin, S., '"Negative" and "Positive" Harmonisation of Labour Law in the European Union', *Columbia Journal of European Law*, 8 (2002), 389.

——and Hepple, B., 'Indirect Discrimination: Interpreting Seymour Smith', *Cambridge Law Journal*, 58/2 (1999), 399.

——Deakin, S., and Hobbs, R., 'Fog in the Channel, Continent Isolated: Britain as a Model for EU Social and Economic Policy?', *Industrial Law Journal*, 34 (2002), 35.

Barnard, N., '"A New Governance" Approach to Economic, Social and Cultural Rights in the EU' in T. Hervey and J. Kenner (eds), *Economic and Social Rights under the EU Charter of Fundamental Rights: A Legal Perspective* (Oxford: Hart Publishing, 2003).

Beechey, V., *Unequal Work* (London: Verso, 1987).

——'Women's Employment in Contemporary Britain' in V. Beechey and E. Whitlegg (eds), *Women in Britain Today* (Oxford: Oxford University Press, 1986).

Bell, M., 'The Right to Equality and Non-Discrimination' in T. Hervey and J. Kenner (eds), *Economic and Social Rights under the EU Charter of Fundamental Rights: A Legal Perspective* (Oxford: Hart Publishing, 2003).

Bengoetxea, J., *The Legal Reasoning of the European Court of Justice* (Oxford: Oxford University Press, 1993).

——McCormick, N., and Soriano, L. M., 'Integration and Integrity in the Legal Reasoning of the European Court of Justice' in G. De Búrca and J. Weiler (eds), *The European Court of Justice* (Oxford: Oxford University Press, 2001).

Bourke, J. 'Using the Law to Support Work/Life Issues: The Australian Experience', *Journal of Gender, Social Policy and the Law*, 12/1 (2004), 19.

——'Caregiver discrimination in Australia in law and litigation'. Presentation at Working time, discrimination and the law: the family responsive workplace in Europe and the United States Conference, American University Washington College of Law; Washington, DC, 21–22 March 2005.

Bredimas, A., *Methods of Interpretation and Community Law* (Amsterdam: North Holland, 1978).

Browne, J., Deakin, S., and Wilkinson, F., 'Capabilities, Social Rights and European Market Integration' in R. Salais and R. Villeneuve (eds), *Europe and the Politics of Capabilities* (Cambridge: Cambridge University Press, 2004).

Bubeck, D., *Care, Justice and Gender* (New York: Oxford University Press, 1995).

——'Justice and the Labor of Care' in E. Feder Kittay and E. Feder (eds), *The Subject of Care: Feminist Perspectives on Dependency* (New York: Rowan and Littlefield, 2002).

Burchardt, T., *Time and Income Poverty* (LSE: Centre for Analysis of Social Exclusion, 2008) available at <http://sticerd.lse.ac.uk/dps/case/cr/CASEreport57.pdf>.

Burrows, N., 'Opting in to the Opt-out: The UK and European Social Policy', *Web Journal of Current Legal Issues*, 4 (1997) available at <http://webjcli.ncl.ac.uk/1997/issue4/burrows4.html>.

——'The New Employment Chapter and Social Policy Provisions of the Amsterdam Treaty' in J. Usher (ed), *The State of the European Union* (Harlow: Longman, 2000).

——and Robison, M., 'An Assessment of the Recast of Community Equality Laws', *European Law Journal*, 13/2 (2007), 186.

Busby, N., 'Only a Matter of Time', *Modern Law Review*, 64/3 (2001), 489.

——'Equal Pay and Contracting Out: *Lawrence v Regent Office Care Ltd*', *Edinburgh Law Review*, 7/2 (2003), 233.

——and Christie, D., 'The Regulation of Temporary Agency Work in the European Union', *The Cambrian Law Review*, 36 (2005), 15.

Cappelletti, M., 'The Law Making Power of the Judges and its Limits', *Monash University Law Review*, 8 (1981), 15.

Caracciolo di Torella, E., 'A Critical Assessment of the EC Legislation Aiming at Reconciling Work and Family Life: Lessons from the Scandinavian Model' in H. Collins, P. Davies, and P. Ridout (eds), *Legal Regulation of the Employment Relation* (London: Kluwer Law International, 2000).

——'Childcare, Employment and Equality in the EC: First (False) Steps of the Court, *European Law Review*, 25 (2000), 310.

Cockburn, C., *In the Way of Women: Men's Resistance to Sex Equality in Organisations* (London: Macmillan, 1991).

Collins, H., 'The Productive Disintegration of Labour Law', *Industrial Law Journal*, 26/4 (1997), 295.

——Review of S. Deakin and F. Wilkinson, 'The Law of the Labour Market: Industrialisation, Employment and Legal Evolution', *Industrial Law Journal*, 35 (2006), 105.

Comité des Sages (chaired by Maria de Lourdes Pintasilgo), *For a Europe of Civic and Social Rights* (Brussels: Office for Official Publications of the European Communities, 1996).

Conaghan, J., 'Contesting the Terrain' in A. Morris and T. O'Donnell (eds), *Feminist Perspectives on Employment Law* (London: Cavendish, 1999).

——'Work, Family, and the Discipline of Labour Law' in J. Conaghan and K. Rittich (eds), *Labour Law, Work and Family* (Oxford: Oxford University Press, 2005).

——and Rittich, K. (eds), *Labour Law, Work and Family* (Oxford: Oxford University Press, 2005).

Cornell, D., 'Beyond Tragedy and Complacency', *Northwestern University Law Review*, 81 (1987), 693.

——'The Doubly Prized World: Myth, Allegory And The Feminine', *Cornell Law Review*, 75 (1990), 644.

Craig, C., Garnsey, E., and Rubery, J., *Payment Structures in Smaller Firms: Women's Employment in Segmented Labour Markets* (London: Department of Employment, 1984).

Craig, P., and De Búrca, G., *EU Law Text, Cases and Materials* (Oxford: Oxford University Press, 2003).

Crompton, R. (ed), *Restructuring Gender Relationships and Employment: The Decline of the Male Breadwinner* (Oxford: Oxford University Press, 1999).

——*Employment and the Family* (Cambridge: Cambridge University Press, 2006).

Davies, A. C. L., 'One Step Forward, Two Steps Back? The Viking and Laval Cases in the ECJ', *Industrial Law Journal*, 37/2 (2008), 126.

Davies, P. and Freedland, M., *Khan-Freund's Labour and the Law* (London: Stevens and Sons, 1983).

——and Freedland, M., 'Employees, Workers and the Autonomy of Labour Law' in H. Collins, P. Davies, and R. Rideout (eds), *Legal Regulation of the Employment Relation* (London: Kluwer Law International, 2000).

de Beauvoir, S., *The Second Sex*, H. M. Parshley (trans) (New York: Vintage, 1949).

Deakin, S., 'Social Rights in a Globalised Economy' in P. Alston (ed), *Labour Rights as Human Rights* (Oxford: Oxford University Press, 2005).

——and Browne, J., 'Social Rights and Market Order: Adapting the Capability Approach' in T. Hervey and J. Kenner (eds), *Economic and Social Rights under the EU Charter of Fundamental Rights* (Oxford: Hart Publishing, 2003).

——and Wilkinson, F., *The Law of the Labour Market: Industrialisation, Employment and Legal Evolution* (Oxford: Oxford University Press, 2005).

Dickens, L., 'Problems of Fit: Changing Employment and Labour Regulation', *British Journal of Industrial Relations*, 42/4 (2004), 595.

Dréze, J., and Sen, A., *India: Development and Participation* (Oxford: Oxford University Press, 2002).

Dworkin, R., *Taking Rights Seriously* (London: Duckworth, 1978).

——'Liberalism' in *A Matter of Principle* (Oxford: Clarendon Press, 1985).

——*Law's Empire* (London: Fontana Press, 1986).

——*Sovereign Virtue: The Theory and Practice of Equality* (Cambridge MA: Harvard University Press, 2000).

——'What is Equality? Part II: Equality of Resources', *Philosophy and Public Affairs*, 10 (1981), 283–345, reprinted in *Sovereign Virtues. The Theory and Practice of Equality* (Harvard University Press, 2000).

Edwards, D., 'How the Court of Justice Works', *European Law Review*, 20 (1995), 539.

Ellis, E., *EU Anti-Discrimination Law* (Oxford: Oxford University Press, 2005).

Equal Opportunities Commission, *Women: Europe's Competitive Edge* (Manchester: EOC, 2005).

Esping-Andersen, G., Gaillie, D., Hemerijck, A., and Myles, J., *Why We Need a New Welfare State* (Oxford: Oxford University Press, 2002).

European Commission, *Proposal on Parental Leave and Leave for Family Reasons*, COM (83) 686 final OJ 1983 C 333/6.

——*Growth, Competitiveness and Employment*, COM (1993) 700 Final.

——*Affirming Fundamental Rights in the European Union: Time to Act* (Brussels: European Commission 1999).

——*European Employment and Social Policy: A Policy for People* (D-G for Education and Culture, 2000).

——*Communication on the Charter of Fundamental Rights of the European Union*, COM (2000) 599 final.

——*Employment and Social Policies: A Framework for Investing in Quality* (Luxembourg: Office for Official Publications of the European Communities, 2001).

——*Communication on Certain Arrangements for the Debate on the Future of the European Union*, COM (2001) 178 final of 25 April 2001.

——*Communication from the Commission to the Council, the European Parliament, The European Economic and Social Committee and the Committee of the Regions updating and simplifying the Community acquis*, COM (2003) 71, Final.

——*Report on Equality Between Men and Women*, COM (2004) 115 final.

——*Roadmap for Equality Between Men and Women 2006–2010, Communication from the Commission to the Council, the European Parliament and the Social Committee and Committee of the Regions, A Roadmap for Equality between Men and Women*, COM (2006) 92.

——*Health and Long-Term Care in the European Union*, Special Eurobarometer 283 (Luxembourg, 2007).

——*Work Programme for 2008*, COM (2007) 640.

——*Proposal for a directive of the European Parliament and the Council amending Council Directive 93/85/EEC on the introduction of measures to encourage improvements in the safety and health at work of pregnant workers and those who have recently given birth or are breastfeeding*, COM (2008) 600/4.

——*A Better Work-Life Balance: Stronger Support for Reconciling Professional, Private and Family Life*, COM (2008) 635 final.

——*Reconciliation between Work, Private and Family Life in the European Union* (Brussels: 2009).

——*Strategy for Equality Between Women and Men*, COM (2010) 491 final. Bulletin of the European Communities, Supplement 2/74.

European Council, Presidency Conclusions of the Lisbon European Council of 23rd and 24th March 2000, available at <http://www.europarl.europa.eu/summits/lis1_en.htm> accessed 7 December 2010.

European Foundation for the Improvement of Living and Working Conditions, *Quality of Women's Work and Employment: Tools for Change* (Luxembourg: Office for Official Publications of the European Communities, 2002).

——*Childcare Services in the EU—What Future?* (2006), available at <http://www.eurofound.europa.eu/emcc/content/source/eu06015a.htm?p1=ef_publication&p2=null> accessed 7 December.

——*Working Time Options over the Life Course: New Work Patterns and Company Strategies* (Dublin: Eurofound, 2006).

Eurostat, *The Life of Women and Men in Europe: A Statistical Portrait* (Luxembourg: Office for Official Publications of the European Communities, 2000).
Everling, U., 'The Court of Justice as a Decisionmaking Authority' in Michigan Law Review Association, *The Art of Governance: Festschrift zu Ehren von Eric Stein*, 156 (1987), 163.
——'Zur Begründung der Urteile des Gerichtshofes der Europäischen Gemeinschaften', *Europarecht*, 29 (1994), 127.
Ewing, K., 'Democratic Socialism and Labour Law', *Industrial Law Journal*, 24/2 (1995), 103.
Fagan, C., and Burchell, B., European Foundation for the Improvement of Living and Working Conditions, *Gender, Jobs and Working Conditions in the European Union* (Luxembourg, Office for Official Publications of the European Communities, 2002).
Filmer, R., *Patriarcha and Other Writings*, J. P. Sommerville (ed) (Cambridge: Cambridge University Press, 1991).
Fineman, M., *The Autonomy Myth: A Theory of Dependency* (New York: The New Press, 2004).
Fredman, S.,'European Community Discrimination Law: A Critique', *Industrial Law Journal*, 21/2 (1992), 119.
——*Women and the Law* (Oxford: Oxford University Press, 1997).
——'Labour Law in Flux: The Changing Composition of the Workforce', *Industrial Law Journal*, 26/4 (1997), 337.
——'Women at Work: The Broken Promise of Flexicurity', *Industrial Law Journal*, 33/4 (2004), 299.
——'The Ideology of New Labour Law' in C. Barnard, S. Deakin, and G. Morris (eds), *Essays in Honour of Bob Hepple* (Oxford: Hart Publishing, 2004).
——'Disability Equality: A Challenge to the Existing Anti-Discrimination Paradigm?' in C. Gooding and A. Lawson (eds), *Disability Rights in Europe* (Oxford: Hart Publishing, 2004).
——'Precarious Norms for Precarious Workers' in J. Fudge and R. Owens, *Precarious Work, Women and the New Economy: The Challenge to Legal Norms* (Oxford: Hart Publishing, 2006).
——'Transformation or Dilution: Fundamental Rights in the EU Social Space', *European Law Journal*, 12/1 (2006), 41.
Fudge, J., 'The New Discourse of Labor Rights: From Social to Fundamental Rights?', *Comparative Labour Law and Policy Journal*, 30 (2007), 29.
——and Owens, R. (eds), *Precarious Work, Women and the New Economy: The Challenge to Legal Norms* (Oxford: Hart Publishing, 2006).
Fukuda Parr, S., and Shiva Kumar, A. K., *Readings in Human Development* (Delhi: Oxford University Press, 2003).
Gershuny, J., *Changing Times: Work and Leisure in Post-Industrial Society* (Oxford: Oxford University Press, 2000).
Gilligan, C., *In a Different Voice: Psychological Theory and Women's Development* (Cambridge: Harvard University Press, 1982).
Giullari, S., and Lewis, J., *The Adult Worker Model Family, Gender Equality and Care: The Search for New Policy Principles, and the Possibilities and Problems of a Capabilities Approach*, United Nations Research Institute, Social Policy and Development Programme (2005) Paper No. 19.
Goetschy, J., 'The European Employment Strategy: Genesis and Development', *European Journal of Industrial Relations*, 5/2 (1999), 117.

Hakim, C., 'The Myth of Rising Female Employment', *Work, Employment and Society*, 7 (1993), 97.

Hare, R. M., *Moral Thinking: Its Levels, Method and Point* (Oxford: Oxford University Press, 1981).

Hayek, F., *Law, Legislation and Liberty, Vol. II* (London: Routledge and Keegan, 1982).

Hegewisch, A., *Flexible Working Policies: A Comparative Review* (Equality and Human Rights Commission, 2009).

Hepple, B., 'The Crisis in EEC Labour Law', *Industrial Law Journal*, 18 (1987), 129.

——'The Future of Labour Law', *Industrial Law Journal*, 24 (1995), 4.

——'Introduction' to *Social and Labour Rights in a Global Context: International and Comparative Perspectives* (ed B. Hepple) (Cambridge: Cambridge University Press, 2002).

——'For the greater good', *The Guardian*, 23 November 2004.

——*Rights at Work: Global, European and British Perspectives* (London: Sweet and Maxwell, 2005).

——Coussey, M., and Choudhury, T., *Equality: A New Framework* (Oxford: Hart Publishing, 2000).

Hervey, T., *European Social Law and Policy* (London: Longman, 1998).

——'The "Right to Health" in European Union Law', in T. Hervey and J. Kenner (eds), *Economic and Social Rights under the EU Charter of Fundamental Rights: A Legal Perspective* (Oxford: Hart Publishing, 2003).

——and Kenner, J. (eds), *Economic and Social Rights under the EU Charter of Fundamental Rights: A Legal Perspective* (Oxford: Hart Publishing, 2003).

——and Shaw, J., 'Women, Work and Care: Women's Dual Role and Double Burden in EC Sex Equality Law', *Journal of European Social Policy*, 8 (1998), 43.

Hobbes, T., *The Leviathan* (1651), R. Tuck (ed), (Cambridge: Cambridge University Press, 1991).

Hoskyns, C., *Integrating Gender: Women, Law and Politics in the European Union* (London: Verso, 1996).

Hunt, J., 'Fair and Just Working Conditions' in T. Hervey and J. Kenner (eds), *Economic and Social Rights under the EU Charter of Fundamental Rights: A Legal Perspective* (Oxford: Hart Publishing, 2003).

Hutchinson, A. C., 'The Law Emperor?' in *Reading Dworkin Critically* (Oxford: Berg, 1992).

Hyman, R., 'The Europeanisation—or the Erosion—of Industrial Relations?', *Industrial Relations Journal*, 32/4 (2002), 280.

Jacobs, F., 'Is the Court of Justice of the European Communities a Constitutional Court?' in D. Curtin and D. O'Keeffe (eds), *Constitutional Adjudication in European Community and National Law* (London: Butterworths, 1992), 25.

James, G., 'The Work and Families Act 2006: Legislation to Improve Choice and Flexibility?', *Industrial Law Journal*, 35/3 (2006), 272.

——*The Legal Regulation of Pregnancy and Parenting in the Labour Market* (London: Routledge Cavendish, 2009).

Kahn-Freund, O., 'Industrial Relations and the Law—Retrospect and Prospect', *British Journal of Industrial Relations*, 7 (1969), 301.

——'The Impact of Constitutions of Labour Law', *Cambridge Law Journal* (1976), 240.

——'Blackstone's Neglected Child: the Contract of Employment', *Law Quarterly Review*, 93 (1978).

Keeling, D. T., 'In Praise Of Judicial Activism, But What Does It Mean and Has the European Court of Justice Ever Practiced It?' in C. Gialdino (ed) *Scritti in Oncore di G.F. Mancini* (Milan: Bellini, 1998).

Kenner, J., 'Economic and Social Rights in the EU Legal Order' in T. Hervey and J. Kenner (eds), *Economic and Social Rights under the EU Charter of Fundamental Rights: A Legal Perspective* (Oxford: Hart Publishing, 2003).

Kilpatrick, C., 'Community or Communities of Courts in European Integration? Sex Equality Dialogues Between UK Courts and the ECJ', *European Law Journal*, 4/2 (1998), 121.

Kittay, E. Feder, *Love's Labor, Essays on Women, Equality and Dependency* (New York: Routledge, 1999).

——'A Feminist Public Ethic of Care Meets the New Communitarian Family Policy', *Ethics*, 111/3 (2001).

——'When Caring is Just and Justice is Caring', in E. Feder Kittay and E. Feder (eds), *The Subject of Care: Feminist Perspectives on Dependency* (New York: Rowan and Littlefield, 2002).

Koopmans, T., The Roots of Judicial Activism, in F. Matscher and H. Petzold (eds), *Protecting Human Rights: The European Dimension, Studies in Honour of Gerard J. Wiarda* (Kluwer, 1988).

——'The Theory of Interpretation and the Court of Justice' in D. O'Keeffe and A. Bavasso (eds), *Liber Amicorum in Honour of Lord Slynn of Hadley, Vol 1, Judicial Review in European Union Law* (London: Kluwer International Law, 2000).

Koukoulis-Spiliotopoulos, S., 'The Amended Equal Treatment Directive 2002/73: An Expression of Constitutional Principles/Fundamental Rights', *Maastricht Journal*, 12 (2005), 327.

Kutscher, H., *Methods of Interpretation as Seen by a Judge of the Court of Justice* (Luxembourg, 1976).

Lacey, N., 'Theories of Justice and the Welfare State', *Social and Legal Studies*, Vol 1 (1992), 323.

——'Feminist Legal Theory and the Rights of Women' in K. Knopp (ed), *Gender and Human Rights* (Oxford: Oxford University Press, 2004).

Le Feuvre, N., and Andriocci, M., *Employment Opportunities for Women in Europe, A report of the EU-funded project 'Employment and Women's Studies: The Impact of Women's Studies Training on Women's Employment in Europe'* (Luxembourg: European Commission, 2003).

Lester, A., 'The Uncertain Trumpet. References to the European Court of Justice from the United Kingdom: Equal Pay and Equal Treatment without Sex Discrimination' in H. G. Schermers (ed), *Article 177 EEC: Experiences and Problems* (The Hague: TMV Asser Instituut, 1987).

Lewis, J., 'The Decline of the Male Breadwinner Model: Implications for Work and Care', *Social Politics*, 8/2 (2001), 152.

——'Work/Family Reconciliation, Equal Opportunities and Social Policies: The Interpretation of Policy Trajectories at the EU Level and the Meaning of Gender Equality', *Journal of European Public Policy*, 13/3 (2006), 420.

——Campbell, M., and Huerta, C., 'Patterns of Paid and Unpaid Work in Western Europe: Gender, Commodification, Preferences and the Implications for Policy', *Journal of European Social Policy* (2008), 18.

Locke, J., *Two Treatises of Government*, P. Laslett (ed) (Cambridge: Cambridge University Press, 1988).

Lynch, K., and Walsh, J., 'Love, Care and Solidarity: What is and is Not Commodifiable' in K. Lynch, J. Baker, and M. Lyons (eds), *Affective Equality: Love, Care and Injustice* (Basingstoke: Palgrave MacMillan, 2009).
——Baker, J., and Lyons, M. (eds), *Affective Equality: Love, Care and Injustice* (Basingstoke: Palgrave MacMillan, 2009).
——Baker, J., Cantillon, S., and Walsh, J., 'Which Equalities Matter? The Place of Affective Equality in Egalitarian Thinking' in K. Lynch, J. Baker, and M. Lyons (eds), *Affective Equality: Love, Care and Injustice* (Basingstoke: Palgrave MacMillan, 2009).
MacIntyre, A., *After Virtue: A Study in Moral Theory* (London: Duckworth, 1984).
MacKinnon, C. A., *Feminism Unmodified: Discourses on Life and Law* (Cambridge: Harvard University Press, 1987).
Marshall, T. H., *Citizenship and Social Class and other Essays* (Cambridge: Cambridge University Press, 1950, reprinted 1992).
Masselot, A., and Caracciolo di Torella, E., 'Pregnancy, Maternity and the Organisation of Family Life: An Attempt to Classify the Case Law of the European Court of Justice', *European Law Review*, 26/3 (2001), 239.
Matsuda, M., 'Liberal Jurisprudence and Abstracted Visions of Human Nature: a Feminist Critique of Rawls' A Theory of Justice', *New Mexico Law Review*, 16 (1986), 613.
McCann, D., *Regulating Flexible Work* (Oxford: Oxford University Press, 2008).
McCrudden, C., 'Equality Legislation and Reflexive Regulation: A Response to the Discrimination Law Review', *Industrial Law Journal*, 36 (2007), 255.
McGlynn, C., 'Ideologies of Motherhood in European Community Sex Equality Law', *European Law Journal*, 6 (2000), 39.
——'Reclaiming a Feminist Vision: The Reconciliation of Paid Work and Family Life in European Union Law and Policy', *Columbia Journal of European Law*, 7 (2001), 241.
——'Work, Family and Parenthood: The European Union Agenda' in J. Conaghan and K. Rittich (eds), *Labour Law, Work and Family* (Oxford: Oxford University Press, 2005).
Meagher, G., 'Is it Wrong to Pay for Housework?', *Hypatia*, 18/2 (2002), 52.
Mill, J. S., *The Subjection of Women* (London: Longman, 1869).
Mückenberger, U., and Deakin, S., 'From Deregulation to a European Floor of Rights: Labour Law, Flexibilisation and the European Single Market', *Zeitschrift für ausländisches und internationales Arbeits- und Sozialrecht*, 3 (1989), 53.
Nussbaum, M., 'Human Functioning and Social Justice: In Defense of Aristotelian Essentialism', *Political Theory*, 20/2 (1992), 202.
——'Human Capabilities, Female Human Beings' in M. Nussbaum and J. Glover (eds), *Women, Culture and Development: A Study of Human Capabilities* (Oxford: Oxford University Press, 1995).
——*Sex and Social Justice* (New York: Oxford University Press, 1999).
——*Women and Human Development: The Capabilities Approach* (Cambridge: Cambridge University Press, 2000).
——'The Future of Feminist Liberalism' in E. Feder Kittay and E. Feder, *The Subject of Care: Feminist Perspectives on Dependency* (New York: Rowan and Littlefield, 2002).
——'Capabilities and Social Justice', *International Studies Review*, 4/2 (2002), 123.
——'Capabilities as Fundamental Entitlements: Sen and Social Justice', *Feminist Economics*, 9 (2003) 3, 33.
O'Donovan, K., *Sexual Divisions in Law* (London: Weidenfeld and Nicolson, 1985).
Okin, S. Moller, *Women in Western Political Thought* (Princeton: Princeton University Press, 1979).
——*Justice, Gender and the Family* (New York: Basic Books, 1989).

——'On Plato' in M. L. Shanley and C. Pateman (eds), *Feminist Interpretations and Political Theory* (Cambridge: Polity Press, 1991).

O'Neill, P., *The European Court of Justice: a Case Study in Judicial Activism* (London: European Policy Forum, 1995).

Oppenheim, F., 'Egalitarianism as a Descriptive Concept' in L. Pojman and R. Westmoreland (eds), *Equality: Selected Readings* (Oxford: Oxford University Press, 1997).

Organisation for Economic Co-operation and Development, *Employment Outlook* (Paris: OECD, 2002).

Paoli, P., and Merllié, D., European Foundation for the Improvement of Living and Working Conditions, *Third European Survey on Working Conditions 2000* (Luxembourg: Office for Official Publications of the European Communities, 2001).

Pateman, C., *The Sexual Contract* (Cambridge: Polity Press, 1988).

Peers, S., and Ward, A., *The European Union Charter of Fundamental Rights* (Oxford: Hart Publishing, 2004).

Pennings, F., *European Social Security Law* (Oxford: Hart, 2010).

Phillips, A., and Taylor, B., 'Sex and Skill: Notes towards a Feminist Economics', *Feminist Review*, 6 (1980), 79.

Plato, *The Republic*, R. Waterfield (trans) (Oxford: Oxford University Press, 1993).

Polachek, S. W., and Siebert, W. S., *The Economics of Earnings* (Cambridge: Cambridge University Press, 1993).

Pollicino, O., 'Legal Reasoning of the Court of Justice in the Context of Equality: Between Judicial Activism and Self-restraint', *German Law Journal*, 5/3 (2004), 286.

Rasmussen, H., *On Law and Policy in the European Court of Justice: A Comparative Study of Judicial Policymaking* (Copenhagen: Martinus Nijhoff, 1986).

——'Between Self Restraint and Activism: A Judicial Policy for the European Court', *European Law Review*, 13 (1988), 28.

Rawls, J., *A Theory of Justice* (Oxford: Oxford University Press, 1972).

——The Dewey Lectures, 'Kantian Constructivism in Moral Theory', *The Journal of Philosophy*, 77 (1980), 515.

——*Political Liberalism* (New York: Columbia University Press, 1996).

Raz, J., *The Morality of Freedom* (Oxford: Clarendon Press, 1986).

Rees, T., *Mainstreaming Equality in the European Union: Education, Training and Labour Market Policies* (London: Routledge, 1998).

Rousseau, J.-J., '*Emile*' (1762) A. Bloom (trans) (Penguin, 1991).

Salais, R., and Villeneuve, R. (eds), *Europe and the Politics of Capabilities* (Cambridge: Cambridge University Press, 2004).

Sandel, M., *Liberalism and the Limits of Justice* (Cambridge: Cambridge University Press, 1982).

Scanlon, T., *What We Owe to Each Other* (Cambridge: Harvard University Press, 1999).

Schepel, H. (2000), 'Reconstructing Constitutionalization: Law and Politics in the European Court of Justice', *Oxford Journal of Legal Studies*, 20/3 (2000), 457.

Sen, A., 'Personal Utilities and Public Judgments: Or What's Wrong With Welfare Economics?', *The Economic Journal*, 89 (1979), 537.

——*Rights and Capabilities in Resources, Values and Development* (Cambridge MA: Harvard University Press, 1984).

——*Commodities and Capabilities* (New Delhi: Oxford University Press, 1987).

——'Well-being, Agency and Freedom', *The Journal of Philosophy*, LXXXII/4 (1987), 169.

Sen, A., 'The Standard of Living' in *The Standard of Living*, G. Hawthorn (ed) (Cambridge: Cambridge University Press, 1987).

——*Commodities and Capabilities* (New Delhi: Oxford University Press, 1987).

——'Gender and Co-operative Conflicts' in *Persistent Inequalities*, I. Tinker (ed), (Oxford: Oxford University Press, 1990).

——*Inequality Re-examined* (Oxford: Clarendon Press, 1992).

——'Capability and Well-being' in *The Quality of Life*, M. Nussbaum and A. Sen (eds) (Oxford: Clarendon Press, 1993).

——Editorial: Human Capital and Human Capability, *World Development*, 25/12 (1997), 1959.

——*Development as Freedom* (New York: Knopf, 1999).

——*The Idea of Justice* (London: Allen Lane, 2009).

Shanks, M., 'The Social Policy of the European Communities', *Common Market Law Review*, 14 (1977), 375.

Shaw, J., 'Twin-Track Social Europe—The Inside Track' in D. O'Keefe and P. Twomey (eds), *Legal Issues of the Maastricht Treaty* (London: Wiley, 1994).

Standing, G., *Global Labour Flexibility: Seeking Distributive Justice* (Basingstoke: MacMillan, 1999).

——'Globalisation, Labour Flexibility and Insecurity: The Era of Market Regulation', *European Journal of Industrial Relations*, 3/1 (1999), 7.

Supiot, A., 'The Transformation of Work and the Future of Labour Law in Europe: A Multidisciplinary Perspective', *International Labour Review*, 138/1 (1999), 32.

——*Beyond Employment: Changes in Work and the Future of Labour Law in Europe* (Oxford: Oxford University Press, 2001).

——'Governing Work and Welfare in a Global Economy' in J. Zeitlin and D. Trubeck (eds), *Governing Work and Welfare in the New Economy: European and American Experiments* (Oxford: Oxford University Press, 2003).

Swanson, J., *The Public and The Private in Aristotle's Political Philosophy* (Ithaca, NY and London: Cornell University Press, 1992).

Szyszczak, E., *EC Labour Law* (Harlow: Longman, 2000).

Teubner, G., 'Juridification: Concepts, Aspects, Limits, Solutions' in G. Teubner (ed), *Juridification of Social Spheres: A Comparative Analysis in the Areas of Labor, Corporate, Antittrust and Social Welfare Law* (Berlin: Walter de Gruyter, 1987).

Tronto, J., *Moral Boundaries: A Political Argument for an Ethic of Care* (New York: Routledge, 1993).

——'Time's Place', *Feminist Theory*, 4/2 (2003), 119.

Waddington, L., and Hendriks, A., 'The Expanding Concept of Employment Discrimination in Europe: From Direct and Indirect Discrimination to "Reasonable Accommodation" Discrimination', *The International Journal of Comparative Labour Law and Industrial Relations*, 18/4 (2002), 403.

——*Implementing and Interpreting the Reasonable Accommodation Provision of the Framework Employment Directive: Learning from Experience and Achieving Best Practice*, EU Network of Experts on Disability Discrimination (Brussels: European Commission, 2004).

Wajcman, J., 'Feminism Facing Industrial Relations in Britain', *British Journal of Industrial Relations*, 38/2 (2000), 183.

Wasserstrom, R., 'Racism, Sexism and Preferential Treatment: an Approach to the Topics', *University of California Los Angeles Law Review*, 24 (1977), 581.

Wedderburn, L., *The Worker and the Law* (London: Sweet & Maxwell, 1986).

——*Labour Law and Freedom: Further Essays in Labour Law* (London: Lawrence & Wishart, 1995).

——'Labour Law 2008: 40 Years On', *Industrial Law Journal*, 36/4 (2007), 397.

West, R., 'The Right to Care' in E. Feder Kittay and E. Feder (eds), *The Subject of Care: Feminist Perspectives on Dependency* (New York: Rowan and Littlefield, 2002).

Wincott, D., 'Beyond Social Regulation? New Instruments and/or a New Agenda for Social Policy at Lisbon?', *Public Administration*, 81/3 (2003), 533.

Wintemute, R., 'When is Pregnancy Discrimination Indirect Discrimination?', *Industrial Law Journal*, 27 (1998), 23.

Wollstonecraft, M., *A Vindication of the Rights of Women*, originally published in 1792 (Prometheus Books, reprinted 1989).

Zeitlin, J., *The Open Method of Co-ordination and the Future of the European Employment Strategy*, Presentation to the Employment and Social Affairs Committee of the European Parliament on the first five year evaluation of the Employment Guidelines, 8 July 2000.

Index

The manufacturer's authorised representative in the EU for product safety is Oxford University Press España S.A. of El Parque Empresarial San Fernando de Henares, Avenida de Castilla, 2 - 28830 Madrid (www.oup.es/en or product.safety@oup.com). OUP España S.A. also acts as importer into Spain of products made by the manufacturer.
Printed and bound by CPI Group (UK) Ltd, Croydon, CR0 4YY
14/09/2026
02216307-0006